The Development Dimension

Sector Financing in the SDG Era

OECD

BETTER POLICIES FOR BETTER LIVES

This work is published under the responsibility of the Secretary-General of the OECD. The opinions expressed and arguments employed herein do not necessarily reflect the official views of OECD member countries.

This document, as well as any data and any map included herein, are without prejudice to the status of or sovereignty over any territory, to the delimitation of international frontiers and boundaries and to the name of any territory, city or area.

Please cite this publication as:
OECD (2018), *Sector Financing in the SDG Era*, The Development Dimension, OECD Publishing, Paris.
https://doi.org/10.1787/9789264307711-en

ISBN 978-92-64-30770-4 (print)
ISBN 978-92-64-30771-1 (pdf)

Series: The Development Dimension
ISSN 1990-1380 (print)
ISSN 1990-1372 (online)

The statistical data for Israel are supplied by and under the responsibility of the relevant Israeli authorities. The use of such data by the OECD is without prejudice to the status of the Golan Heights, East Jerusalem and Israeli settlements in the West Bank under the terms of international law.

Photo credits: © Cover design S.Coic ; Cover icons adapted from Noun project: Prosymbols, M. Caury, I. Papa and Rudez studio ; Bubble background adapted from dreamstime.com.

Corrigenda to OECD publications may be found on line at: *www.oecd.org/publishing/corrigenda*.

Foreword

Measuring sectors without borders

Why do we measure where finance for development goes? When a student enters their first classroom, does it matter to them how the school was funded? No. Does finance for development matter for our ability to achieve a better world by 2030? Yes.

In 2015, world leaders adopted the 2030 Agenda for Sustainable Development including its 17 goals and 169 targets. These goals and targets include eradication of poverty, equal access to quality education and achieving a sharp decline in the global maternal mortality ratio, to name a few. To understand if we are on track to meet these goals, and where there are gaps – those that *will* affect citizens – we need to measure where development finance is flowing.

However, the challenge exists today in how to measure development finance to the UN Sustainable Development Goals (SDGs). The SDGs rightly break down silos among sectors. The SDGs result from lessons learned from the preceding set of Millennium Development Goals that sustained systemic change cannot be achieved through single-sector goals and approaches. A fundamental feature of the current 2030 Agenda is that it emphasises the complexity and interconnectedness of the different dimensions required to achieve development. It challenges the traditional sector-based approach to looking at education, health or water and sanitation as separate areas. Sectors were traded for terms like "the gender-education-health nexus," and "the climate-land-energy-water nexus."

Three years into the implementation of the SDGs, this report takes stock of the impact of the new agenda on sector policies and for the analysis of sector financing. In the SDG era, providers are required to take a closer look at the various interactions across sectors and adapt strategies to fit the new multidimensional approach. This approach includes supporting global public goods and cross-cutting areas.

We start by broadening the lens on development finance. We need to look at flows beyond official development assistance (ODA) and include other official flows (OOF) – philanthropy, and private funds mobilised. We also need to include tracking funding patterns and trends. With this broader scope, this paper addresses development actors beyond traditional development co-operation providers, and attempts to answer the following questions: What are the sector data gaps? How can sector data be improved? Where do we stand on finance flows by sector, both overall, and by countries most in need? What are the implications of the 2030 Agenda on the use of financial instruments and the use of different channels of delivery?

We have found that, while the SDGs call for "ODA-and-beyond" to meet the cross-cutting ambitions of the 2030 Agenda, we do not yet have the right dashboard in place to monitor progress. This paper is a first step towards further analysis of sector financing, highlighting what is missing, and where the development community should go next. As outlined in the executive summary, the 35% increase in official development finance between 2012 and 2016 means that adopting a smart sectoral approach to SDG finance is essential. Taking this one step further, the findings of this report will inform the development of the first-ever measurement framework for how all official development finance supports the SDGs. Such a framework is total official support for sustainable development (TOSSD), which is currently being developed by an international task force, with the objective of making official development finance more transparent, and ultimately, more effective.

Jorge Moreira da Silva

Director

OECD Development Co-operation Directorate

Acknowledgements

This report was prepared under the direction of Jorge Moreira da Silva, Director of the OECD Development Co-operation Directorate (DCD). It was managed and edited by Guillaume Delalande, Development Finance Policy Analyst and Team Lead, under the overall supervision of Haje Schütte, Head of the Financing for Sustainable Development Division of the DCD and Olivier Cattaneo, Manager of the Policy Analysis and Strategy Unit.

Special thanks go to the authors. Chapter 1 was drafted by Guillaume Delalande, based on the four other chapters. Chapter 2 was drafted by Guillaume Delalande. Chapter 3 was co-drafted by Guillaume Delalande and Emilio Chiofalo, Policy Analyst. Chapter 4 was drafted by Cecilia Piemonte, Statistician. Chapter 5 was drafted by Emilio Chiofalo.

The report was supported by a technical core team: Pierre Blanchard and Valérie Thielemans prepared the dataset, with input from Cécile Sangaré and Tomáš Hos.

The OECD Public Affairs and Communication Directorate produced the publication. Special thanks go to Anne-Lise Prigent and Stacey Bradbury for editorial advice and inputs. Scriptoria copy-edited the report. It was proofread by Stacey Bradbury and the cover design was by Stephanie Coic.

Thanks to Erin Renner Cordell for communication, editorial and media relations support, and to Susan Hodgson, Clare Lannigan and Elise Le Marec for administrative support.

This report has also benefited from comments and contributions from the following: Yasmin Ahmad, Irene Basile, Aussama Bejraoui, Julia Benn, Marisa Berbegal-Ibañez, Pierre Blanchard, Thomas Boehler, Juan Casado-Asensio, Olivier Cattaneo, John Egan, Fredrik Ericsson, Tishka Hope Francis, Valérie Gaveau, Giorgio Gualberti, Jenny Hedman, Tomáš Hos, Jieun Kim, Zeki Kocaata, Frans Lammersen, Kaori Miyamoto, Rachel Morris, Gladys Bindura Mutangadura, Aimée Nichols, Nadine Piefer, Arnaud Pincet, Martin Rivero, Cécile Sangaré, Haje Schütte, Rachel Scott, Jens Sedemund, Henri-Bernard Solignac-Lecomte, Cushla Thompson, Valérie Thielemans, Piera Tortora, Juho Uusihakala, Ann Zimmerman and Rosie Zwart.

Table of contents

Tables

Figures

Boxes

Abbreviations and acronyms

AAAA	Addis Ababa Action Agenda
AfDB	African Development Bank
AIDS	Acquired immunodeficiency syndrome
AsDB	Asian Development Bank
BIO	Belgian Investment Company for Developing Countries
BMI-SBI	Société Belge d'Investissement International
BMGF	Bill & Melinda Gates Foundation
CDB	Caribbean Development Bank
CAGR	Compounded annual growth rate
CDC	CDC Group Plc, formerly the Commonwealth Development Corporation
CIV	Collective investment vehicle
COFIDES	Compañía Española de Financiación del Desarrollo
CRS	Creditor Reporting System
CSO	Civil society organisation
DAC	Development Assistance Committee
DFI	Development finance institution
DFID	Department for International Development
DRM	Domestic resource mobilisation
EBRD	European Bank for Reconstruction and Development
EIB	European Investment Bank
ESS	Environmental and social standard
EU	European Union
FC	Fragile context
FDI	Foreign direct investment
FMO	Nederlandse Financierings-Maatschappij voor Ontwikkelingslanden N.V.
G20	Group of Twenty
GDP	Gross domestic product

GEEREF	Global Energy Efficiency and Renewable Energy Fund
GCF	Green Climate Fund
GEF	Global Environment Facility
GPG	Global public good
HIPC	Heavily indebted poor country
HIV	Human immunodeficiency virus
IATI	International Aid Transparency Initiative
IADB	Inter-American Development Bank
IDA	International Development Association
IBRD	International Bank for Reconstruction and Development
ICT	Information and Communication Technologies
IFC	International Finance Corporation
ILO	International Labour Organisation
IMF	International Monetary Fund
IsDB	Islamic Development Bank
ITC	International Trade Centre
LDC	Least developed country
LIC	Low-income country
LLDC	Landlocked developing country
LMIC	Lower middle-income country
MDB	Multilateral development bank
M&E	Monitoring and evaluation
MENA	Middle East and North Africa
MIGA	Multilateral Investment Guarantee Agency
NGO	Non-governmental organisation
ODA	Official development assistance
ODC	Other developing country
ODF	Official development finance
OECD	Organisation for Economic Co-operation and Development
OeEB	Oesterreichische Entwicklungsbank AG
OOF	Other official flows
OPIC	Overseas Private Investment Corporation
PD/GG	Participatory development and good governance
PEPFAR	President's Emergency Plan for AIDS Relief

PSD	Private sector development
PSE	Private sector engagement
RMNCH	Reproductive, maternal, newborn and child health
SDG	Sustainable Development Goal
SEGIB	Secretaría General Iberoamericana
SIDA	Swedish International Development Cooperation Agency
SIDICSS	Sistema Integrado de Datos de Iberoamérica sobre Cooperación Sur-Sur y Triangular
SIDS	Small island developing state
SIFEM	Swiss Investment Fund for Emerging Markets
SIMEST	Società Italiana per le Imprese all'Estero
SME	Small and medium-sized enterprise
SSC	South-South co-operation
STI	Science, technology and innovation
TA	Technical assistance
TC	Triangular co-operation
TOSSD	Total official support for sustainable development
UAE	United Arab Emirates
UN	United Nations
UNCTAD	United Nations Conference on Trade and Development
UNEP	United Nations Environment Programme
UNHCR	United Nations High Commissioner for Refugees
UMIC	Upper middle-income country
UNDP	United Nations Development Programme
UNDS	United Nations Development System
UNICEF	United Nations Children's Fund
USAID	United States Agency for International Development
USD	United States dollar

Executive summary

In September 2015, international leaders agreed on a new global development agenda comprising 17 Sustainable Development Goals (SDGs) and 169 targets to be achieved by 2030: "Transforming our World: The 2030 Agenda for Sustainable Development".

Providers of development co-operation face a new challenge as they embark on this agenda with growing financial commitments. They primarily design and implement their interventions in developing countries as inputs by sector (e.g. health, education, energy or agriculture). However, the SDGs have multisector expected outcomes (e.g. no poverty, reduced inequalities or sustainable cities and communities). Shifting their focus to the latter thus requires assessing the impact of the resources they invest in each sector against specific SDGs.

Yet doing so is extremely complex. First, because comprehensive, detailed and comparable information from development co-operation providers on their sector activities, including detailed project descriptions, is sometimes missing. Second, because the links between sectors and the SDGs, and, indeed, between the SDGs themselves, are intricate. To use SDG 4, on quality education, as an example: providers can support the achievement of this SDG by investing in the education sector (e.g. building schools and training teachers). They can also do that by investing in the energy sector (e.g. increasing access to electricity in rural areas), which will enable children to study in the evening, and might also support SDG 7, on affordable and clean energy. And third, because this new focus on outcomes requires that providers engage with partner countries to identify their respective SDG priorities, align country programmes with the indicators identified at country level, and target resources appropriately.

This report aims to help development co-operation providers better grasp the implications of the 2030 Agenda for their sector strategies, so that they can effectively support the SDGs by choosing the right instruments, channels and financing approaches. It provides them with an unprecedented, comprehensive picture of official development finance (ODF) allocations by sector by bringing together data for the period 2012-16 on sector financing by country, type of instrument and delivery channel. The analysis includes not only official development assistance, but also other official flows and resources mobilised from the private sector by official development interventions. The report looks into potential data gaps and the challenge of matching the traditional typologies of donors' investments by sector with the expected multisector outcomes framed by the SDGs. It also reviews the sector composition of financial flows to specific income groups and countries most in need, such as least developed countries and small island developing states. Finally, the report takes stock of the use of specific approaches, such as sector budget support or pooled funding.

The report's main conclusions are the following:

- Overall, **ODF increased by 35% in real terms between 2012 and 2016, benefiting all sectors** in developing countries. In 2016, ODF by bilateral and multilateral providers of development co-operation amounted to USD 293.6 billion.
- **Development co-operation providers mobilise private finance only in a handful of sectors**. An estimated USD 22.7 billion of private finance was mobilised every year by official development interventions during the period 2012-16, but, unexpectedly, private finance is hardly mobilised by official interventions in sectors such as water, agriculture, or transport and storage.
- **All providers of development co-operation should make their sector financing information more detailed, more comprehensive and more comparable** to respond to the new, multifaceted SDG framework. In that regard, the total official support for sustainable development measurement framework (TOSSD) is an opportunity for them to make official development finance more transparent.
- **Providers of development co-operation have to map the impact of each sector intervention against each goal, align with the SDG targets defined by each partner country, and appropriately target their interventions**. Support for global public goods will also help, as these are enablers for achieving development gains in multiple sectors.
- **Providers of development co-operation need to look more closely at the specific challenges in each country, especially for countries most in need**. For example, in LLDCs, providers do not sufficiently prioritise infrastructure.
- **Adopting a smart, sector approach to transition finance is essential, but demands new research**. This publication takes an initial look at the benefits of analysing transition finance gaps from a sector perspective.
- **The use of debt instruments to support the commercial and infrastructure sectors is growing, calling for increased attention to fiscal sustainability in countries most in need**. While grants by development co-operation providers are increasing moderately, loans have increased three times faster than grants in recent years. Debt vulnerability is becoming a concern in the most vulnerable economies. The number of developing countries in debt distress or at high risk of debt distress doubled from 12 to 24 between 2013 and 2017.
- **While channels of delivery may vary, depending on sector priorities and strategies, development effectiveness and good donorship need to guide development partners' efforts**. For example, in the social and humanitarian sectors, bilateral providers need to implement good funding practices with civil society organisations and multilaterals implementing projects in the most challenging contexts. This is particularly true for those highly dependent on bilateral resources.

Chapter 1. Overview

This chapter provides an overview of the main highlights of this publication. It is structured around four main sections, corresponding to the four substantive chapters. It provides an overview of official development finance (ODF) allocations for the period 2012-16 by sector, including not only official development assistance (ODA), but also other official flows (OOF) and resources mobilised from the private sector by official development finance interventions. The chapter provides data on sector financing by country, type of instrument and channel of delivery. It looks into potential data gaps and the challenge of matching the traditional typologies of donors' investments by sector with their expected, multisector outcomes, as framed by the Sustainable Development Goals (SDGs). The chapter also provides policy makers and sectoral experts with some insights into the implications of the 2030 Agenda for the sectoral strategies of development co-operation providers.

In September 2015, international leaders agreed on a new global development agenda comprising the 17 Sustainable Development Goals (SDGs) and 169 targets to be achieved by 2030: *"Transforming our World: The 2030 Agenda for Sustainable Development"* (United Nations, 2015[1]).

The SDGs are highly intertwined with sectors, such as health, education, energy or agriculture. Hence, measuring official development finance (ODF) flowing to sectors is critical to designing efficient development strategies in the SDG era. Yet, this exercise is complex, and this report is a first attempt to provide a comprehensive picture of ODF allocations by sector. The analysis includes not only official development assistance (ODA), but also other official flows (OOF) and resources mobilised from the private sector by official development interventions. It provides unique data for the period 2012-16 on sector financing by country, type of instrument and channel of delivery.[1] It looks into potential data gaps and the challenge of matching the traditional typologies of donors' investments by sector with their expected, multi-sectoral outcomes, as framed by the SDGs. The report provides policy makers and sectoral experts with some insights into the implications of the 2030 Agenda for the sectoral strategies of development co-operation providers.

When analysing specific sector allocations, this report focuses on the portion of ODF that is *sector allocable* using the following broad sector groupings and sub-sectors (*non-sector allocable* contributions are those that are not susceptible to allocation by sector, such as general budget support, actions relating to debt, humanitarian aid and internal costs in the donor country). The broad sector groupings and sub-sectors used in this publication are:

- **Social** – this comprises education, health, government and civil society, and other social services.
- **Infrastructure** – this includes water, transport and storage, communications and energy.
- **Production** – this encompasses agriculture, industry, mining and construction, and trade and tourism.
- **Banking and business** – these two sectors are grouped into a single sector grouping.
- **Multisector** – this comprises both the environment sector and multisector activities. General environmental protection activities are classified in the multisector grouping and cover activities related to conservation, protection or amelioration of the physical environment without sector allocation. As a result, these activities do not reflect the totality of the donors' investments targeting environment, but only the part that cannot be allocated to a single sector.

This chapter is structured around four main sections, corresponding to the four substantive chapters of the publication, thus providing an overview of the main messages and findings emerging from the publication.

1.1. Comprehensive, comparable and detailed sectoral data is the basis for effective financing strategies in the Sustainable Development Goal era

In the last decades, the development finance landscape has seen the emergence of a large number of new actors and new instruments, making it challenging to monitor development finance data holistically. Actors beyond traditional official providers, such as private companies and funds, philanthropic foundations and civil society organisations (CSOs) have become key partners in supporting the global development agenda. This has changed the perspective on the instruments and modalities of development co-operation.

Overall, the profusion of sources and databases on external flows makes it hard to easily collate a picture of financing to a given sector (apart from ODF – see below). The diversity of scope, definitions and reporting methods across databases and data providers makes the presentation of a financing picture on a given sector or the comparison of sectoral information across data sources highly challenging. However, many initiatives are taking place to gradually develop a comprehensive sectoral picture, both for official and private development finance.

1.1.1. All providers of development co-operation need to make their sector financing information more detailed and comparable to respond to the new multifaceted SDG framework

The closely intertwined nature of the SDGs makes it challenging to establish a direct and robust link between the SDGs and traditional sectors (such as health, energy, education or agriculture). Providers who wish to contribute to better analyses of sectoral information in the SDG era need to make their sectoral data public and more detailed, focusing on three main tasks:

- **Ensuring the accuracy of the sectoral purpose of the activities**. For example, in the Organisation for Economic Co-operation and Development Creditor Reporting System (OECD CRS[2]), activities need to be reported against sector codes. These provide a strong basis for sectoral analyses. However, if not done appropriately the recording of the sectoral purpose of activities can lead to faulty analyses. In order to avoid this issue, the OECD has put in place many automated checks on reporting. Every year, it manually verifies for accuracy approximately 250 000 records to ensure the consistency of sector codes, for example, against project descriptions.
- **Improving the granularity of sectoral information.** For example, in July 2016, members of the Development Assistance Committee (DAC) of the OECD agreed to introduce a system of "multiple sector codes" in the OECD CRS. This system will allow recording an activity against up to ten sector codes, thus reflecting the reality of many development projects that actually benefit several sectors. This is becoming even more important in an SDG era where the Goals are highly intertwined with sectors.
- **Increasing the availability of detailed descriptive information.** The OECD CRS provides fields for reporting both short and long descriptions of projects. Appropriate descriptions allow the project to be put into context. They provide details on a wide range of dimensions, such as the objectives, the beneficiaries, and the implementation strategy of the project, which are key to analyse ODF and to inform sector strategies of development co-operation providers.

The international community could also find ways to make sectoral data more comparable. From a sectoral perspective, one particular area of attention is to expand the picture of financing of official providers, particularly Arab and other emerging providers, such as the People's Republic of China (hereafter "China"), Brazil and India, so that they gradually publish more and more information, including disaggregated data by sectors. Broader international co-operation flows from providers beyond the membership of the

DAC were estimated at around USD 300 billion in 2014[3]. In the infrastructure sector, estimated combined disbursements for China, India and Arab development partners accounted for 14% of total ODF for infrastructure in 2014. Data for a very large portion of this financing is currently unavailable publicly and the overall financing from these providers might be much bigger than current estimations. For example, going forward, Arab providers could continue (e.g. United Arab Emirates, Kuwait and Saudi Arabia) or start (e.g. Qatar, Oman and Bahrain) publishing information on their development finance efforts, including at the sector level. Traditional providers also ought to seek more engagement with South-South and triangular co-operation providers, as well as with other providers beyond the DAC, including Brazil, China, India, South Africa, Mexico and Costa Rica. Such engagement would help achieve a more comprehensive picture of the financing for development landscape across sectors worldwide.

1.1.2. TOSSD represents a major opportunity for all development partners to make sectoral data more comprehensive and comparable

The concept of total official support for sustainable development (TOSSD)[4] first emerged in 2014 in the course of work undertaken by the OECD DAC to align its statistical system with today's development finance landscape. The new framework aims to provide greater transparency about the full array of officially supported bilateral, multilateral and South-South finance provided in support of sustainable development. TOSSD was first recognised internationally in the Addis Ababa Action Agenda in July 2015 (United Nations, 2015[2]).[5] Its statistical features have been developed since July 2017 by an International Task Force[6] comprising about 25 development policy and statistical experts. Emerging providers are also present as observers to the Task Force.

Figure 1.1. TOSSD: two pillars to capture more information on sustainable development

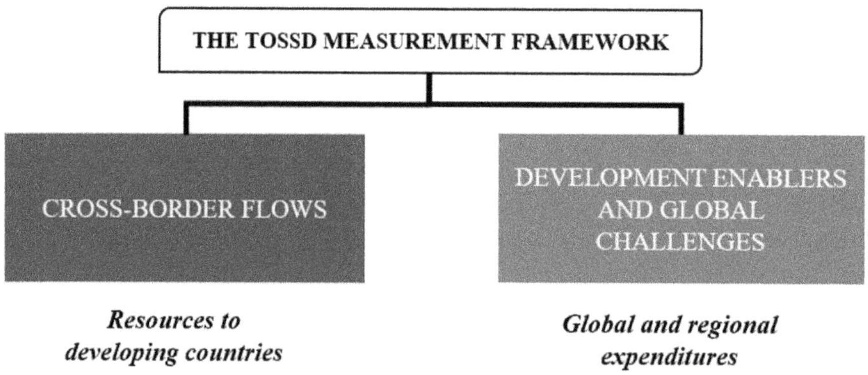

Source: Extracted from the International TOSSD Task Force webpage (accessed 31 October 2018), http://www.oecd.org/dac/financing-sustainable-development/development-finance-standards/tossd-task-force.htm

TOSSD is envisaged as a two-pillar framework (See Figure 1.1) that would capture both cross-border flows to developing countries (Pillar I) and the resources that support development enablers and address global challenges at the regional and global levels (Pillar II). While both pillars will provide information relevant for sectoral analyses, the second pillar has the potential to unveil some sectoral information currently missing in international statistics. This includes support to international tribunals (in the justice sector) or activities supporting oceans in international waters (in the environment sector), two areas that are not well captured in existing databases.

The TOSSD framework will capture all resources in support of SDG-related investments (Table 1.1), including grants, loans and equity investments. It will also include amounts mobilised from the private sector, which will help create incentives to mobilise more resources from the private sector.[7] A number of "satellite" indicators will complement the TOSSD framework to put official resources into context, including private flows at market terms and remittances, and information on private finance for development coming from private foundations.

Thus, TOSSD represents a major opportunity for all development co-operation providers to make sectoral data more comprehensive and comparable, thus providing greater transparency on ODF flows.

Table 1.1. The emerging framework of TOSSD

Types of flows	Description
A. Grants	Including grants and technical assistance
B. Financial transactions	Including debt instruments and equity investments
Total official flows (A+B)	In gross terms
C. **Resources mobilised from the private sector**	Private resources mobilised by official development interventions, regardless of the country of origin of the funds
Envisaged "satellite" indicators	
D. Private flows at market terms	Foreign direct investment and other securities, including bonds
E. Private philanthropy	Provided by private philanthropic foundations for development
F. Remittances	

Source: Compilation based on information available at http://www.oecd.org/dac/financing-sustainable-development/development-finance-standards/tossd-task-force.htm, (Delalande and Gaveau, 2018[3]) and (Delalande, Halvorson-Quevedo and Sangaré, 2018[4])

1.2. In a context of growing official development finance, the integrated nature of the Sustainable Development Goals agenda requires rethinking sector financing approaches

1.2.1. ODF is growing and benefitting all sectors

In 2016, ODF by bilateral and multilateral providers of development co-operation amounted to USD 293.6 billion – a growth of 35% between 2012 and 2016 in real terms. Of this increase, 64% was support from bilateral providers (46% from DAC providers and 18% from non-DAC providers) and 36% came from multilateral institutions. Overall, ODF grew at an average rate of 7.8% per year during this period in real terms.

Sector-allocable ODF, which is the portion of ODF that can be analysed by sector[8], represented about USD 224 billion in 2016. The breakdown of ODF across broad sector categories has not changed much in the last five years, reflecting the stability of sectoral allocation policies by official providers (Figure 1.2). ODF to broad sector groupings is broken down into three tiers, with "Social sectors" and "Infrastructure" representing two-thirds (34% respectively on average during the period for each of the two groupings). The last third is shared by the production sectors (14% of ODF on average). "Banking and business" and "Multisector" activities represented approximately 9% of ODF during the period 2012-16 (Figure 1.2).

Figure 1.2. The growth in ODF is benefitting all sector groupings

ODF by broad sector grouping, 2012-16, 2016 constant prices, USD billion commitments

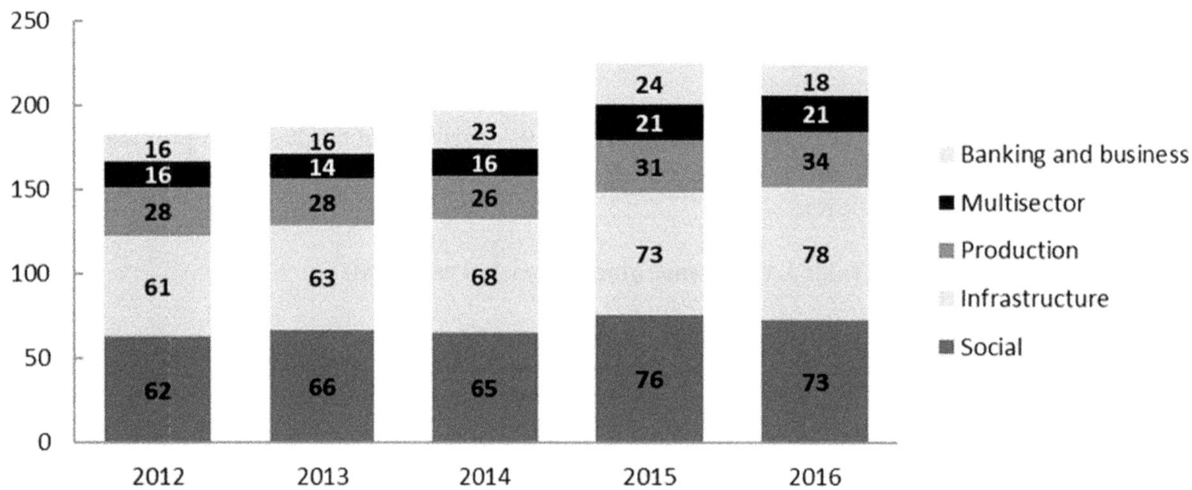

Source: (OECD, 2018[5]), "International development statistics (database)", http://www.oecd.org/dac/financing-sustainable-development/development-finance-data/idsonline.htm.

StatLink https://doi.org/10.1787/888933855390

1.2.2. Development partners only mobilise private finance in a handful of sectors

Providers increasingly mobilise private finance for development. Since 2012, amounts mobilised by official development interventions are estimated to have more than doubled, from USD 15 billion in 2012 to an estimated USD 33 billion in 2016.

From a sectoral perspective, the mobilisation of private finance takes place in many different sectors and, unsurprisingly, in much bigger volumes in sectors where prospects of financial return for the private sector are high. On average for the period 2012-16, more than 80% of the total private finance mobilised took place in four sectors, "banking and business", "energy", "industry" and "mining and construction" (Figure 1.3). Private finance is hardly mobilised in social sectors (e.g. health, education and government, and civil society), even though these sectors do present some potential to attract the private sector. Surprisingly however, other sectors, where the potential for mobilising resources could be considered as high, given the traditional involvement of the private sector, do not show a high level of private finance mobilised by official providers. This is, for example, the case in "water", "agriculture" and the "transport and storage" sectors.

Figure 1.3. Private finance is only mobilised in a handful of sectors

ODF and private finance mobilised through official development finance interventions by individual sectors, average 2012-16, 2016 constant prices, USD billion commitments

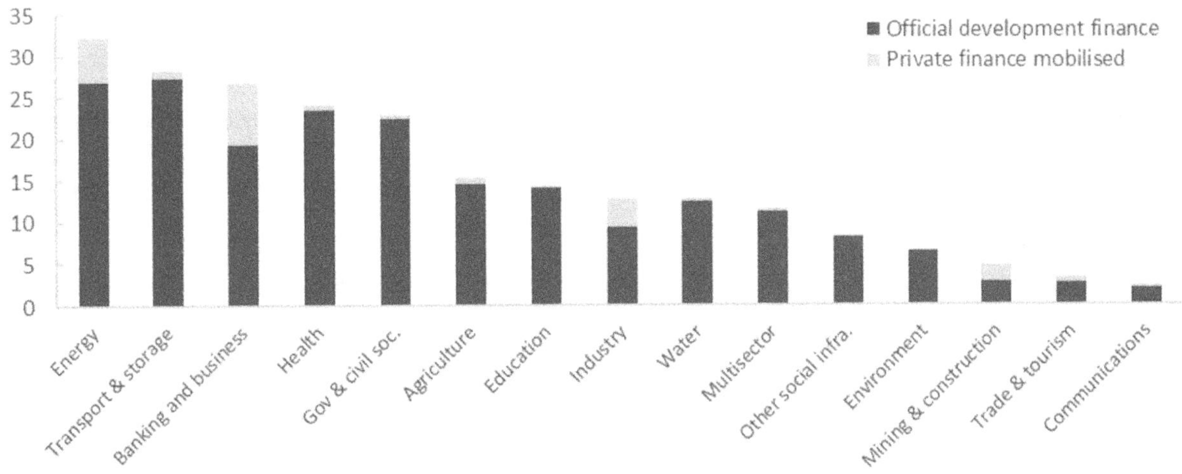

Source: (OECD, 2018[5]), "International development statistics (database)", http://www.oecd.org/dac/financing-sustainable-development/development-finance-data/idsonline.htm and (OECD, 2016[6]), "OECD DAC survey on amounts mobilised from the private sector by official development finance interventions 2012-2015", http://www.oecd.org/dac/financing-sustainable-development/development-finance-standards/mobilisation.htm.

StatLink https://doi.org/10.1787/888933855447

1.2.3. The SDGs are expected results, not sectors of intervention. Providers of development co-operation need to adjust their sector financing strategies to align with partner country targets

The SDGs represent an integrated and complex development framework that goes beyond sectors. To adjust to this new framework, providers need to adapt their sector financing strategies.

Thus, support for traditional sectors is only one among several strategies and approaches for development partners to carry out development co-operation in the new context of the 2030 Agenda. At the global level, development partners can contribute to the SDGs by supporting global public goods. At country level, they can complement their country sectoral approaches with other strategies using themes rather than sectors (e.g. private sector development) or by mainstreaming cross-cutting approaches (e.g. gender equality).

In practice, strategic and programmatic design and implementation requires (see Figure 1.4):

- prioritising areas that align with developing countries needs and priorities
- developing sectoral and thematic country programmes that align objectives and results expected with SDG targets
- monitoring and evaluating results using frameworks that are aligned with the SDGs

Figure 1.4. How can donors align sector financing strategies with the Sustainable Development Goals?

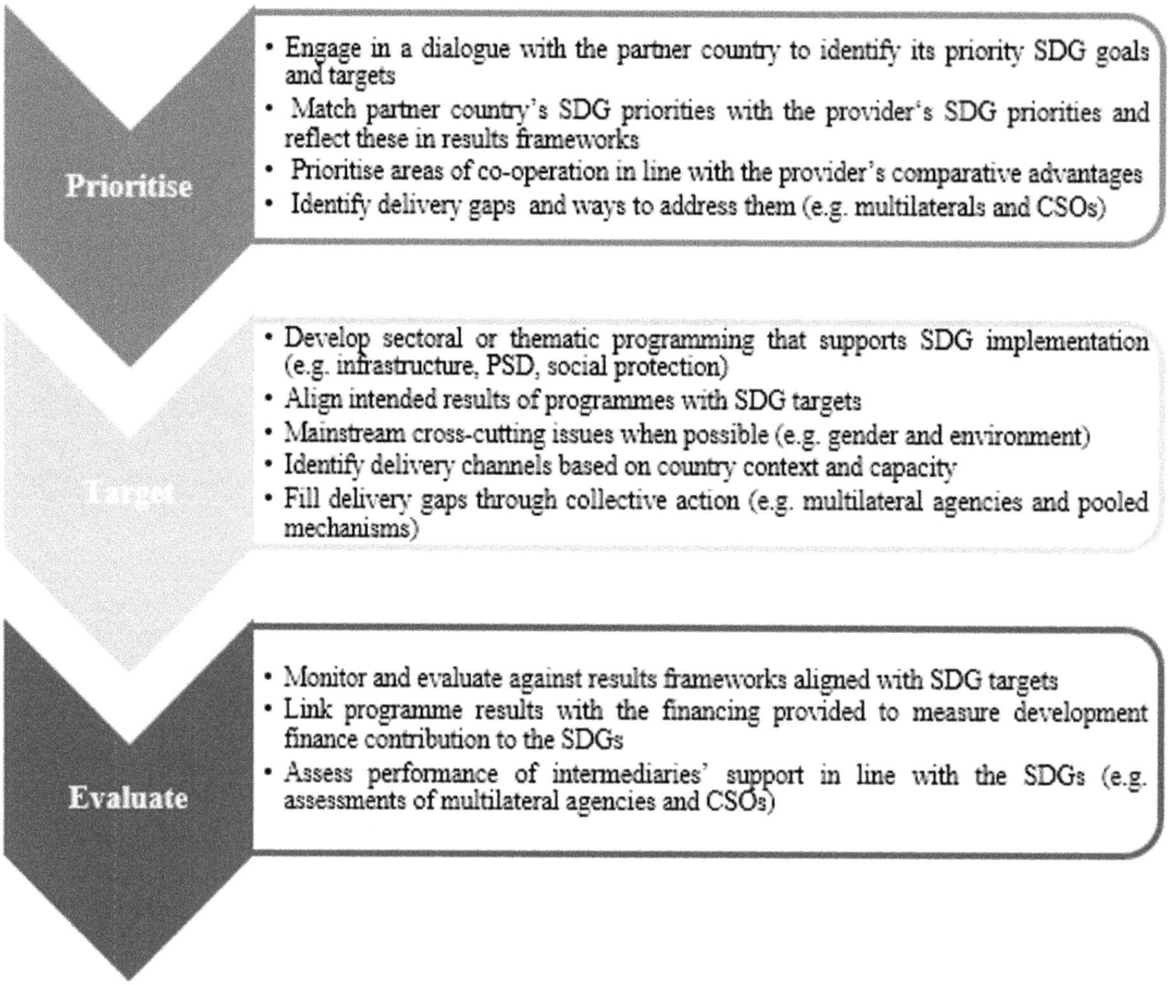

Source: Authors

1.2.4. Resources targeting the SDGs have to be distributed appropriately across sectors and countries

Getting financing strategies right will be indispensable to meeting SDG financing needs in developing countries, which are estimated at between USD 3 and 4 trillion a year (UNCTAD, 2014[7]). The new comprehensive, integrated and, mostly unfunded development agenda points to the importance of both the quantity of financing and the appropriate targeting of this financing. This means:

- mobilising sufficient financing volumes
- ensuring a balanced targeting of resources (sectoral/thematic areas, country allocation, type of beneficiaries, type of instrument and concessionality level, channel of implementation, etc.)

- focusing on impact (short-term and long-term results, public and private mobilisation effect, alignment with local needs, integration of cross-cutting issues, etc.).

Development partners need to co-ordinate their activities to ensure a balanced distribution of resources across sectors to achieve all the SDGs. For example, sectors presenting clear business opportunities (e.g. information and communications technology and energy) attract more private investment than those that have traditionally been serviced by the public sector (e.g. health and education). Bilateral and multilateral development partners need to ensure that sufficient resources are provided both for sectors that present business opportunities and those that support non-commercial initiatives, such as public sector and/or CSO projects, particularly in social sectors.

1.3. Sector financing in the Sustainable Development Goals era needs to adapt to different country contexts

In recent years, the OECD DAC has been working to develop co-operation approaches tailored to a wide variety of country contexts. These include different income categories (low-income countries [LICs], lower middle-income countries [LMICs], and upper middle-income countries [UMICs]). The DAC has also focused on specific groups of countries most in need (least developed countries [LDCs], landlocked developing countries [LLDCs], small island developing states [SIDS] and countries in fragile contexts [FCs]). When relevant, the above country groupings are compared with "Other developing countries" (ODCs), which includes all countries on the OECD DAC list of ODA recipients (OECD, 2018[8]) excluding those in the country grouping under study. Comparing country groupings to ODCs highlights the extent to which development finance patterns in the country groupings differ from those in the rest of the developing countries outside this grouping.

1.3.1. As countries climb the income per capita ladder, concessional resources decline, and non-concessional resources increase

The key consideration when a country develops is to ensure a long-lasting impact of its development finance efforts. This implies a progressive mobilisation of domestic and private resources in a sound macroeconomic context (e.g. debt sustainability) towards independence from ODA while avoiding economic and development setbacks. As countries climb on the income per capita ladder, the relative weights of the different financing resources change. ODA resources decline, while OOF, private and domestic revenue mobilisation resources grow, with different patterns, and remittances show a parabolic trend (growing, reaching a peak, and then declining).

As such, while this report focuses on ODF, the observations made should be seen in the overall context of a wider set of flows comprised of both official and private flows for development. With regards to ODF, as countries pursue their development pathways, it appears clearly that ODA tends to decrease and OOF tend to increase (Figure 1.5). Thus, ODA represents 93% of flows to LICs, where OOF represent the remaining 7%. The ODA portion falls to 64% in LMICs – OOFs then account for 36% in this category. In UMICs, the breakdown trend between ODA and OOF is almost the opposite of that in LMICs, with ODA reaching 34% of total official flows and OOFs 66%.

Figure 1.5. Concessionality of ODF decreases as countries develop economically

Share of ODA and OOF in total ODF by income and sector groupings, average 2012-16, 2016 constant prices, USD billion commitments.

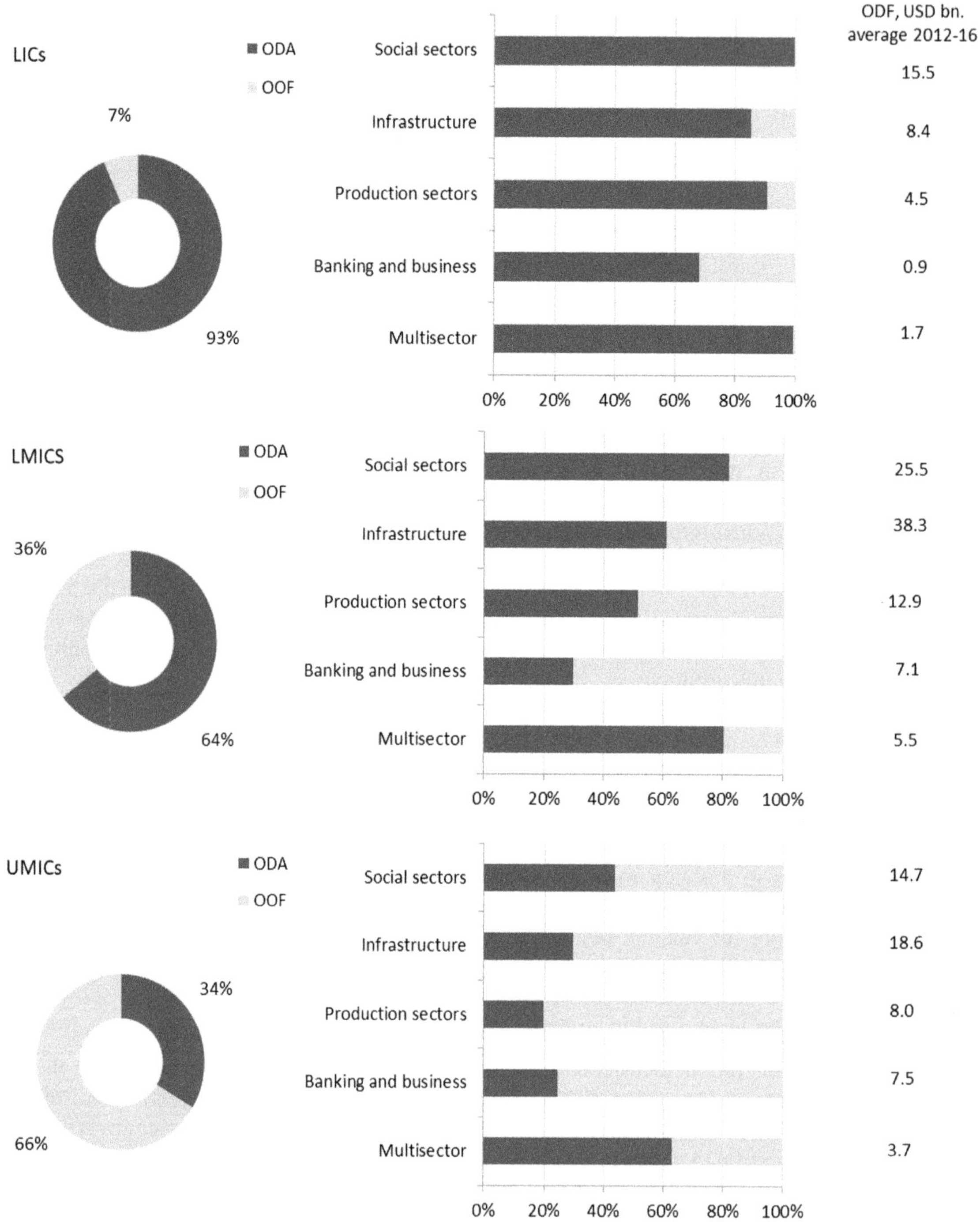

Source: (OECD, 2018[5]) "International development statistics (database)", OECD, Paris, http://www.oecd.org/dac/financing-sustainable-development/development-finance-data/idsonline.htm.

StatLink https://doi.org/10.1787/888933855751

Looking at a more detailed picture of sectors, the report also reveals important findings for providers of development co-operation, including:

- **Allocations of OOF to the "education" and "health" sectors in LMICs appear much lower than in the other social sectors**. The share of OOF in LMICs amounts to only 6% in health and 12% in education, as opposed to 28% in the government and civil society sector, with other social sectors at 34%. Making more resources available for education and health can boost economic productivity by tackling the root causes of the "middle-income trap".
- **Agriculture faces considerable challenges in attracting OOF compared to other productive sectors, across all developing country income categories**. Only 6% of ODF to LICs is in the form of OOF. As countries develop, this proportion remains far below that in the other productive sectors. The share of OOF in agriculture reaches 57% in the UMIC status, when other productive sectors reach around 90%.

1.3.2. LDCs are highly funded by concessional finance, with the social sectors and infrastructure attracting most of the donor efforts

The LDC category contains 47 developing countries[9], representing 13% of the world's population and 38% of the world's extreme poor. These countries are categorised as having long-term structural handicaps that require special attention.

Total ODF to LDCs amounted to USD 45 billion during the period 2012-16. Concessional finance represented 91% or USD 40.8 billion (see Figure 1.6). The social sectors and infrastructure attracted most of the donor efforts (these two sectors represented 77% of total ODF to LDCs, mainly in the form of concessional flows). More granular sector allocation analysis reveals that health, followed by the government and civil society sectors, are the two social sectors most supported by providers of development co-operation.

While this publication focuses on providing an overview of sector financing, the analysis carried out raised a number of questions related to LDC financing. These require further study. For example, is the low level of OOF explained by the specific needs of LDCs in terms of concessional finance? Or could it be that donors do not wish to carry out OOF operations because they first need to maximise their ODA levels to meet their ODA commitments? Are social and/or economic vulnerabilities, the other two factors, in addition to GNI per capita, that determine the LDC status such that they justify low levels of OOF in certain sectors (Alonso, 2014[9])?[10] Or is it that LDCs' risk ratings are so high that it makes it simply prohibitive for them to borrow? Finally, could this situation reflect debt sustainability issues that prohibit borrowing from responsible lenders?

Figure 1.6. Least developed countries are highly funded by concessional finance

Share of ODA and OOF in total ODF (left hand chart) and share of ODA and OOF in total ODF by sector groupings (right hand chart) in LDCs, average 2012-16, 2016 constant prices, USD commitments

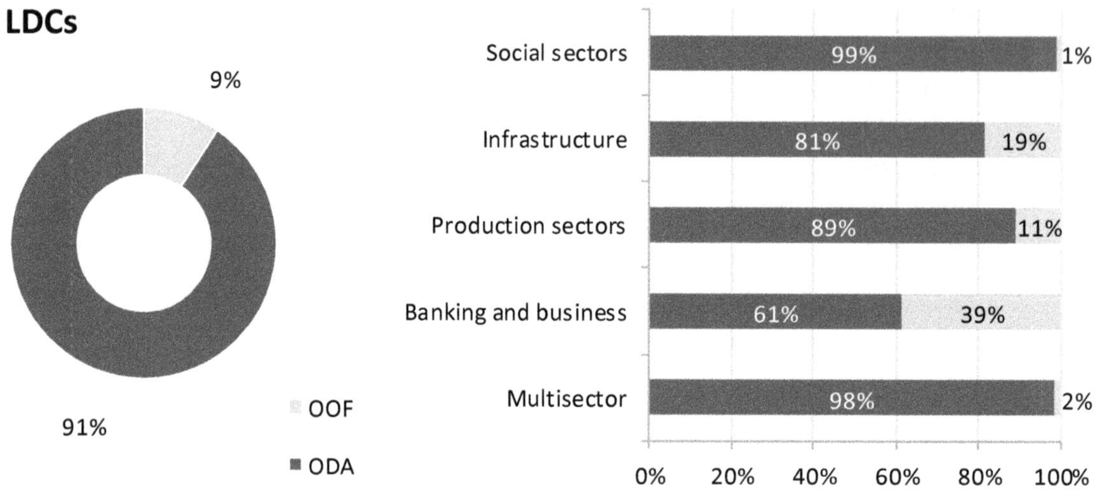

Source: (OECD, 2018[5]), "International development statistics (database)", http://www.oecd.org/dac/financing-sustainable-development/development-finance-data/idsonline.htm.

StatLink https://doi.org/10.1787/888933855789

1.3.3. In LLDCs, providers do not prioritise infrastructure

Among developing countries, the LLDC category is a grouping of 32 countries[11] that face particular challenges related to their lack of direct access to the sea and geographical isolation from international markets. For these countries, imports and exports of goods and services need to transit through other countries, which generates higher trade costs and major logistical and infrastructure challenges (e.g. changes in transport modes, and international road and rail connections with neighbours' networks) that impose serious constraints on their development.

Infrastructure is the main sector where LLDCs need assistance in order to overcome their isolation and facilitate their path to development. Providers' sectoral allocations to LLDCs are mainly focused on the social sectors with infrastructure being only the second most supported sector grouping. Total ODF to the social sectors represented USD 13 billion during the period 2012-16 (41% of total ODF to LLDCs). Support to infrastructure amounted to USD 10.3 billion (33% of total ODF to LLDCs) (Figure 1.7). Also, LLDCs get a similar share of their ODF going to key infrastructure sectors in comparison to ODCs (33% compared to 34% for ODCs). Providers should therefore carefully consider increasing their support on hard and soft infrastructure investment in LLDCs.

Figure 1.7. Providers need to redouble efforts towards infrastructure investments in landlocked developing countries

Share of ODA and OOF in LLDCs by sector groupings, and shares of ODF by sector groupings in LLDCs and ODCs, average 2012-16, 2016 constant prices, USD commitments

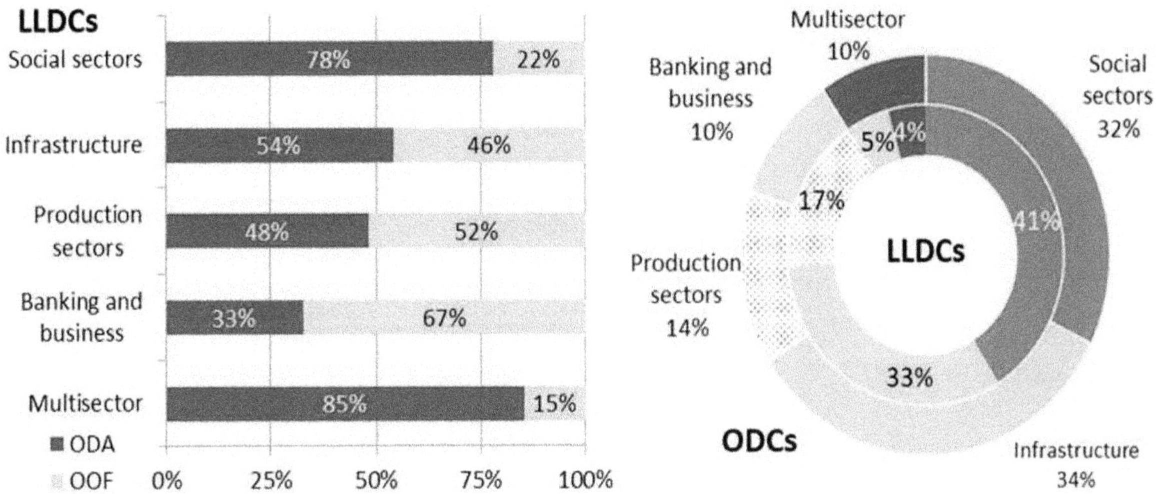

Note: The double centred pie chart at the right shows, in the inner circle, total ODF to LLDCs and, in the outer circle, total ODF to all ODCs.
Source: (OECD, 2018[5]), "International development statistics (database)", OECD, Paris, http://www.oecd.org/dac/financing-sustainable-development/development-finance-data/idsonline.htm.

StatLink https://doi.org/10.1787/888933855827

1.3.4. In SIDS, for almost all sectors, non-concessional finance is lower than in ODCs, at any income category

The OECD DAC identifies 35 countries[12] as SIDS, located across different geographic areas. SIDS share a number of structural challenges and geophysical constraints that result in disproportionately large economic, social and environmental challenges. These structural features have a determinant impact on SIDS' ability to access finance (OECD, 2018[10]) (OECD/The World Bank, 2016[11]).

During 2012-16, SIDS received each year on average USD 4.3 billion in official concessional finance from bilateral and multilateral donors[13]. A particularly salient aspect of SIDS financing is that, for almost all sub-sectors, non-concessional finance is lower for SIDS than for ODCs in any income category (see column 'share of OOF' in Table 1.2).

Table 1.2. SIDS find it difficult to follow a virtuous transition path towards more other official flows

ODF by sector in LMIC- and UMIC-SIDS vs. ODCs, average 2012-16, USD million commitments, 2016 prices

LMIC-SIDS	ODA	OOF	Total ODF	Share of OOF	Other LMICs	ODA	OOF	Total ODF	Share of OOF
Social sectors					**Social sectors**				
Education	201.3	0.0	201.3	0%	Education	5 064.7	716.1	5780.7	12%
Health	218.1	0.0	218.1	0%	Health	7 439.1	471.1	7 910.2	29%
Gov. & civil soc.	333.1	3.3	336.4	1%	Gov. & civil soc.	5 290.4	2 204.3	7 494.7	6%
Other social	51.6	0.0	51.6	0%	Other social	2 313.6	1 209.7	3 523.3	34%
Infrastructure					**Infrastructure**				
Water	91.3	0.7	92.0	1%	Water	4 525.0	1 915.7	6 440.7	30%
Energy	77.9	36.2	114.1	32%	Energy	8 348.8	7 464.3	15 813.1	47%
Transport & storage	320.6	98.0	418.7	23%	Transport & storage	9 683.1	4 816.7	14 499.8	33%
Communications	15.3	7.7	23.0	34%	Communications	303.2	553.7	856.9	65%
Production sectors					**Production sectors**				
Agriculture	114.2	2.1	116.3	2%	Agriculture	4 871.7	1 459.1	6 330.8	23%
Industry	2.6	1.8	4.4	41%	Industry	874.9	3 343.5	4 218.4	79%
Mining & construction	1.1	5.0	6.1	81%	Mining & construction	378.9	1 229.8	1 608.8	76%
Trade & tourism	9.7	0.0	9.7	0%	Trade & tourism	390.9	261.4	652.3	40%
Banking & business	23.6	9.5	33.0	29%	**Banking & business**	2 085.0	4 959.3	7 044.4	70%
Multisector	164.3	0.0	164.3	0%	**Multisector**	4 229.4	1 076.4	5 305.8	20%
UMIC-SIDS	**ODA**	**OOF**	**Total ODF**	**Share of OOF**	**Other UMICs**	**ODA**	**OOF**	**Total ODF**	**Share of OOF**
Social sectors					**Social sectors**				
Education	149.5	101.0	250.4	40%	Education	1 810.4	1 674.1	3 484.4	48%
Health	126.0	156.0	282.0	55%	Health	1 347.2	1 268.8	2 616.0	49%
Gov. & civil soc.	162.6	166.2	328.8	51%	Gov. & civil soc.	2 082.7	2 924.6	5 077.3	58%
Other social	40.8	116.8	157.6	74%	Other social	645.4	1 858.0	2 503.3	74%
Infrastructure					**Infrastructure**				
Water	144.6	25.4	170.0	15%	Water	817.1	2 352.2	3 169.3	74%
Energy	145.7	121.0	266.7	45%	Energy	1 869	4 155	6 024	69%
Transport & storage	117.1	178.3	295.4	60%	Transport & storage	2 100.9	5 824.9	7 925.8	73%
Communications	25.8	26.3	52.1	51%	Communications	173.3	490.4	663.7	74%
Production sectors					**Production sectors**				
Agriculture	112.6	18.2	130.7	13%	Agriculture	897.5	1 327.9	2 225.4	60%
Industry	18.9	12.5	31.3	40%	Industry	322.9	3 543.3	3 866.2	92%
Mining & construction	2.1	12.3	14.4	86%	Mining & construction	127.1	706.7	833.8	85%
Trade & tourism	18.6	39.0	57.6	68%	Trade & tourism	66.8	822.7	889.5	92%
Banking & business	36.6	197.3	233.9	84%	**Banking & business**	1 782.3	5 809.9	7 592.2	77%
Multisector	244.0	9.1	253.1	4%	**Multisector**	2 056.8	1 351.8	3 408.6	40%

Source: (OECD, 2018[5]) "International development statistics (database)", OECD, Paris, http://www.oecd.org/dac/financing-sustainable-development/development-finance-data/idsonline.htm.

StatLink https://doi.org/10.1787/888933856017

1.3.5. In fragile contexts, providers of development co-operation use guarantee instruments much more than in other developing countries

The OECD DAC defines fragility as the combination of exposure to risk and insufficient capacity of the state, system and/or communities to manage, absorb or mitigate those risks. The fragility framework used in this report is based on OECD work and is built around five dimensions – economic, environmental, political, societal, and security (OECD, 2016[12]) (OECD, 2018[13]). Using this fragility framework, the 2018 OECD *States of Fragility Report* identifies 58 contexts of fragility (28 are LICs, 26 LMICs and 4 UMICs), including 15 in extreme fragility.

Because of the nature of the FCs grouping, and the many variables considered, the final list of FCs is very diverse. As a result, compiling sectoral statistics for this group of 58 FCs does not appear sufficiently robust. As a way to advance the policy discussion on interventions in FCs, this subsection provides an overview on the use of various financial instruments, including risk-management instruments, recognising that FCs are often perceived as riskier areas by both public and private actors.

As shown in Figure 1.8, 22% of all private finance mobilised by ODF interventions target FCs. When looking at the composition of instruments used to mobilise this finance in fragile and non-FCs, it appears that providers extensively use guarantees in FCs. Of the amounts mobilised in FCs, 65% are done so using guarantee instruments, as against only 38% in non-FCs. This figure is encouraging as it shows that providers effectively consider the risk perceived by the private sector and use appropriate instruments, such as guarantees, to address it.

Figure 1.8. Amounts mobilised in fragile contexts using guarantee instruments, against similar amounts mobilised in non-fragile contexts

Share of amounts mobilised from the private sector by ODF interventions and share of instruments used to mobilise private finance in FCs and non-FCs, average 2012-16, 2016 constant prices, USD commitments

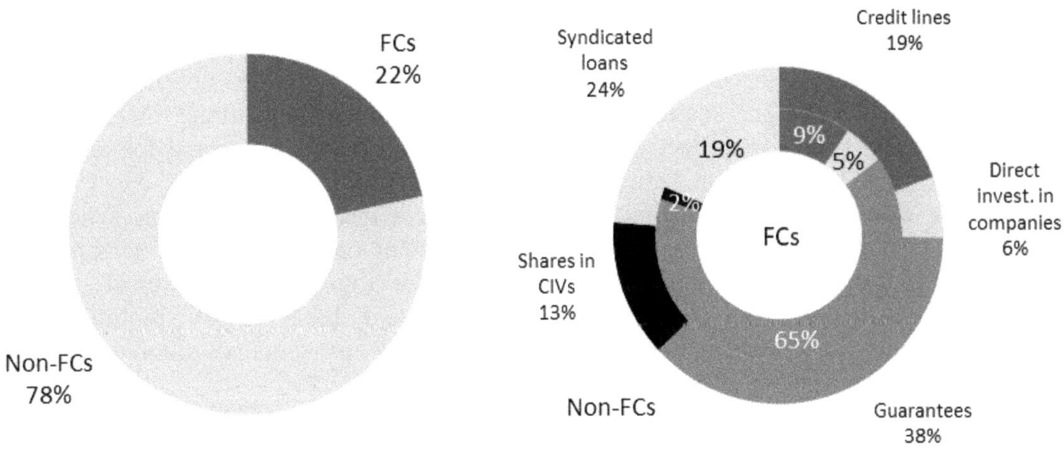

Note: the double pie chart on the right shows FCs in the inner circle and all ODCs in the outer circle.
Source: (OECD, 2018[5]), "International development statistics (database)", OECD, Paris, http://www.oecd.org/dac/financing-sustainable-development/development-finance-data/idsonline.htm and (OECD, 2016[6]), "OECD DAC survey on amounts mobilised from the private sector by official development finance interventions 2012-2015", http://www.oecd.org/dac/financing-sustainable-development/development-finance-standards/mobilisation.htm with estimates for 2016.

StatLink https://doi.org/10.1787/888933855903

1.4. Development partners can effectively support the Sustainable Development Goals by choosing instruments, channels and financing approaches appropriately

1.4.1. Providers of development co-operation have at their disposal a wide array of development finance instruments to implement their sector strategies

ODF is provided using five main groups of instruments:

- **Grants:** transfers in cash and in kind where no legal debt is incurred.
- **Debt instruments:** transfers in cash and in kind where legal debt is incurred (e.g. loans, bonds and other securities) or could be incurred when certain events occur (e.g. reimbursable grants).
- **Equity:** a share in the ownership of a company or a collective investment scheme.
- **Mezzanine finance:** hybrid instruments, such as subordinated loans and preferred equity, that present risk profiles between senior loans and equity.
- **Guarantees/insurance:** risk-sharing agreements under which the guarantor agrees to pay to the lender/investor part or the entire amount due on a loan, equity or other instrument in the event of non-payment by the borrower or loss of value in case of investment.

While grants, debt instruments, equity investment and mezzanine finance are funded positions (i.e. there is an upfront transfer of resources), guarantees and insurance are unfunded. This means that the transfer of resources occurs only under certain conditions, mainly if a default of payment occurs.

1.4.2. The interest and resources to promote commercial solutions that can close important financing gaps in infrastructure, climate change and social services are growing

Amounts mobilised from the private sector are still small when compared to the USD trillions that are needed to close the financing gaps to achieve the SDGs. In fact, according to a recent survey conducted by the OECD, the amounts mobilised from the private sectors from guarantees, syndicated loans, credit lines, direct investment in companies and shares in collective investment vehicles (CIV) accounted for an annual average of USD 20.3 billion between 2013 and 2015 (OECD, 2016[6]). Most of this financing was mobilised through guarantees and debt instruments, such as syndicated loans and credit lines, in areas with clear commercial opportunities, such as energy, banking, industry, and mining and construction (see Figure 1.9). Conversely, equity instruments, such as direct investment in companies and shares in CIV, mobilised less financing from the private sector compared to the other instruments, although they are used by a greater number of institutions.

Figure 1.9. Amounts mobilised from the private sector by official development finance interventions are still small and concentrated in a few sectors

Amounts mobilised from the private sector by selected ODF interventions by sector, average 2012-15, current prices, USD billion commitments

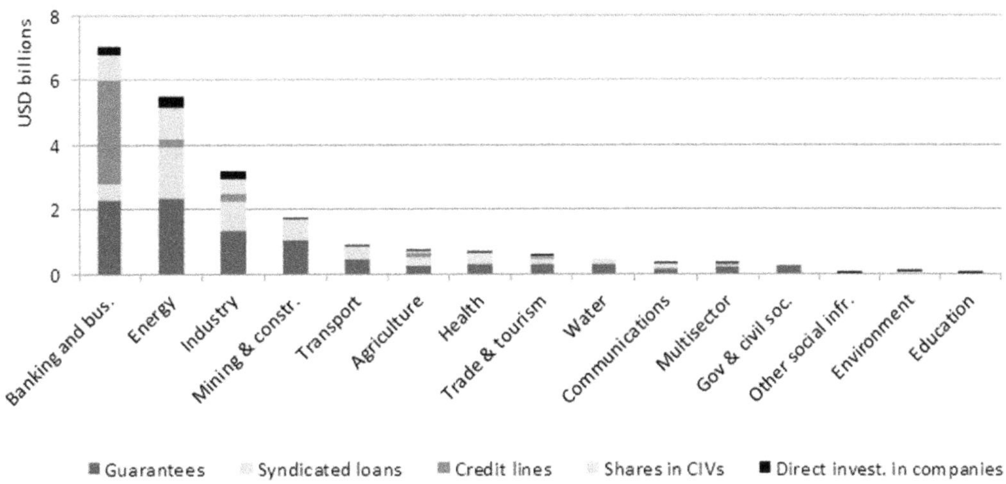

Source: (OECD, 2016[6]) "OECD DAC survey on amounts mobilised from the private sector by official development finance interventions 2012-2015", http://www.oecd.org/dac/financing-sustainable-development/development-finance-standards/mobilisation.htm.

StatLink https://doi.org/10.1787/888933856074

Albeit still relatively small, private amounts mobilised by ODF are set to grow considerably in the coming years. This is because of the increasing lending capacity of development finance institutions (DFIs) and multilateral development banks (MDBs), as well as an increasing interest in commercial solutions for development. The Addis Ababa Action Agenda, the Paris Agreement and intergovernmental processes at meetings of the Group of 20 (G20) and UN clearly show a widespread political commitment to promoting commercial solutions to close important financing gaps in the infrastructure, climate change and social services[(United Nations, 2015[2]); (G20, 2017[14]); (OECD, 2017[15])]. Political commitment to increase private finance is reflected in unprecedented capital reforms by MDBs to increase lending capacity, including joint targets at the G20 level (AIIB et al., 2017[16]). In the same vein, the financial capacity of bilateral DFIs is expanding considerably. For example, European Development Finance Institutions' annual commitments increased from USD 11 billion in 2005 to USD 36 billion in 2015 (EDFI, 2016[17]). This increase was mainly driven by government replenishments and reinvested earnings, suggesting a continuing upward trend in the short to medium term. This trend is compounded by widespread interest of bilateral donors in providing commercial solutions for development, including through blended finance funds and facilities.

1.4.3. The use of debt instruments to support the infrastructure and commercial sectors requires attention to fiscal sustainability in countries most in need

While grants are increasing moderately, at a compounded annual growth rate (CAGR) of 2%, loans increase at a CAGR of 7%, i.e. three times faster than grants (see Figure 1.10).

In volume terms, the trend reflects a widespread boost in non-concessional loans by MDBs and a global upsurge in infrastructure finance by both bilateral and multilateral providers. This includes loans to LDCs and other LICs, which is reshaping the ODF architecture across income groups and sectors. While in 2012 two-thirds of sector-allocable ODF to LDCs and other LICs were in the form of grants, these instruments only accounted for slightly more than half in 2016. This trend was driven by minor increases in grants in most sectors and an important rise of concessional and non-concessional loans for the infrastructure and social sectors. In middle-income countries, there is an important upward trend of non-concessional debt, which is boosting resources for infrastructure and production sectors in LMICs, and financing for every allocable sector, including social sectors, in UMICs.

Figure 1.10. Loans are playing a bigger role in most sectors in the development finance architecture, particularly in infrastructure

Shares of concessional and non-concessional loans in total ODF from bilateral and multilateral development partners (left hand chart) and total of concessional and non-concessional loans by sector groupings (right hand chart), 2012-16, 2016 prices, USD billion commitment

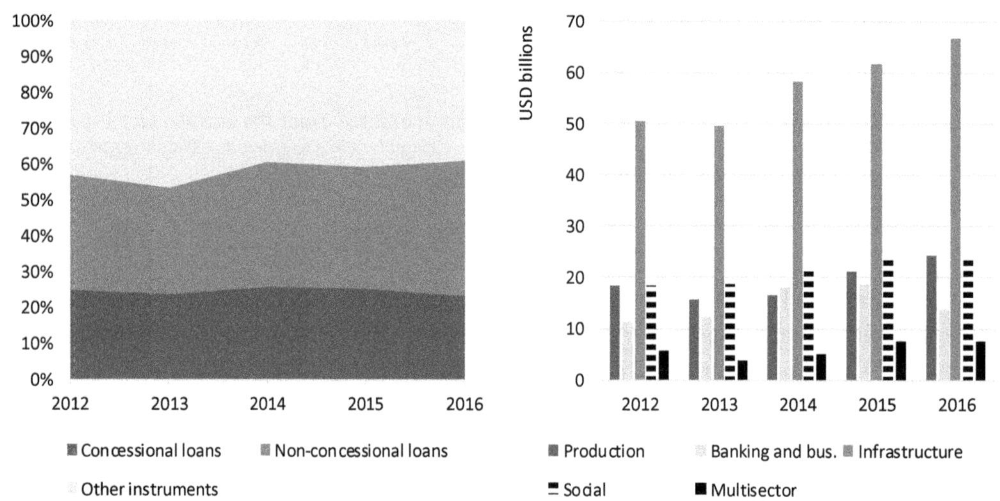

Source: (OECD, 2018[5]), " International development statistics (database)", http://www.oecd.org/dac/financing-sustainable-development/development-finance-data/idsonline.htm.

StatLink https://doi.org/10.1787/888933856169

1.4.4. Around 8% of sector-allocable ODF is implemented using sector budget support and 4 % is channelled using pooled funding

In a context where the 2030 Agenda calls for increased policy coherence and more co-ordinated approaches, development partners allocate most of their sectoral financing for specific projects rather than as sector budget support and pooled funding (Figure 1.11). Around 8% of sector-allocable ODF is implemented using sector budget support and 4 % is channelled using pooled funding.

Figure 1.11. Project-type interventions are prevalent in most sectors

ODF volumes for sectoral programmes by type of intervention (left hand chart) and shares of ODF for sectoral programmes by type of intervention and sector grouping (right hand chart), annual average 2012-2016, 2016 prices, USD billion commitment

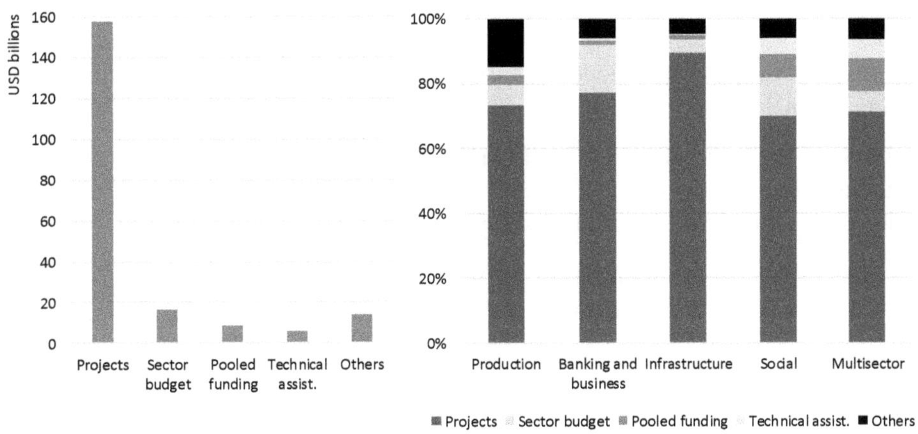

Source: (OECD, 2018[5]), "International development statistics (database)", http://www.oecd.org/dac/financing-sustainable-development/development-finance-data/idsonline.htm.

StatLink https://doi.org/10.1787/888933856207

Sector budget support is about loans, grants and technical assistance provided for the implementation of national sector strategies of recipient governments (e.g. energy, health and education). Resources are generally provided through the recipient government's system, usually the ministry of finance. They are then channelled to the sector ministry or public agency responsible for budget execution (Williamson and Dom, 2010[18]).

There are both proponents and opponents of sectoral budget support. Proponents point out that this type of financing increases national ownership, aligns with domestic sectoral strategies, and allows for harmonisation among donors. Opponents emphasise that it can lead to corruption and misappropriation of funds in contexts with high political and fiduciary risks. Nevertheless, a comprehensive review of general and sector budget support evaluations of donors suggests that evidence is needed to confirm the assumed risks of corruption of budget support (Orth et al., 2017[19]).

Pooled funding mechanisms are financing vehicles that earmark or blend resources to support sector, integrated or system-wide programming and implementation. Providers contribute resources to an autonomous account, managed jointly with other providers and/or the recipient, or through more complex fund structures similar to multilateral institutions. Supporters of pooled funding mechanisms indicate that these mechanisms offer the opportunity to increase the quantity and the quality of financing for a cross-cutting and integrated development agenda (OECD, 2015[20]). This is achieved by consolidating scattered earmarked funding, promoting innovation, fostering policy coherence and co-ordination, and increasing financial mobilisation. However, pooled funding mechanisms can also increase transaction costs and fragmentation. They also need governance mechanisms that ensure country ownership and co-ordination and require donor-financing streams that are predictable and flexible.

1.4.5. National interests of bilateral donors to support their companies can hinder appropriate sectoral allocations

Ensuring the achievement of the 2030 Agenda will require supporting appropriate sectoral allocations based on country needs. Contrary to this, tied aid, which is ODA that can only be used to buy goods and services from the provider country, can stifle appropriate sectoral allocations of resources. This is the case if aid is motivated by the interest of supporting the provider's national companies rather than the local needs of developing countries.

DAC countries have improved significantly in reducing formal restrictions in their procurement processes in the last decade. DAC members have committed to untying bilateral ODA to the greatest extent as suggested by:

- a 2001 DAC recommendation on untying aid to LDCs, which was extended to non-LDC heavily indebted poor countries in 2008
- the aid effectiveness principles agreed in Paris and reiterated in Busan and Nairobi
- the indicators used in DAC peer reviews and the Global Partnership for Effective Development Co-operation monitoring exercises.

OECD data shows that the share of tied ODA to LDCs and non-LDC heavily indebted poor countries importantly decreased in the period 2005-15 – from 30% to 12% of bilateral ODA (which includes both sector-allocable and non-sector allocable ODA) (OECD, 2018[21]).

However, the untying agenda still requires attention, especially in certain sectors. For example, of the USD 69 billion of sector-allocable ODA commitments formally tied by DAC countries in 2012-16, 58% are in the social sectors. Moreover, two-thirds of ODA procured by DAC countries in 2015-16 were awarded to companies from the donor country in competitive procurement.

1.4.6. While channels of delivery may vary depending on sectoral priorities and strategies, development effectiveness and good donorship need to guide development partners' efforts

Development partners use different channels depending on their priorities, knowledge and recipient country needs. The main channels of delivery include recipient governments, CSOs, donor agencies, multilateral institutions, research institutions and the private sector. While bilateral development partners implement most of their ODF using channels other than recipient governments, particularly in the social sectors, multilateral development partners channel most of their financing to them. In fact, only a third of concessional and non-concessional finance from bilateral development partners reporting to the DAC was channelled to recipient country governments between 2012 and 2016, mainly for infrastructure in middle income countries (Figure 1.12). About half of bilateral development finance within sectors is implemented by donor agencies (17%), CSOs (14%), multilateral organisations (10%) and research institutes (4%).

Figure 1.12. Large portions of bilateral development finance are provided beyond national governments, particularly in the social sectors

ODF from bilateral development partners by channel and groups of sectors (2012-2016).

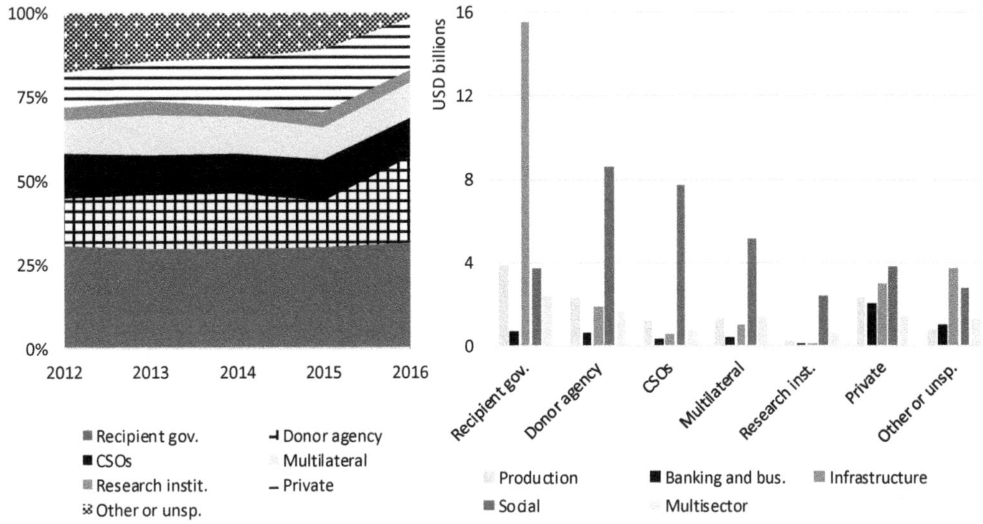

Note: (OECD, 2018[5]), "International development statistics (database)", OECD, Paris, http://www.oecd.org/dac/financing-sustainable-development/development-finance-data/idsonline.htm.

StatLink https://doi.org/10.1787/888933856264

In the most challenging contexts, bilateral development partners prioritise implementation through external agencies, such as CSOs and multilateral agencies rather than their own agencies. Moreover, as shown in Figure 1.13, DAC countries channel significantly higher amounts for humanitarian assistance through CSOs and multilateral organisations than through their donor agencies and other channels. Amounts channelled by DAC countries through multilateral agencies and CSO for humanitarian assistance are increasing significantly. The largest increases in funding are through multilateral channels. This doubled from USD 5 billion in 2012 to USD 10 billion in 2016.

This increasing delegation by bilateral development partners of their ODA to multilateral organisations and CSOs in priority sectors and challenging contexts raises the question of establishing effective funding polices and partnerships among donor and intermediaries. This is particularly evident for CSOs and multilaterals that are very reliant on bilateral donor assistance to fund their budgets. They may feel constrained to accept resources for operations that are not entirely aligned with their mandate and strategy. This challenge is particularly prominent for the United National Development System, as 80% of the revenue of its agencies and institutions are in the form of piecemeal earmarked contributions.

Figure 1.13. DAC countries channel most of their official development assistance for humanitarian programmes through multilateral organisations and civil society organisations

DAC countries' ODA for humanitarian programmes by channel, 2012-16 annual average, 2016 prices, USD billion commitment

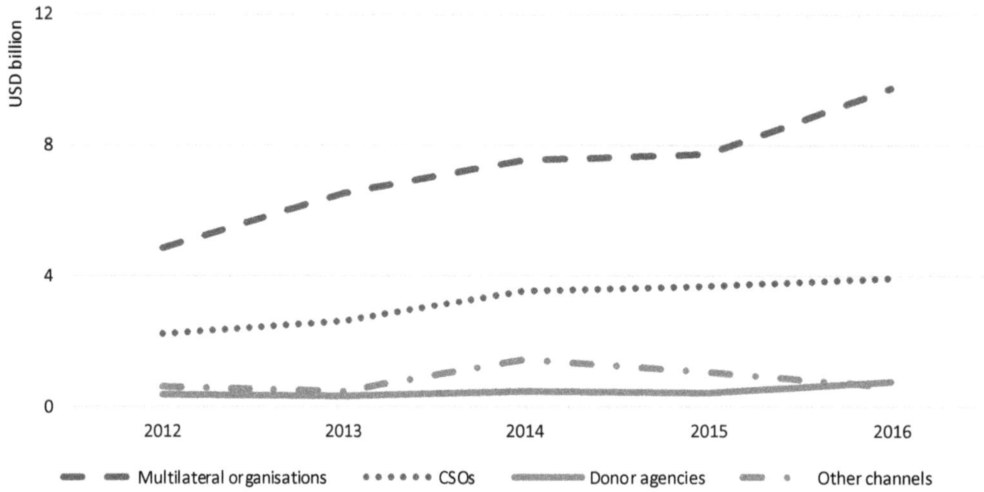

Source: (OECD, 2018[5]), "International development statistics (database)", OECD, Paris, http://www.oecd.org/dac/financing-sustainable-development/development-finance-data/idsonline.htm.

StatLink https://doi.org/10.1787/888933856321

Notes

[1] The statistical data for Israel are supplied by and under the responsibility of the relevant Israeli authorities. The use of such data by the OECD is without prejudice to the status of the Golan Heights, East Jerusalem and Israeli settlements in the West Bank under the terms of international law.

[2] The (OECD, 2018[22]) "Creditor Reporting System" is the authoritative database for official development finance (ODF) data. It provides statistical information on official and private concessional and non-concessional resources to developing countries by bilateral and multilateral ODF providers reporting to the OECD DAC, as well as a growing number of private foundations, representing every year approximately 250 000 records. The OECD DAC statistical directives govern the collection of these data, covering all definitions and methodologies and ensuring the comparability of information, including on sectors. OECD DAC statistics are publicly available free of charge.

[3] Based on OECD estimates, around 96% of this total relates to finance from the Chinese Export-Import Bank and the China Development Bank. In volume terms, the largest category of broader international co-operation instruments comprises activities that have a principally commercial purpose. This finance can include concessional and non-concessional loans for promoting the provider country's exports and profitable equity investments or financial inputs with specific expected returns, such as natural resources.

[4] For more information on TOSSD, please see: http://www.oecd.org/dac/financing-sustainable-development/development-finance-standards/tossd.htm.

[5] See paragraph 55 of the Addis Ababa Action Agenda (United Nations, 2015[2]).

[6] For more information, see: http://www.oecd.org/dac/financing-sustainable-development/development-finance-standards/tossd-task-force.htm.

[7] For more information on the work of the International TOSSD Task Force, see: http://www.oecd.org/dac/financing-sustainable-development/development-finance-standards/tossd-task-force.htm.

[8] Some providers' contributions are not susceptible to allocation by sector, such as general budget support, actions relating to debt, humanitarian aid and internal costs in the donor country.

[9] LDCs: Afghanistan, Angola, Bangladesh, Benin, Bhutan, Burkina Faso, Burundi, Cambodia, Central African Republic, Chad, Comoros, Democratic Republic of the Congo, Djibouti, Eritrea, Ethiopia, Gambia, Guinea, Guinea-Bissau, Haiti, Kiribati, Lao People's Democratic Republic (hereafter "Lao PDR"), Lesotho, Liberia, Madagascar, Malawi, Mali, Mauritania, Mozambique, Myanmar, Nepal, Niger, Rwanda, São Tomé and Principe, Senegal, Sierra Leone, Solomon Islands, Somalia, South Sudan, Sudan, Timor-Leste, Togo, Tuvalu, Uganda, United Republic of Tanzania, Vanuatu, Yemen and Zambia.

[10] Nevertheless, when looking at OOF loans, Bangladesh was able to benefit from considerable volumes from the Asian Development Bank in recent years: 20 loans delivered in the period 2012-16 for a total of USD 2.8 billion, mainly spent on energy and transport and storage.

[11] Afghanistan, Armenia, Azerbaijan, Bhutan, Plurinational State of Bolivia, Botswana, Burkina Faso, Burundi, Central African Republic, Chad, Kingdom of Eswatini, Ethiopia, Former Yugoslav Republic of Macedonia, Kazakhstan, Kyrgyzstan, Lao PDR, Lesotho, Malawi, Mali, Republic of Moldova, Mongolia, Nepal, Niger, Paraguay, Rwanda, South Sudan, Tajikistan, Turkmenistan, Uganda, Uzbekistan, Zambia, Zimbabwe.

[12] As for other country groupings, there are several definitions of SIDS. The United Nations identifies 52 countries or territories under this grouping. They first defined a SIDS grouping in 1992, then came others such as the European Union with ACP (Africa, Caribbean and Pacific), and the World Trade Organisation with the economic vulnerability index (Small Vulnerable Economies). The World Bank has been applying a small island exception in determining IDA eligibility since 1985.

[13] Including the regional groupings Oceania and West Indies.

References

AIIB et al. (2017), *Joint MDB Statement of Ambitions for Crowding in Private Finance*, https://www.bundesfinanzministerium.de/Content/DE/Downloads/G20-Dokumente/Hamburg_Genannte_Berichte/Joint-MDB-Statement-of-Ambitions.pdf?__blob=publicationFile&v=1. [16]

Alonso, J. (2014), *LDC and Other Country Groupings: How useful are current approaches to classify countries in a more heterogenous developing world?*, UNDESA, Department of Economics and Social Affairs, http://www.un.org/en/development/desa/policy/cdp/cdp_background_papers/bp2014_21.pdf. [9]

Delalande, G. and V. Gaveau (2018), "Senegal's Perspective on TOSSD", *OECD Development Co-operation Working Papers*, No. 43, OECD Publishing, Paris, http://dx.doi.org/10.1787/4144f82a-en. [3]

Delalande, G., R. Halvorson-Quevedo and C. Sangaré (2018), "The Philippines' Perspective on TOSSD", *OECD Development Co-operation Working Papers*, No. 42, OECD Publishing, Paris, http://dx.doi.org/10.1787/6ecaa5ac-en. [4]

EDFI (2016), *Investing to Create Jobs, Boost Growth and Fight Poverty*, EDFI, Brussels, https://www.deginvest.de/DEG-Documents-in-English/Download-Center/EDFI-Flagship-Report-2016.pdf. [17]

G20 (2017), *Principles of MDBs' strategy for crowding-in Private Sector Finance for growth and sustainable development*, http://www.bundesfinanzministerium.de/Content/DE/Downloads/G20-Dokumente/principles-on-crowding-in-private-sector-finance-april-20.pdf?__blob=publicationFile&v=2. [14]

OECD (2018), *"2018 Report on the DAC Untying Recommendation"*, https://www.oecd.org/dac/financing-sustainable-development/development-finance-standards/DCD-DAC(2018)12-REV2.en.pdf. [21]

OECD (2018), *"International development statistics (database)"*, OECD, Paris, http://www.oecd.org/dac/financing-sustainable-development/development-finance-data/idsonline.htm. [5]

OECD (2018), *"OECD DAC List of ODA Recipients"*, OECD, Paris, http://www.oecd.org/dac/financing-sustainable-development/development-finance-standards/daclist.htm. [8]

OECD (2018), *"Creditor Reporting System"*, OECD, Paris, https://stats.oecd.org/Index.aspx?DataSetCode=crs1. [22]

OECD (2018), *Making Development Co-operation Work for Small Island Developing States*, OECD Publishing, Paris, http://dx.doi.org/10.1787/9789264287648-en. [10]

OECD (2018), *States of Fragility 2018*, OECD Publishing, Paris, http://dx.doi.org/10.1787/9789264302075-en. [13]

OECD (2017), *"DAC High Level Communiqué, 31 October 2017"*, https://www.oecd.org/dac/DAC-HLM-2017-Communique.pdf. [15]

OECD (2016), *"OECD DAC survey on amounts mobilised from the private sector by official development finance interventions 2012-2015"*, OECD, Paris, http://www.oecd.org/dac/financing-sustainable-development/development-finance-standards/mobilisation.htm. [6]

OECD (2016), *States of Fragility 2016: Understanding Violence*, OECD Publishing, Paris, http://dx.doi.org/10.1787/9789264267213-en. [12]

OECD (2015), *Multilateral Aid 2015: Better Partnerships for a Post-2015 World*, OECD Publishing, Paris, http://dx.doi.org/10.1787/9789264235212-en. [20]

OECD/The World Bank (2016), *Climate and Disaster Resilience Financing in Small Island Developing States*, OECD Publishing, Paris, http://dx.doi.org/10.1787/9789264266919-en. [11]

Orth, M. et al. (2017), *What we know about the effectiveness of budget support. Evaluation Synthesis*, https://www.deval.org/files/content/Dateien/Evaluierung/Berichte/2017/DEval_Synthesen_Bericht_2017_EN_bffinal.pdf. [19]

UN DESA (2017), *The Sustainable Development Goals Report 2017*, UN, New York, http://dx.doi.org/10.18356/4d038e1e-en. [23]

UNCTAD (2014), *"World Investment Report 2014: Investing in the SDGs, an Action Plan"*, United Nations Conference on Trade and Development, Geneva, http://unctad.org/en/PublicationsLibrary/wir2014_en.pdf. [7]

United Nations (2015), *"Addis Ababa Action Agenda of the Third International Conference on Financing for Development"*. [2]

United Nations (2015), *"Transforming our World: The 2030 Agenda for Sustainable Development"*, United Nations, New York, NY, https://sustainabledevelopment.un.org/post2015/transformingourworld/publication. [1]

Williamson, T. and C. Dom (2010), *Sector Budget Support in Practice: Good Practice Note*, https://www.odi.org/sites/odi.org.uk/files/odi-assets/publications-opinion-files/5802.pdf. [18]

Chapter 2. Getting good sectoral data on development finance

Recognising that effective financing strategies cannot be achieved without comprehensive, comparable and detailed data, this chapter looks at current initiatives to improve sectoral development finance information. After a short section looking at the evolution of the data landscape, the second section provides an overview of the initiatives currently underway to provide an increasingly comprehensive and qualitative picture of sectoral development finance data in response to the Addis Ababa Action Agenda, with the measurement of an ever larger set of flows, providers and modalities. The third section then provides insights into the critical articulation between sectors traditionally used for data reporting and the Sustainable Development Goals (SDGs). The fourth section builds on the dual recognition that the financing picture of sectors cannot improve without the participation of all actors and the standardisation of development finance information across providers. This section, therefore, unpacks the potential for sectoral analyses of the new statistical framework of total official support for sustainable development, designed to track external resources in support of sustainable development by providers of development co-operation.

Key messages

Key messages to development co-operation providers emerging from this chapter include:

- **In order to analyse Sustainable Development Goals (SDG) financing, all providers of development co-operation could focus on making their sector financing information more detailed to respond to the new multifaceted SDG framework.** Since a direct and robust link between the SDGs and traditional sector classifications appears challenging, more detailed information on sectors, including detailed project descriptions, will be required to cater for the analysis of an increasingly complex landscape, and for accommodating a wider range of analytical needs.
- **The international community could find ways to make sectoral data more comparable.** For example, going forward, Arab providers could continue (e.g. United Arab Emirates, Kuwait, Saudi Arabia) or start (e.g. Qatar, Oman, Bahrain) publishing information on their development finance efforts, including at the sector level. Traditional providers ought to seek more engagement with South-South and triangular co-operation providers, as well as with other providers beyond the Development Assistance Committee (DAC). This includes such providers as Brazil, the People's Republic of China (hereafter "China"), India, South Africa, Mexico or Costa Rica. Such engagement would help achieve a more comprehensive picture of the financing for development landscape across sectors worldwide.
- **The total official support for sustainable development (TOSSD) represents a major opportunity for all development co-operation providers to make sectoral data more comprehensive, and shape a new measure of development finance in support of sustainable development**. The framework aims to capture all official and officially supported resources in support of sustainable development. These would include official resources, including beyond official development assistance (other official flows) and private finance mobilised by official development interventions.
- **In developing countries, co-ordination mechanisms could be extended to include all major actors of development finance.** These would include emerging providers (e.g. China, India and Brazil) and private philanthropic foundations, such as the Bill & Melinda Gates Foundation and its implementing partners, and other international and domestic foundations. A more comprehensive, shared picture of the financing landscape will enable new forms of dialogue, co-ordination and mutual learning between all providers of finance for sustainable development. This, in turn, could facilitate innovation.

2.1. Setting the scene: A complex data landscape on development finance

2.1.1. A wide and highly fragmented data landscape makes it challenging to obtain a comprehensive mapping of sector financing

In the last decades, the development finance landscape has seen the emergence of a large number of new actors and new instruments. This has made it challenging to monitor development finance data holistically. Actors beyond traditional official providers, such as private companies and funds, philanthropic foundations and civil society organisations (CSOs), have become key partners in supporting the global development agenda. They have changed the perspective on the instruments and modalities of development co-operation. Work commissioned by the OECD in 2014 to capture the broad landscape of external development finance data to developing countries (see Box 2.1) revealed a very wide and fragmented landscape (Prada and al., 2014[1]). The emerging picture is comprised of more than two hundred databases (see Figure 2.1). These for example:

- focus on specific geographical dimensions (e.g. regional databases, such as the South-South Cooperation Database by the Ibero-American Secretariat[1])
- are dedicated to specific sectors (e.g. the World Bank's Private Participation in Infrastructure Database[2])
- are related to specific instruments (e.g. The Joint External Debt Hub - JEDH[3]) or types of flows (e.g. the Foreign Direct Investment [FDI] Market[4])
- cover thematic and policy related issues (such as the "Climate Funds Update" database[5]).

Figure 2.1. The landscape of databases on external finance is complex

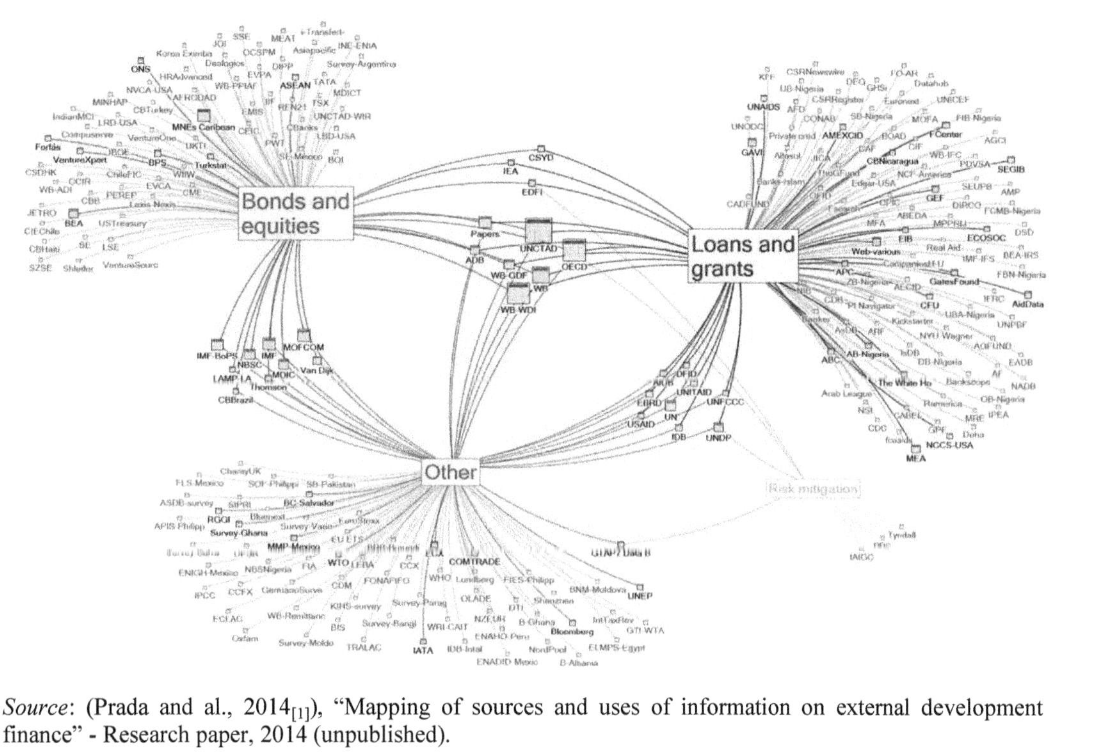

Source: (Prada and al., 2014[1]), "Mapping of sources and uses of information on external development finance" - Research paper, 2014 (unpublished).

Box 2.1. The definition of development finance data

Whereas the broad concept of "financing for development", as reflected in the Addis Ababa Action Agenda (United Nations, 2015[21]) covers a comprehensive range of financing sources, the term "development finance" is narrower in scope. The defining criterion for development finance is the intentionality of the flow, i.e. it is based on an explicit development mandate or purpose. At the international level, this comprises official development finance (ODF). ODF is concessional and non-concessional bilateral, and multilateral finance in support of development. Development Finance also includes private development finance, which embraces private funds that are extended with a development motivation, e.g. financing provided by philanthropic organisations for development purposes in developing countries. There are also domestic flows in developing countries that can fall under this concept, even if, in the context of this publication, the focus will be on external ODF, and a subset of private development finance for which data are available, namely private philanthropy, as well as private finance mobilised through official development interventions. On this basis, the term "development finance data" relates to data that describe and characterise the financial flows, terms and conditions of development finance.

Source: Adapted from Box 6.1 in (OECD, 2017[3]).

Going forward, with the "Big Data" movement, complexity of information, including on sectors, will continue to increase. In recent years, the global data architecture has experienced a fundamental change, with the volume of data increasing exponentially. In 2014, the United Nations estimated that 90% of the data in the world had been created in the last two years (United Nations, 2014[4]) and would increase by 40% each year (United Nations, 2018[5]). The Big Data movement offers promising avenues for development and for facilitating access to information to a wider share of the world population. Many examples across a wide range of SDGs are now available on the potential contributions of Big Data to development. These include the monitoring of food security (SDG 2) or infectious diseases (SDG 3) and using mobile phones (UN Global Pulse, 2017[6]). The "Blockchain", though still at its infancy, also has the potential to revolutionise some sectors, such as financial services (IFC, 2017[7]), and is starting to be used in the development world (Stanford GSB, 2018[8]) (UN OICT, 2017[9]).

Overall, the profusion of databases on external flows makes it hard to easily collate a picture of financing to a given sector (apart from ODF – see Section 2.2). The diversity of scope, definitions and reporting methods across databases and data providers makes the presentation of a financing picture on a given sector or the comparison of sectoral information across data sources highly challenging. But many initiatives are taking place to gradually develop a comprehensive sectoral picture for both official and private development finance.

2.2. The state of play on sectoral official and private finance data for development

For ODF[6], the most comprehensive sector financing picture currently available is provided through the OECD Creditor Reporting System (OECD CRS) (See Box 2.2).[7] The OECD Creditor Reporting System provides robust statistical information for four sets of providers – bilateral DAC members, bilateral non-DAC providers, multilateral organisations and private foundations. Sectoral data challenges faced by these four communities differ substantially.

Box 2.2. The OECD Creditor Reporting System

The OECD Creditor Reporting System is the authoritative database for official development finance (ODF) data. It provides statistical information on official and private concessional and non-concessional resources to developing countries by more than 90 bilateral and multilateral ODF providers and a growing number of private foundations. Every year these represent approximately 250 000 records. The OECD DAC statistical directives govern the collection of these data, covering all definitions and methodologies and ensuring the comparability of information, including on sectors. OECD DAC statistics are publicly available free of charge.

Note: The OECD Creditor Reporting System is available at: https://stats.oecd.org/Index.aspx?DataSetCode=CRS1
Source: (OECD, 2017[3]) , (OECD, 2018[10]) and compilation by the author.

2.2.1. Official providers need to ensure regular investment in their statistical capacity to allow for accurate sector financing information

OECD providers that are members of the DAC are required to provide the OECD with data on their official and private resource flows to developing countries according to the OECD DAC statistical directives. While information reported by these providers are the backbone of the information provided on development co-operation globally, these providers still face numerous challenges and are working to constantly improve the quality of their sectoral information. To monitor these efforts, every year the DAC is carrying out an assessment of DAC members' reporting on development finance to the OECD Creditor Reporting System [see for example (Ahmad and Nichols, 2017[11])], which regularly highlights several elements critical to sectoral analyses.[8]

The first and most important requirement for good sectoral data reporting is the **accurate recording of the sectoral purpose of activities**. In the OECD CRS, activities need to be reported against sector codes available in the OECD DAC sector classification (see Box 2.3)[9]. If development activities are not properly recorded against sector codes, this can result in faulty analyses. To avoid this issue, the DAC Secretariat has put in place automated checks on reporting and manually verifies approximately 250 000 records for accuracy every year. This is to ensure the consistency of sector codes, for example, against project descriptions. The misreporting of activities against sectors codes can occur for different reasons. For many providers, the reporting of activities is carried out by a large number of decentralised desk officers. This can result in uneven reporting practices within a single donor. The limited availability of staff dedicated to statistical reporting for quality assurance, or a high staff turnover, can also represent challenges to ensure accurate reporting.

Another big challenge for sectoral analyses of external official finance is that activities are, for most providers, currently assigned to only one sector code, while many projects tend to target several sectors at the same time. In order to tackle this issue, in July 2016[10], DAC members agreed to introduce a system of "multiple sector codes" in the CRS that will allow **improved granularity of sectoral information.** This system makes it possible to record an activity against up to ten sector codes, thus reflecting the reality of many development projects that actually benefit several sectors. By offering the possibility to record an activity against several sectors, this system is also likely to reduce the amounts of aid recorded as "multisector" (see Box 2.3 and Chapter 3) and make DAC sector statistics more relevant going forward. Finally, the multiple-sector code system will also help providers better reflect their efforts in responding to the SDGs, which are multifaceted in nature.

Another critical element for sectoral analyses is the availability of detailed **descriptive information** for activities recorded in the system, which remains a challenge for many providers of development co-operation reporting to the DAC. The DAC CRS provides fields for reporting both short and long descriptions of projects. Short descriptions (which are limited to 150 characters) generally contain project titles that are particularly valuable to users who undertake sectoral studies. Long descriptions help put the project further into context, providing details on a wide range of dimensions, such as the objectives, the beneficiaries, or the implementation strategy of the project. The information in long descriptions allows the Secretariat to check the accuracy and consistency of purpose coding. In addition, descriptive information is valuable in detailed sectoral studies. It allows users to carry out research on specific topics (sectors or themes) not identified in existing classifications (e.g. disability), using keyword searches[11]. A quick review of the evolution of both long and short descriptions for the period 2013-17[12] shows no major changes in the quality of descriptions. Half of the DAC membership provided "meaningful and good descriptive" information over this 5-year period. Still, in 2017, about one-quarter of the membership provided the same information in short and long descriptions for more than 20% of their activities. This shows the importance of providers making additional efforts to provide more detailed information beyond short descriptions.

Box 2.3. The OECD DAC sector classification

The OECD DAC sector classification[1] includes the following broad sector categories:

- *social infrastructure and services* (covering the sectors of education, health, population policies/reproductive health, water and sanitation, government and civil society, and other social infrastructure and services)
- *economic infrastructure and services* (covering transport and storage, communications, energy, banking and financial services, and business and other services)
- *production* sectors (covering agriculture, forestry, fishing, industry, mining, construction, trade and tourism)
- *multisector/cross-cutting* (covering general environmental protection, other multisector elements, including urban and rural development)
- *non-sector allocable* (for contributions not susceptible to allocation by sector, such as general budget support, actions relating to debt, humanitarian aid and internal costs in the donor country).

Each of these broad sector categories is then broken down into specific "CRS purpose codes", against which providers are required to report, as shown in the example below (Table 2.1).

The sector/purpose codes in the DAC CRS classification are selected by answering the question: "Which specific area of the recipient's economic or social structure is the transfer intended to foster"? The sector classification, therefore, does not refer to the type of goods or services provided by the donor. For example, education activities in a specific sector, such as education in agricultural techniques, would be reported under Agriculture, not Education.

Table 2.1. Example of a sector classification in the OECD Creditor Reporting System for banking and financial services

240		Banking and financial services
24010	Financial policy and administrative management	Finance sector policy, planning and programmes; institution capacity building and advice; financial markets and systems
24020	Monetary institutions	Central banks
24030	Formal sector financial intermediaries	All formal sector financial intermediaries; credit lines; insurance, leasing, venture capital, etc. (except when focused on only one sector).
24040	Informal/semi-formal financial intermediaries	Micro credit, savings and credit co-operatives, etc.
24081	Education/training in banking and financial services	

[1] Available at: http://www.oecd.org/dac/financing-sustainable-development/development-finance-standards/purposecodessectorclassification.htm.

Source: (OECD, 2018[10]) and (OECD, 2018[12])

2.2.2. Efforts to include non-DAC providers in the global statistical system could be stepped up as these providers have the potential to greatly improve the sectoral picture of development finance

From a sectoral perspective, one particular area for attention is to expand the picture of the financing of official providers, particularly Arab and other emerging providers such as China, Brazil and India, so that they gradually publish more and more information, including disaggregated data by sector. Broader international co-operation flows from providers beyond the membership of the DAC were estimated at around USD 300 billion in 2014 (Benn and Luijkx, 2017[13]). In the infrastructure sector, estimated combined disbursements for China, India and Arab development partners accounted for 14% of total ODF for infrastructure in 2014 (Miyamoto and Chiofalo, 2016[14]). Data for a very large portion of this financing is currently unavailable publicly (See Box 2.4) and the overall financing from these providers might be much bigger than current estimates. For example, a pilot study (Delalande and Gaveau, 2018[15]) carried out in 2016 showed that China was extending several lending operations to Senegal[13] that year, including two loans totalling about USD 1.3 billion to finance road infrastructure. This is almost the equivalent of a single year's total ODA to Senegal.[14]

Box 2.4. A partial picture of official development finance, including by sector

The OECD DAC collects annually a large amount of information on official development finance. However, there are still several major providers who do not yet make public the financial information on their development co-operation activities, including by sector. This greatly affects the picture currently available on sectors. The first reason for this lack of availability of information is capacity-related, as it is sometimes challenging for certain large co-operations to collect, collate, and publish this information. The second reason is that some providers, mainly South-South co-operation providers, consider that financial information does not adequately reflect the quality of the intervention or its impact on the developing country. Finally, another important reason is that some providers are fearful of the reaction of their populations to publicity on the support provided to other countries while these same providers face major social challenges at home, including sometimes significant poverty rates.

Providers beyond the DAC increasingly report to the DAC statistical systems, improving the development finance picture, including by sector. In 2012, only two such countries were reporting at the activity level to these systems. Six years later, nine countries reported voluntarily on their development co-operation activity by activity. The nine included some of the now largest bilateral providers of development co-operation, such as the United Arab Emirates and Kuwait[15]. This has, for example, helped to build a much more complete picture on the "transport and storage" sector where non-DAC providers (mainly Kuwait and the United Arab Emirates) have multiplied more than threefold their support between 2012 and 2016.[16]

Going forward, the main focus for non-DAC providers from a sectoral perspective would be to strive to provide activity-level information, including with robust sector-coding, rather than the provision of aggregate data (Berbegal and Benn, 2017[16]). For example, Saudi Arabia has reported to the OECD since the 1970s, but only at the aggregate level. So far, this has prevented any meaningful analyses on sectors, despite the significant amount of financing provided by the country. However, in 2018, Saudi Arabia officially launched, through KSrelief, the Saudi Aid Platform (Saudi Arabia, 2018[17]). This is a database that contains activity-level information on Saudi Arabia's aid contributions. The launch of this database represents a major transparency undertaking by Saudi Arabia to provide critical information, including by sector, on the country's development co-operation.

2.2.3. Thanks to strong data partnerships, the picture on financing of sectors by multilateral providers is improving

Over the last few years, there has been much improvement in the reporting by multilateral institutions (Berbegal and Benn, 2017[16]). For example, in 2016-17, the Caribbean Development Bank reported activity-level data for commitments in CRS format for the first time, including by sector codes. For the first time in 2016, the United Nations Environment Programme also reported its aid disbursements by programme themes mapped to the CRS sector codes.

The main challenge in the reporting of multilateral institutions is that the data, including that on sectors, are often submitted in non-standard formats, which requires extensive work by the OECD DAC Secretariat before they can be uploaded to the CRS database. In fact, while most bilateral DAC providers record their activities in their own internal systems against the DAC sector classification, this is not the case for many multilateral organisations that have their own sector classifications (e.g. World Bank, African Development Bank and Asian Development Bank)[17]. To ensure that the information published in the OECD CRS is comparable across all providers, bilateral and multilateral, the OECD has worked with each provider to produce a mapping of their internal sector classifications against the OECD DAC classification. These mappings are regularly updated to ensure that the information published on sectors in the CRS is fully harmonised across providers. Furthermore, for this group of providers, there is room for significant improvement in the use of policy markers (See Box 2.5), although good progress is being made on the climate-related policy markers.

Box 2.5. The contribution of policy markers to sectoral analyses

The "marker" system in the OECD CRS allows for the identification of activities targeted to a specific policy objective. The system covers eight policy areas – gender equality and women's empowerment; aid to the environment; participatory development and good governance (PD/GG); trade development; reproductive, maternal, new-born and child health (RMNCH); disaster risk reduction; nutrition; and support to people with disabilities – as well as four areas related to the objectives of the Rio Conventions – biodiversity, climate change mitigation, climate change adaptation and desertification. When reporting to the OECD DAC, providers can "flag" their activities against these specific markers, thus providing information on the degree to which members implement these policies in their aid programmes. The marker system can be very useful from a sectoral perspective, for example, when analysing support to the environment, one of the three fundamental pillars of the 2030 Agenda.

Source: (OECD, 2018[10]), "Converged statistical reporting directives for the Creditor Reporting System (CRS) and the annual DAC questionnaire" https://one.oecd.org/document/DCD/DAC/STAT(2018)9/FINAL/en/pdf.

2.2.4. Private finance to sectors: collecting information on philanthropic giving and the private finance mobilised should be just a first step to responding to the Addis Ababa Action Agenda

Private finance for development mainly comprises finance by private philanthropic foundations and CSOs. Other private flows, such as private flows at market terms (e.g. FDI) and remittances, are important to put ODF data, including that on sectors, into context. Another dimension of private finance currently being developed by the OECD DAC is the measurement of private finance mobilised by ODF interventions. This helps identify those sectors in which private finance is being mobilised by public efforts (see below and Section 2.4).

Private foundations provide significant contributions to critical sectors and are recognised for their flexibility and capacity for innovation, as well as for their ability to leverage additional funds through multi-stakeholder partnerships (United Nations, 2015[2]). However, in terms of availability of information on activities carried out by these actors, there are very few central repositories that provide a wide-ranging view on philanthropic giving by sector, other than the Foundation Center[18] and the efforts made by the OECD (See Section 2.4). While, overall, financing by private foundations may not be high compared to traditional providers (See Chapter 3), funding from the Bill & Melinda Gates Foundation shows the impact that private foundations can have on critical sectors, such as health (see Section 2.4). At this stage, to further include the contributions of philanthropic giving into sectoral analyses, current efforts should be sustained to expand the scope of publicly and freely available information on philanthropic giving. This will ensure that data are published along internationally agreed sectoral statistical classifications, such as that of the OECD DAC.

In 2015, funds raised privately by non-governmental organisations were estimated at USD 35 billion, according to data collected by the OECD DAC (Ahmad and Nichols, 2017[11]). However, the current reporting of data on these flows is probably understated. In 2015, for example, half of the membership of the OECD DAC did not report data on net private grants by CSOs and, beyond the OECD DAC, there is no central repository on funds mobilised privately by CSOs. This is despite the International Aid Transparency Initiative[19]. This Initiative makes available information on the funding provided by more than 540 international and national CSOs[20] to developing countries, including data broken down by sector along the OECD DAC sector classification.

Knowledge of private flows at market terms is also critical to put development financing into context. From a sectoral perspective, FDI flows would typically be expected to be much higher in sectors where a relative financial return is possible (e.g. such as production sectors and economic infrastructure sectors) and lower in social sectors. In turn, this would mean that official funds would be expected to be smaller in the former and bigger in the latter. Some of the main databases available online, which can provide information on FDI on a global scale, include the OECD.Stat Database[21], the Investment Map of the International Trade Centre (ITC)[22] or UNCTAD's Statistical Databases[23], even though not all of these databases provide information on FDI by sector.

Regarding remittances, the main source of data currently available is the World Bank Remittances database (World Bank, s.d.[18]), in which the data is not categorised by sector or industry because of the private nature of these flows. However, remittances data can still be useful in analyses that focus on specific sectors – such as health or education – and in specific countries [See for example (Refugee and Migratory Movements Research Unit (RMMRU), 2016[19])].

Measuring private finance mobilised by the official sector in developing countries provides critical information to inform the implementation of the AAAA (United Nations, 2015[2]), which positions private businesses as important actors in delivering on the global ambitions crystalised in the SDGs[24]. From a development perspective, it is, therefore, critical to measure efforts made by the official sector to mobilise these private resources for development. It is also why the OECD has developed a dedicated work stream on this subject[25] and that the present publication integrates amounts mobilised from the private sector through official development interventions (see for example Section 2.4 and Chapter 3). This effort helps improve the picture on where financing is mobilised in support of the SDGs. Additional support and international attention should, therefore, be given to this issue going forward.

Overall, the development finance data landscape shows that capturing broader information on official finance and complementing it with philanthropic data or the private finance mobilised is only a first step in getting a more transparent picture on sector financing. Efforts could be stepped up to get a much wider picture of flows for development from all sources, public and private, as called for in the AAAA.

2.3. Articulating the Sustainable Development Goals and traditional sectors

As the development community has entered the implementation phase of the SDGs, it is important to clarify the relationship between sectors, traditionally used for data reporting, and the SDGs. Understanding this relationship could potentially help improve the measurement of financing channelled towards the goals.[26]

Looking at the 17 SDGs, it quickly appears that only a few SDGs present a strong and relatively straightforward sectoral focus (such as Goal 3 on Health or Goal 4 on Education). Many others relate to multiple sectors (e.g. SDG 1 on Poverty Eradication, SDG 8 on Decent Work and Economic Growth or SDG 10 on Reducing Inequality). To further analyse this issue and improve its own statistical reporting systems, the OECD

DAC has launched a number of initiatives to see how data reported in the CRS could be adjusted to measure financing to the SDGs and how its sector classification could be improved to be useful in this new context of the 2030 Agenda. These initiatives include a pilot exercise to map the SDGs with traditional sectors. Revisions to the DAC sector classification reflect the evolving needs of the development community and, through creation of a specific focus field, will help to tag development activities against the SDGs.

2.3.1. Mapping the SDGs against traditional sectors appears highly challenging

Since 2015, the OECD DAC has been investigating the possibility of mapping the OECD DAC CRS sector codes and the SDGs[27] (Benn and Gaveau, 2015[20]); (Nichols and Thielemans, 2016[21]) (Benn, 2017[22]). The work has confirmed the overall relevance of the OECD current system of sector classifications to monitor SDG-related interventions, but it has also highlighted numerous challenges to strictly mapping the traditional sectors with the SDGs and their related targets.

First, many goals and targets in the SDG framework are very wide in scope. This makes it hard to identify a direct correspondence between an SDG and a traditional sector. Examples of this difficulty would include Goal 1 "End poverty in all its forms everywhere" and target 8.1 on "Economic growth" to which a large portion of development co-operation actually contributes. Conversely, many SDG targets are too narrow to be matched with existing sector codes. For example, the DAC sector code on "*Human rights*" could relate to several detailed human rights-related SDG targets. These include target 5.3 "Eliminate all harmful practices, such as child, early and forced marriage and female genital mutilations", target 8.7 "Take immediate and effective measures to eradicate forced labor, end modern slavery and human trafficking […]" and targets 16.2 and 16.10.

Second, a fundamental challenge in mapping the SDGs to sectors is that the SDGs describe outcomes while sector classifications are defined based on inputs from providers. Even when SDGs and sectors should be relatively easy to match (for example, education or health, where the goals are relatively well delineated and where OECD DAC sector codes are easily identifiable), linking them to each other in a robust way appears highly challenging. An example is the health goal (SDG 3). Target 3.2 reads, "By 2030, end preventable deaths of new-borns and children under 5 years of age, with all countries aiming to reduce neonatal mortality to at least as low as 12 per 1 000 live births and under-5 mortality to at least as low as 25 per 1 000 live births". This target can be linked to two different codes in the OECD DAC CRS classification (code 12220-Basic health care and code 12230-Basic health infrastructure). But not all health activities relate to fighting neonatal mortality. So analysing financing for this issue would require assessing all activities under these two codes to identify activities directly related to child mortality. This can be highly challenging in practice. In this particular case, one could also use the RMNCH marker to identify relevant activities (see Box 2.5).

Overall, the many challenges finally led to the recognition that the classifications would not allow establishment of a direct and robust link between development co-operation sectoral inputs and development outcomes (Benn, 2017[22]).

2.3.2. Sectoral classifications are being improved to reflect the evolving needs of the development community

To keep sectoral tracking of development flows up to date, the DAC regularly carries out adjustments to its sectoral classifications. Such adjustments are suggested based on members' experiences in the field or based upon specific requests from external development actors[28] (see Box 2.6). Over the last years, more than 10 new codes have been created and several adjusted on a wide range of themes, such as investment, non-communicable diseases, humanitarian assistance or nutrition. In parallel to this process, as mentioned in Section 2.2, a "multiple purpose codes" system to record a given activity against several sector codes was recently introduced in the OECD CRS. This will allow greater granularity of data to respond to the multifaceted SDG agenda.

Box 2.6. Adjusting the DAC classification to emerging needs: The case of nutrition

Capturing resources for nutrition is critical to monitoring the progress and commitments towards the World Health Organisation 2025 targets for nutrition[1] and SDG 2 ("End hunger, achieve food security and improved nutrition and promote sustainable agriculture").

The CRS purpose code for basic nutrition[2] (12240) is commonly used by the global nutrition community as a proxy for investments in nutrition-specific interventions. These would be direct, high-impact nutrition interventions that address the immediate determinants and causes of undernutrition. However, the basic nutrition purpose code was not well-aligned with the international and scientific consensus on the definition of nutrition-specific interventions. For example, the basic nutrition code included school feeding and household food security, which are not typically considered nutrition specific. These inclusions were leading to an overestimation of nutrition-specific investments and a misinterpretation of progress towards nutrition scale up.

In that context, the non-governmental organisation "Action Contre la Faim", with the support of France, initiated a proposal to the DAC Working Party on Development Finance Statistics to redefine the scope of the basic nutrition purpose code. This led to the creation of two new separate codes for school feeding and household food security, thereby improving the quality of nutrition-related activities. The new codes will be implemented in 2019 for 2018 flows.

1 See: http://www.who.int/nutrition/global-target-2025/en/.

2 Which covers direct feeding programmes (maternal feeding, breastfeeding and weaning foods, child feeding and school feeding); determination of micro-nutrient deficiencies; provision of vitamin A, iodine, iron, etc.; monitoring of nutritional status; nutrition and food hygiene education; and household food security.

2.3.3. Scoping the possibility of tagging individual activities to the SDGs

In 2018, the DAC has approved the introduction of a voluntary SDG reporting field in the CRS database (Gualberti, Benn and al., 2018[23]) with reporting scheduled to start in 2019 on 2018 flows. The SDG data field will allow establishing linkages between the activities and the goals and targets to which the activities are contributing. The presence of this field in the database will permit bilateral and multilateral development partners reporting to the DAC to tag activities against specific SDG goals or targets. This would greatly help in better tracking financing to the 2030 Agenda. Also, it would help to shift the logic of the current system, which is mainly based on the classification of the purposes and sectors of intervention of the activities (inputs), towards a new system that will also capture a large set of targets along with the purposes and sectors. The development of this SDG focus field will also contribute to the reporting against the emerging framework for the SDG era called TOSSD (see Section 2.4.).

2.4. Unpacking total official support for sustainable development's potential for sectoral analyses

The development landscape is characterised by highly fragmented development finance information (see Section 2.1). Getting a better understanding of where SDG financing is targeted, including by sector, requires the international community to come together and standardise information across providers of development co-operation. This is the ambition of the TOSSD framework. It is a statistical framework specifically designed to track resources towards the SDGs and to provide transparency on development resource flows, including beyond ODA.

After a short presentation of the TOSSD framework, this section sheds light on key areas where TOSSD can provide critical information for sectoral analyses (specifically the inclusion of amounts mobilised from the private sector, the inclusion of data by emerging providers and data on private philanthropy, as a satellite indicator).

2.4.1. TOSSD: A statistical standard for the SDG era

The concept of total official support for sustainable development (TOSSD)[29] first emerged in 2014 in the course of work undertaken by OECD DAC to align its statistical system with today's development finance landscape. The new framework aims to provide greater transparency about the full array of officially-supported bilateral, multilateral and South-South finance provided in support of sustainable development (OECD, 2017[24]). TOSSD was first recognised internationally in the AAAA in July 2015 (United Nations, 2015[2]). Its statistical features have been under development since July 2017 by an International Task Force[30] consisting of about 25 development policy and statistical experts. Emerging providers are also present as observers to the Task Force.

TOSSD is envisaged as a two-pillar framework (See Figure 2.2). Pillar I would capture cross-border flows to developing countries. Pillar II would capture resources that support development enablers and address global challenges at the regional and global levels. While both pillars will provide information relevant for sectoral analyses, Pillar II has the potential to unveil some sectoral information currently missing in international statistics. This includes support to international tribunals (in the justice sector) or activities supporting oceans in international waters (in the environment sector), two areas that are not well captured in existing databases.

Figure 2.2. TOSSD: two pillars to capture more information on sustainable development

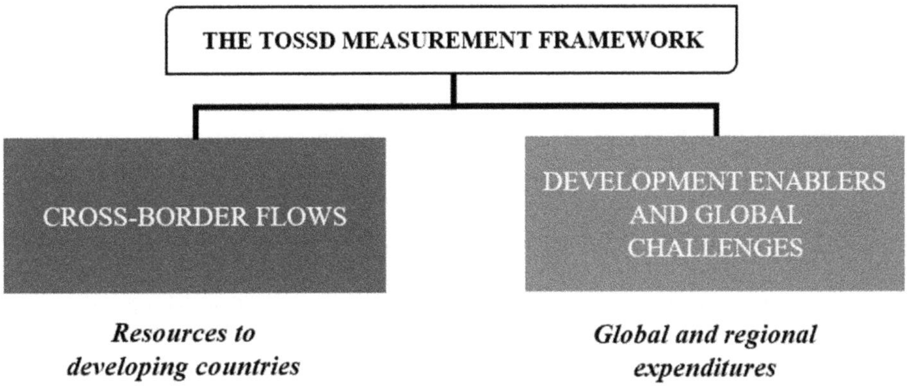

Source: Extracted from the International TOSSD Task Force webpage (accessed 31 October 2018), http://www.oecd.org/dac/financing-sustainable-development/development-finance-standards/tossd-task-force.htm.

The TOSSD framework will capture all resources in support of SDG-related investments (Table 2.2) including grants, loans and equity investments. It will also include the amounts mobilised from the private sector, which will help create incentives to mobilise more resources from the private sector.[31]

A number of "satellite" indicators will complement the TOSSD framework to put official resources into context. These will include private flows at market terms and remittances along with information on private finance for development coming from private foundations.

Table 2.2. The emerging framework of TOSSD

Types of flows	**Description**
A. Grants	Including grants and technical assistance
B. Financial transactions	Including debt instruments and equity investments
Total official flows (A+B)	In gross terms
C. **Resources mobilised from the private sector**	Private resources mobilised by official development interventions, regardless of the country of origin of the funds
Envisaged "satellite" indicators	
D. Private flows at market terms	FDI and other securities, including bonds
E. Private philanthropy	Provided by private philanthropic foundations for development
F. Remittances	

Source: Compilation based on information available at http://www.oecd.org/dac/financing-sustainable-development/development-finance-standards/tossd-task-force.htm, (Delalande and Gaveau, 2018[15]) and (Delalande, Halvorson-Quevedo and Sangaré, 2018[25]).

2.4.2. TOSSD can help the development community to deliver on its promise to mobilise the private sector for the SDGs

The AAAA positions private businesses as critical actors in delivering on the global ambition crystallised in the SDGs[32]. But how will the development community know if it delivers on its promise to mobilise the private sector towards the SDGs?

The TOSSD framework will help to respond to this question. It will build on the work started by the OECD DAC in 2013 to establish an international standard to measure the volume of private finance mobilised through ODF interventions[33] (Figure 2.3). So far, methodologies to measure the amounts mobilised have been developed for seven leveraging mechanisms (representing most of the instruments used to mobilise private finance) – guarantees, syndicated loans, shares in collective investment vehicles, credit lines, direct investment in companies, grants and loans in co-financing arrangements, and project finance. A recent survey (Benn, Sangaré and Hos, 2017[26]) showed that the main sectors in which private finance was mobilised were the banking sector, followed by the energy and the industry sectors. These data provide a new view on where private finance is mobilised in critical SDGs and sectors. They also invite the development community to reflect on how to improve the granularity of sectoral information as, in some cases, the information provided may relate to the sectoral allocation of the first channel of delivery (e.g. banks, funds), rather than the ultimate beneficiary sector of the financial transaction.

Figure 2.3. Private finance is mostly mobilised in industry, mining, construction, energy and banking and business

Average 2012-16, 2016 constant prices, USD billion commitments

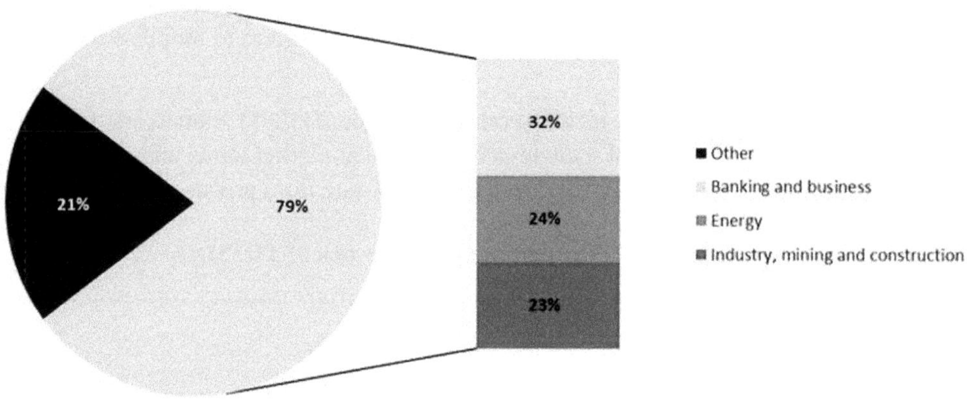

Source: (OECD, 2016[27]), "OECD DAC survey on amounts mobilised from the private sector by official development finance interventions 2012-2015". Estimates for the year 2016. See also the Annex at the end of this document.

StatLink https://doi.org/10.1787/888933855333

In order to reflect the new trend, this report uses the data collected on the amounts mobilised alongside ODF information to provide a cross-sectoral overview of officially supported resources in support of the SDGs.

Beyond the measurement of how much private finance is mobilised towards the SDGs, another critical aspect for developing countries and the development community at large is how sectoral financing packages actually come together in targeted sectors. TOSSD will provide data that identifies all the actors involved in a given financing package. This will greatly help to bring additional transparency to these financing packages. From a developing country perspective, this information will contribute to an understanding of how countries put together financing packages (See Box 2.7). In order to fully harness the potential of TOSSD data, however, it will be important that the international community complements these data with appropriate tools that can allow for visual representations of financing packages.

Box 2.7. TOSSD: How do sector financing packages come together in the 2030 era?

In 2016 and 2017, the OECD carried out two country pilots in Senegal (Delalande and Gaveau, 2018[15]) and the Philippines (Delalande, Halvorson-Quevedo and Sangaré, 2018[25])) to gather the perspectives of developing countries on TOSSD. These pilots revealed that TOSSD could greatly contribute to a greater transparency of financing packages in key sectors. This would be particularly so in countries where financing is scarce, or the risk perceived as highest. In these contexts, putting together financing packages sometimes requires more financing engineering than in countries where money is more easily available. TOSSD would inform developing countries and providers alike about how different financing packages come together in different sectors.

For example, Figure 2.4 shows the financing package of a toll highway project between Dakar and Diamniadio, a city located about 30 kms from the Senegalese capital. TOSSD would help capture information that is currently not available in the DAC Creditor Reporting System by collecting data on the contributions of the private company Eiffage and the Compagnie bancaire de l'Afrique occidentale (CBAO – the Banking Company of West Africa) to this financing package.

Figure 2.4. The Dakar–Diamniadio toll highway project

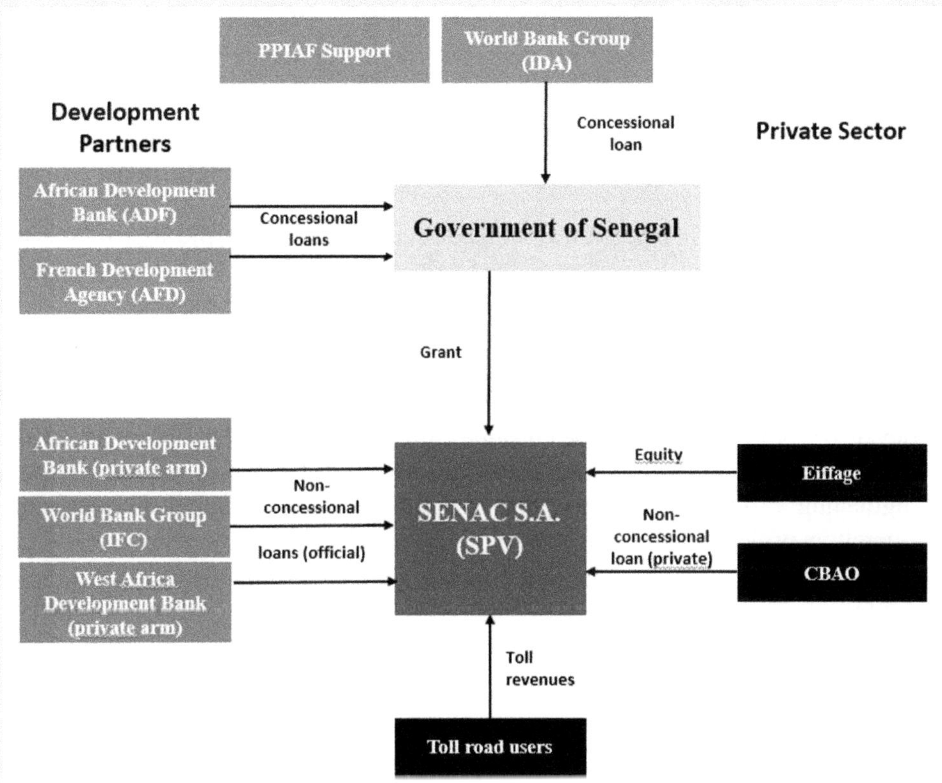

Note: PPIAF – Public-Private Infrastructure Advisory Facility; SENAC – a Senegalese concession company set up by Eiffage.
Source: Updated through country-level interviews from Figure 1 in (OECD, 2014[28])

2.4.3. TOSSD can help trigger policy dialogue with emerging providers while filling-in critical sectoral data gaps coming from non-traditional providers

TOSSD aims to capture resources from all providers, including South-South and triangular co-operation providers, whatever the modality used by these providers. To consider the perspective of these providers in TOSSD, the International TOSSD Task Force is, for example, developing a methodology to measure in-kind technical co-operation in the TOSSD framework, a modality that is central to these providers.[34]

The sectoral implications of this work are numerous. First, by bringing together traditional and emerging providers, TOSSD would help standardise information, including on sectors across a much wider development community, thereby facilitating the analyses of information through a more comprehensive sectoral picture. The latest 2017 Secretaría General Iberoamericana (SEGIB) report on South-South Co-operation in the Ibero-America region (SEGIB, 2017[29]), for example, presents data on 1 475 South-South Co-operation activities. If these activities were available in a format that allowed for the manipulation of these data along the various dimensions available in the report, they could greatly complement information available in the OECD CRS and improve the existing sectoral picture available publicly (See Box 2.8). Seeing the information currently available in the first regional Ibero-American Integrated Data System on South-South and Triangular Co-operation (Sistema Integrado de Datos de Iberoamérica sobre Cooperacíon Sur-Sur y Triangular – SIDICSS) alongside data available in the OECD CRS would provide a very advanced sectoral picture on development co-operation.[35]

Box 2.8. Example of an area of collaboration on sectors with South-South co-operation providers: approaches to institutional strengthening

The latest 2017 SEGIB report on South-South co-operation in the Ibero-América region (SEGIB, 2017[29]), supported by Spain as a main funder for more than a decade, presents data on 1 475 South-South co-operation activities. From a sectoral perspective, the report is mainly based on the OECD Creditor Reporting System sector classifications, but with a methodology that has been adjusted over time to reflect the specificities of South-South co-operation. An interesting feature of the report is that activities are clustered along priority policy areas. The most important priority area for South-South co-operation providers is "institutional strengthening". This represents more than 21% of bilateral South-South co-operation projects and more than 17% of regional South-South co-operation projects. This is an area of action that the OECD Creditor Reporting System is not in a position to capture easily and represents an interesting subject for policy dialogue between the two communities of providers.

In order to capture the evolving nature of some of the interventions by DAC and non-DAC providers, the DAC is also taking a number of initiatives to include a wider range of activities supported by its membership. For example, starting in 2016, the DAC has implemented a "Triangular Co-operation" code in the OECD CRS that allows members to report their bilateral triangular co-operation (Benn and Luijkx, 2015[30]). Germany has been the first member to report information in the OECD CRS using this new code, with 10 programmes for approximately USD 11 million in 2016.[36] Germany has been supporting, for example, projects on climate change, health and governance issues in various regions.

The OECD's Development Co-operation Directorate has also established an online repository of triangular co-operation projects (OECD, 2017[31]). This is based on its 2015 survey of triangular co-operation activities, which collected 450 projects from 62 countries (OECD, 2017[32]), and additional activities that were shared later on. These added up to over 500 triangular initiatives. These activities, currently not recorded in the OECD CRS, represent critical complementary data to that already available in this database. These data facilitate understanding of the current development co-operation landscape by sector. Triangular Co-operation projects may not always have large budgets, but they may have a big impact on partners and the lives of people in the target groups. For instance, a Triangular Co-operation project that Brazil has been implementing with the World Food Programme on human milk banks started working with USD 30 000 and has been scaled up to work in nine Latin American and African countries, reaching millions of people.

An OECD working paper focusing on triangular co-operation in the Middle East and North Africa (MENA) region (Casado-Asensio and Piefer, 2018[33]), helped collect another 53 projects in addition to those in the repository. The paper, confirms that triangular co-operation is happening in regions beyond Latin America. Triangular co-operation in the MENA region is more than a niche modality and represents non-negligible volumes of assistance for 68% of technical co-operation projects in this region having a budget over USD 1 million. This information, currently not available in the CRS, reveals the composition of Arab providers' support to sectors. The focus is on economic infrastructure and services, notably, transport and storage (20% of their co-operation for about USD 700 million), energy (15%), and industry, mining and construction (9%).

Overall, it appears clear that both South-South co-operation and triangular co-operation would provide valuable information if it was seen in conjunction with existing DAC CRS reporting. TOSSD has a strong potential to provide this common framework of reporting and provide an improved sectoral picture of development finance.

2.4.4. TOSSD "satellite" indicators can help expand the global picture on sectors

The TOSSD framework is expected to include the tracking of external financing for development much beyond official finance. It does this by also looking at private finance mobilised through official interventions, as well as other private flows, such as FDI, remittances or private philanthropy (see Table 2.2) This is very much in line with the Addis Ababa Action Agenda (AAAA) (United Nations, 2015[2]).

A good example of the potential contribution of TOSSD to providing increased transparency on sectoral flows for development is the example of private philanthropy, the growth of which was much welcomed at the Third International Conference on Financing for Development in Addis Ababa[37]. The private philanthropy "satellite indicator" of the TOSSD framework would be informed by a regular collection of data on Global Private Philanthropy for Development. This would build on the recent OECD survey[38] that managed to collect activity-level data and detailed information from major philanthropic foundations active in development co-operation. Even though tracking an expanded set of flows does not come without challenges (See Box 2.9), initiatives such as the OECD DAC Survey can fill critical sectoral data gaps and has the potential to change the perspective on some specific SDGs. Prior to this ground-breaking exercise, no publicly available source of data on the activities of private philanthropic foundations in development, aligned with international statistical standards and comparable to traditional aid by sector, was available. The survey revealed a total contribution by private philanthropic foundations of USD 23.9 billion during the period 2013-15, or USD 7.96 billion per year, on average.

Box 2.9. TOSSD will need to overcome some of the barriers in the existing system

TOSSD holds great promise for standardising the information on a wider range of flows from a larger number of providers. However, there is a legitimate risk that some of the challenges faced by the current OECD DAC system (see Sections 2.2 and 2.3 in this chapter) may also be present in the TOSSD framework. When implementing TOSSD, providers could, therefore, pay special attention to a number of key dimensions.

A new architecture involving a wide set of actors: New mechanisms, taking into account political dimensions, will need to be put in place to allow for the participation of all actors. For example, the International TOSSD Task Force[39] is implementing an observer mechanism that allows for the participation of major emerging economies in the process. This mechanism will help to bring their perspectives into the process. A better sectoral picture may come at a cost in the short term. For example, getting data from emerging economies may mean accepting only aggregated sectoral information at first.

Staff capacity: Collecting a wider set of flows requires additional capacity to manage the amount and increased complexity of information that underpin these flows. From a sectoral perspective, knowledge of the SDGs and an understanding of the various financial instruments and partnership modalities with the private sector, will be increasingly important.

Information technology systems: Investment in current systems will be needed to avoid duplication of efforts. DAC providers should, for example, continue investing in the CRS, as this system will remain the backbone of the TOSSD framework (to avoid parallel data collection processes, it is anticipated that the DAC CRS reporting will be used to produce TOSSD data for these providers.) Other systems and strong partnerships should be used to complement the information beyond official information.

The potential of private philanthropy to contribute to the global picture of support to sectors in developing countries is particularly visible in the health and population policies/programmes and reproductive health sectors, as shown in Figure 2.5. Overall, during the period 2012-16, private philanthropy is estimated to have contributed USD 3.3 billion dollars annually to the "health" and "population and reproductive health" sectors in developing countries. This makes private philanthropy the third biggest donor in these two sectors and the largest donor when looking solely at the health sector. Private philanthropic foundations, particularly the Bill & Melinda Gates Foundation, which accounts for an estimated yearly average of USD 2.2 billion of this USD 3.3 billion of contributions to the "health" and "population and reproductive health" sectors, represent important actors in the delivery of SDG 3 – "Ensure healthy lives and promote well-being for all at all ages".

Figure 2.5. Private philanthropy as a whole is the third biggest donor to the health sectors and is critical to achieving SDG 3

Average 2012-16, 2016 constant prices, USD billion commitments

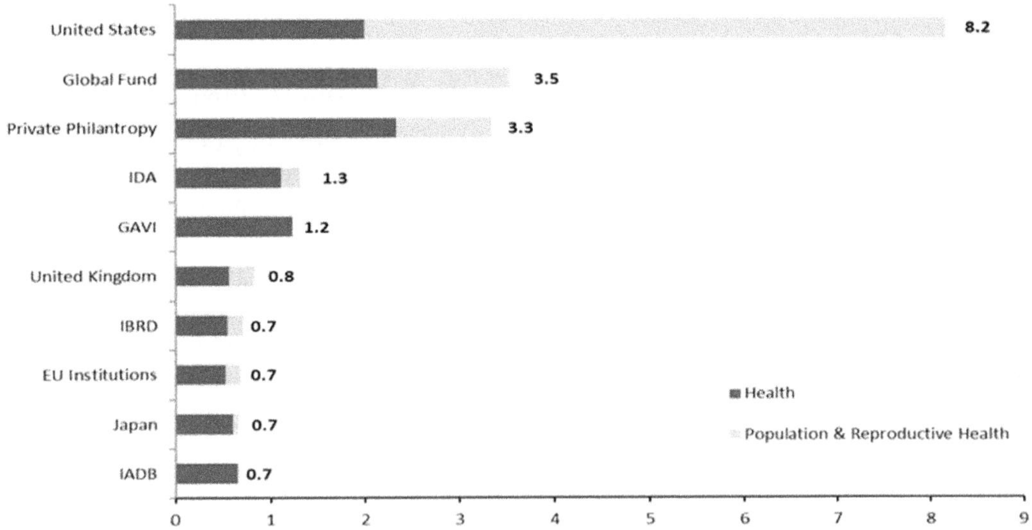

Note: SDG 3 is "Ensure healthy lives and promote well-being for all at all ages".

Source: For ODF, (OECD, 2018[34]), "International development statistics (database)", http://www.oecd.org/dac/financing-sustainable-development/development-finance-data/idsonline.htm. For private philanthropy, calculations based on philanthropic information in (OECD, 2018[35]), Creditor Reporting System, https://stats.oecd.org/Index.aspx?DataSetCode=crs1 and (OECD, 2017[36]), the OECD survey on Private Philanthropy for Development 2013-15 (with estimates for 2012 and 2016). See also the Annex at the end of this document. Assessed/core contributions to multilateral organisations were excluded to avoid double counting.

StatLink https://doi.org/10.1787/888933855352

Notes

[1] See https://www.cooperacionsursur.org/es/recursos/sidicss.html for more information on the Ibero-American Integrated Data System on South-South and Triangular Cooperation (SIDICSS). The latest report using this data is available at http://www.informesursur.org/?lang=en#informe.

[2] The database is available at http://ppi.worldbank.org. The Private Participation in Infrastructure Projects Database records the total investment in infrastructure projects from private participation since 1990. It covers a wide range of infrastructure-related sectors (water, energy, transport and telecommunications), including at activity level.

[3] For more information see: http://www.jedh.org/about.html. The database has been jointly developed by the Bank for International Settlements, the International Monetary Fund (IMF), the Organisation for Economic Co-operation and Development (OECD) and the World Bank (WB). It

brings together external debt data and selected foreign assets from international creditor/market and debtor/national sources.

4 The service tracks cross-border greenfield investment across all sectors and countries worldwide, with real-time monitoring of investment projects, capital investment and job creation.

5 The database is available at: https://climatefundsupdate.org/data-dashboard/. Climate Funds Update is an independent website that provides information on the growing number of international climate finance initiatives designed to help developing countries address the challenges of climate change.

6 For a definition of official development finance see para. 31 in (OECD, 2018[10]).

7 The statistical data for Israel are supplied by and under the responsibility of the relevant Israeli authorities. The use of such data by the OECD is without prejudice to the status of the Golan Heights, East Jerusalem and Israeli settlements in the West Bank under the terms of international law.

8 Other challenges not described in this section, but which may also have implications for the quality of sectoral analyses, include, for example, challenges related to data provided in national languages; the use of acronyms, which makes it hard for the user to interpret the data; or varying levels of aggregation of data, which prevents users from accessing activity-level information – recognising that for some providers, such as the United States, the number of records makes it almost obligatory to aggregate some of the information.

9 In the current system, reporters are required to report their activities against one sector only, even if the activity focuses on more than just one sector. This system is being improved with a "multiple sector coding system" – as described in the same section.

10 This new system will be implemented in 2018 for 2017 flows, with a trial period of three years.

11 For more information on these issues, see (OECD, 2018[10]). Key word searches in particular do not necessarily allow for good analysis of certain topics as these types of searches heavily depend on the quality of descriptive information provided in the data reporting.

12 Through a comparison between Table 2 in [DCD-DAC-STAT(2017)15] and the table in Annex 2 in [DCD/DAC/STAT(2013)4]. The years refer to the year of assessment, 2012 or 2017, not the year of the flows considered.

13 Some of the loans are extended at an interest rate of 2% with a grace period of 9 years and a maturity of 20 years. The concessional character of a loan, from the point of view of the OECD DAC, differs from the one applied in Senegal.

14 All providers reporting to the CRS, in 2015 commitment terms.

15 See also Figure 7.13 on page 156 in (OECD, 2017[3]).

16 Non-DAC providers account for more than 5% of ODF to this sector.

17 For an example of classification by a multilateral organisation, see that of the World Bank at: http://projects.worldbank.org/sector.

18 https://foundationcenter.org/.

19 https://www.iatiregistry.org/.

20 As of 20 June 2018, based on the list provided at https://www.iatiregistry.org/publisher.

21 Available at http://stats.oecd.org/index.aspx, under the section "Globalisation", the OECD.Stat database provides FDI financial flows in main aggregates, by partner country and by industry; FDI

income by partner country and by industry; and FDI positions by main aggregates, by partner country and by industry. FDI information is also available in the OECD IDS online databases (OECD, 2018[34]).

22 The Investment map is available at http://www.intracen.org/itc/market-info-tools/foreign-direct-investment/. It is a web-based tool that helps Investment Promotion Agencies (IPAs) assess which sectors in their countries have successfully attracted Foreign Direct Investment (FDI) and it assists them in the process of prioritizing sectors for investment promotion.

23 Available at http://unctadstat.unctad.org/wds/ReportFolders/reportFolders.aspx; the UNCTADStat provides annual FDI figures (inward and outward flows and stock) since 1970.

24 See in particular paragraphs 35 to 49 in (United Nations, 2015[2]).

25 See: http://www.oecd.org/dac/financing-sustainable-development/development-finance-standards/mobilisation.htm.

26 Every year, the OECD DAC provides the UN with key financing information to develop the Sustainable Development Goals Report. See for example the section on "the Partnerships for the Goals" in (UN DESA, 2017[39]).

27 For a full list of SDGs and targets, see (United Nations, 2017[38]).

28 For more information on how purpose codes are updated, see the "Rules on frequency of updates to purpose codes for DAC Sector Classification" at: http://www.oecd.org/dac/stats/42745930.pdf.

29 For more information on TOSSD, please see: http://www.oecd.org/dac/financing-sustainable-development/development-finance-standards/tossd.htm.

30 See: http://www.oecd.org/dac/financing-sustainable-development/development-finance-standards/tossd-task-force.htm.

31 For more information on the work of the International TOSSD Task Force, see: http://www.oecd.org/dac/financing-sustainable-development/development-finance-standards/tossd-task-force.htm.

32 See in particular paragraphs 35 to 49 of the Addis Ababa Action Agenda (United Nations, 2015[2]).

33 For more information on this OECD work strand, see: http://www.oecd.org/dac/financing-sustainable-development/development-finance-standards/mobilisation.htm.

34 See the papers related to the measurement of technical co-operation in http://www.oecd.org/dac/financing-sustainable-development/development-finance-standards/tossd-task-force.htm.

35 This would also require discussions of the respective methodologies and definitions used in both systems.

36 Data was reported in 2017 on 2016 flows (disbursements, current).

37 See in particular paragraph 42 in the Addis Ababa Action Agenda (United Nations, 2015[2]).

38 For more information on the work strand on private philanthropy at the OECD, see: http://www.oecd.org/dac/financing-sustainable-development/development-finance-standards/beyond-oda-foundations.htm.

39 For more information on the TOSSD Task Force, see http://www.oecd.org/dac/financing-sustainable-development/development-finance-standards/tossd-task-force.htm.

References

Ahmad, Y. and A. Nichols (2017), *"CRS reporting issues in 2016"*, OECD, Paris, http://www.oecd.org/officialdocuments/publicdisplaydocumentpdf/?cote=DCD/DAC/STAT(2017)15&docLanguage=En. [11]

Benn, J. (2017), *"Data collection in the CRS on development co-operation in support of the 2030 Agenda for sustainable development", paper presented to the meeting of the Working Party on Development Finance Statistics (WP-STAT), 20-21 June 2017 - DCD/DAC/STAT(2017)20*, OECD, Paris, http://www.oecd.org/officialdocuments/publicdisplaydocumentpdf/?cote=DCD/DAC/STAT(2017)20&docLanguage=En. [22]

Benn, J. and V. Gaveau (2015), *"Comprehensive review of purpose codes and policy markers in light of the SDGs and post-2015 Agenda", discussion document*, OECD, Paris, http://www.oecd.org/officialdocuments/publicdisplaydocumentpdf/?cote=DCD/DAC/STAT(2015)9&docLanguage=En. [20]

Benn, J. and W. Luijkx (2017), "Emerging providers' international co-operation for development", *OECD Development Co-operation Working Papers*, No. 33, OECD Publishing, Paris, http://dx.doi.org/10.1787/15d6a3c7-en. [13]

Benn, J. and W. Luijkx (2015), *"Update on progress in adapting DAC statistics to non-DAC countries' needs and a proposal for monitoring triangular co-operation through DAC statistics - DCD/DAC/STAT(2015)23"*, OECD, Paris. [30]

Benn, J., C. Sangaré and T. Hos (2017), ""Amounts mobilised from the private sector by official development finance interventions: guarantees, syndicated loans, shares in collective investment vehicles, direct investment in companies, credit lines"", *OECD Development Co-operation Working Papers*, No. 36, OECD Publishing, Paris, http://dx.doi.org/10.1787/8135abde-en. [26]

Berbegal, M. and J. Benn (2017), *"Update on reporting by multilateral organisations, non-DAC countries and private foundations - DCD/DAC/STAT(2017)16"*, OECD, Paris, http://www.oecd.org/officialdocuments/publicdisplaydocumentpdf/?cote=DCD/DAC/STAT(2017)16&docLanguage=En. [16]

Casado-Asensio, J. and N. Piefer (2018), "Breaking Down the Myths of Triangular Co-operation in Middle East and North Africa", *OECD Development Co-operation Working Papers*, No. 41, OECD Publishing, Paris, http://dx.doi.org/10.1787/41102acd-en. [33]

Delalande, G. and V. Gaveau (2018), "Senegal's Perspective on TOSSD", *OECD Development Co-operation Working Papers*, No. 43, OECD Publishing, Paris, http://dx.doi.org/10.1787/4144f82a-en. [15]

Delalande, G., R. Halvorson-Quevedo and C. Sangaré (2018), "The Philippines' Perspective on TOSSD", *OECD Development Co-operation Working Papers*, No. 42, OECD Publishing, Paris, http://dx.doi.org/10.1787/6ecaa5ac-en. [25]

Gualberti, G., J. Benn and al. (2018), *"Proposal to include an SDG Focus field in the CRS database, Formal meeting of the Working Party on Development Finance Statistics (WP-STAT), 13-15 June 2018"*, OECD, Paris, http://DCD/DAC/STAT(2018)41/REV1. [23]

Gualberti, G. and V. Thielemans (2018), *"Inclusion of an SDG Focus Field in the CRS database - Proposal for discussion DCD/DAC/STAT(2018)1"*, OECD, Paris, http://www.oecd.org/officialdocuments/publicdisplaydocumentpdf/?cote=DCD/DAC/STAT(2018)1&docLanguage=En. [37]

IFC (2017), *Opportunities for Private Enterprises in Emerging Markets*, IFC, http://www.ifc.org/wps/wcm/connect/publications_ext_content/ifc_external_publication_site/publications_listing_page/blockchain+report. [7]

Miyamoto, K. and E. Chiofalo (2016), *"Official Development Finance for infrastructure: with a special focus on Multilateral Development Banks", OECD Development Co-operation Working Papers, No. 30*, OECD Publishing, Paris. [14]

Nichols, A. and V. Thielemans (2016), *"Adjusting CRS classification in light of the SDGs - next steps - DCD/DAC/STAT(2016)25"*, OECD, Paris, https://one.oecd.org/document/DCD/DAC/STAT(2016)25/en/pdf. [21]

OECD (2018), *"Converged statistical reporting directives for the CRS and the annual DAC questionnaire - Addendum 1, 2 and 3"*, OECD, Paris, http://www.oecd.org/dac/financing-sustainable-development/development-finance-standards/addenda-converged-statistical-reporting-directives.htm. [12]

OECD (2018), *"International development statistics (database)"*, OECD, Paris, http://www.oecd.org/dac/financing-sustainable-development/development-finance-data/idsonline.htm. [34]

OECD (2018), *"Converged statistical reporting directives for the Creditor Reporting System (CRS) and the annual DAC questionnaire"*, OECD, Paris, https://one.oecd.org/document/DCD/DAC/STAT(2018)9/FINAL/en/pdf. [10]

OECD (2018), *"Creditor Reporting System"*, OECD, Paris, https://stats.oecd.org/Index.aspx?DataSetCode=crs1. [35]

OECD (2017), *"Development Co-operation Report 2017: Data for Development"*, OECD Publishing, Paris, http://dx.doi.org/10.1787/dcr-2017-en. [3]

OECD (2017), *"TOSSD: a new statistical measure for the SDG era"*, OECD, Paris, http://www.oecd.org/dac/financing-sustainable-development/development-finance-standards/Updated%20TOSSD%20Flyer%20with%20TOSSD%20Task%20Force%20inserted%2011%20May%202017.pdf. [24]

OECD (2017), *"OECD Survey on Private Philanthropy for Development 2013-15"*, OECD, Paris, http://www.oecd.org/dac/financing-sustainable-development/development-finance-standards/beyond-oda-foundations.htm. [36]

OECD (2017), "Dispelling the myths of triangular co-operation: Evidence from the 2015 OECD survey on triangular co-operation", *OECD Development Policy Papers*, No. 6, OECD Publishing, Paris, http://dx.doi.org/10.1787/a8b14341-en. [32]

OECD (2017), *Triangular Co-operation*, http://www.oecd.org/dac/dac-global-relations/triangular-cooperation.htm. [31]

OECD (2016), *"OECD DAC survey on amounts mobilised from the private sector by official development finance interventions 2012-2015"*, OECD, Paris, http://www.oecd.org/dac/financing-sustainable-development/development-finance-standards/mobilisation.htm. [27]

OECD (2014), *"Donor Support to Public-Private Partrnerships: the case of the Dakar-Diamniadio Toll Highway Project - COM/DAF/INV/DCD/DAC(2014)4"*, OECD, Paris. [28]

Prada and al. (2014), *"Mapping of sources and uses of information on external development finance" - Research paper*, (FNI), FORO Nacional International, Lima, Peru, http://www.oecd.org/dac/financing-sustainable-development/Mapping%20sources%20of%20information%20on%20external%20developing%20finance%20.pdf. [1]

Refugee and Migratory Movements Research Unit (RMMRU) (2016), *Impact of Remittances on Education and Human Resource Development: Evidence from Bangladesh [RMMRU Policy Brief 15]*, RMMRU, Dhaka, https://assets.publishing.service.gov.uk/media/57a0895c40f0b6497400003a/RMMRU-Policy-Brief-No15_Mar16.pdf. [19]

Saudi Arabia (2018), *"Saudi Aid Platform"*, Saudi Arabia, Riyadh, Saudi Arabia, https://data.ksrelief.org/en/home.aspx. [17]

SEGIB (2017), *"Report on South-South Cooperation in Ibero-América 2017"*, SEGIB, Veracruz, http://www.informesursur.org/?lang=en#informe. [29]

Stanford GSB (2018), *"Blockchain for Social Impact - Moving beyond the hype"*, OECD, Paris, http://www.gsb.stanford.edu/sites/gsb/files/publication-pdf/study-blockchain-impact-moving-beyond-hype_0.pdf. [8]

UN DESA (2017), *The Sustainable Development Goals Report 2017*, UN, New York, http://dx.doi.org/10.18356/4d038e1e-en. [39]

UN Global Pulse (2017), *UN Global Pulse Annual Report 2016*, United Nations, New York, NY, http://unglobalpulse.org/sites/default/files/UNGP%20Report%202016_DIGITAL%20VERSION.pdf. [6]

UN OICT (2017), *"Usage of blockchain in the UN System - A desk review"*, United Nations, https://unite.un.org/sites/unite.un.org/files/session_3_b_blockchain_un_initiatives_final.pdf. [9]

United Nations (2018), *Big Data for Sustainable Development*, http://www.un.org/en/sections/issues-depth/big-data-sustainable-development/index.html (accessed on 7 February 2018). [5]

United Nations (2017), *"Global indicator framework for the Sustainable Development Goals and targets of the 2030 Agenda for Sustainable Development" - A/RES/71/313*, United Nations, New York, NY, https://undocs.org/A/RES/71/313. [38]

United Nations (2015), *"Addis Ababa Action Agenda of the Third International Conference on Financing for Development"*, United Nations, New York, NY, http://www.un.org/esa/ffd/wp-content/uploads/2015/08/AAAA_Outcome.pdf. [2]

United Nations (2014), *"A World that Counts - Mobilising the data revolution for sustainable development"*, United Nations, New York, NY, http://www.undatarevolution.org/wp-content/uploads/2014/11/A-World-That-Counts.pdf. [4]

World Bank (s.d.), *Migration and Remittances Database*, World Bank, Washington, DC., http://www.worldbank.org/en/topic/migrationremittancesdiasporaissues/brief/migration-remittances-data. [18]

Chapter 3. Rethinking sector financing strategies to achieve the Sustainable Development Goals

Recognising that an overview of official finance by Sustainable Development Goal (SDG) is highly challenging given the multifaceted and integrated nature of the SDG agenda (Chapter 2), analyses along traditional sectors represent the strongest basis available to inform interventions targeting the SDGs. The first section of this chapter provides an overview of the main patterns and trends of sector financing by official development finance providers. It builds on an analytical framework that draws on the implications for sectoral analyses of the Addis Ababa Action Agenda, using both official development finance and private finance mobilised through official development interventions. The second section complements the first one by looking in more detail at the current division of labour between bilateral and multilateral providers across sectors. The third section then scopes the sector implications that the new SDG agenda has on providers' sector financing strategies and how they can concretely adjust these financing strategies to reflect the new 2030 Agenda.

Key messages

Key messages to development co-operation providers emerging from this chapter include:

- **Overall, official development finance (ODF) has increased by 35% between 2012 and 2016 in real terms, benefiting all sectors in developing countries.** In 2016, ODF from bilateral and multilateral providers of development co-operation amounted to USD 293.6 billion.
- **Development co-operation providers mobilise private finance only in a handful of sectors.** An estimated USD 22.7 billion of private finance was mobilised every year by official development intervention during the period 2012-16. More than 80% of this was focused in just four sectors – banking and business, energy, industry and mining and construction. Unexpectedly, private finance is hardly mobilised by official interventions in sectors such as water (USD 318 million on average per year between 2012 and 2016) or transport and storage (USD 917 million).
- **The Sustainable Development Goals (SDGs) are expected results, not sectors of intervention.** Providers of development co-operation have to map the impact of each sector intervention against each goal. For instance, a contribution to SDG 4 on education could be supported through direct investment in education (e.g. building schools and training teachers) and/or by increasing electricity access in rural areas (SDG 7) to enable children to study in the evening. Moreover, development partners can support global public goods as these are enablers for achieving development gains in multiple sectors.
- **Since the SDGs are primarily implemented domestically, sector strategies of development partners should align with the SDG targets defined by each partner country.** SDG alignment requires engaging in dialogue with each partner country to identify the SDG priorities and aligning the providers' country programmes with the targets identified. It will also require mainstreaming cross-cutting issues (e.g. gender and environment) as much as possible and finding the best delivery channels based on country context and local capacity. Finally, providers' monitoring and evaluation frameworks need to be aligned with the SDGs to assess their effects and learn from experience.
- **Resources targeting the SDGs have to be distributed appropriately across sectors and countries**, so as not to leave social sectors and the poorest countries, which have more difficulties mobilising financing, unfunded.

3.1. An overview of sector financing by official development partners

This section examines the contribution of official development partners to targeted sectors. In response to the Addis Ababa Action Agenda (AAAA) (United Nations, 2015[1]), it takes a broad view of this contribution. It does this by looking at the development partners' reporting to the Development Assistance Committee's (DAC's) statistical systems during the period 2012-16.[1] These development partners include members of and participants[2] in the DAC and multilateral institutions. This section, like the rest of the publication, also presents official flows using the latest data on private finance mobilised through official development interventions. Thus it presents a global picture of officially supported flows[3] to developing countries, including across sectors.

3.1.1. Official development finance is growing steadily

The share of ODF has grown steadily over the last five years

In 2016, ODF by bilateral and multilateral providers of development co-operation amounted to USD 293.6 billion, which represented a growth of 35% between 2012 and 2016 in real terms (Figure 3.1). Of this increase, 64% was support provided by bilateral providers (46% from DAC providers and 18% from non-DAC providers) and 36% was support provided by multilateral institutions. Overall, ODF grew at an average rate of 7.8% per year over this period in real terms.

Figure 3.1. Official development finance is growing steadily

ODF by type of donor in 2012-16 and amounts mobilised, 2016 constant prices, USD billion commitments

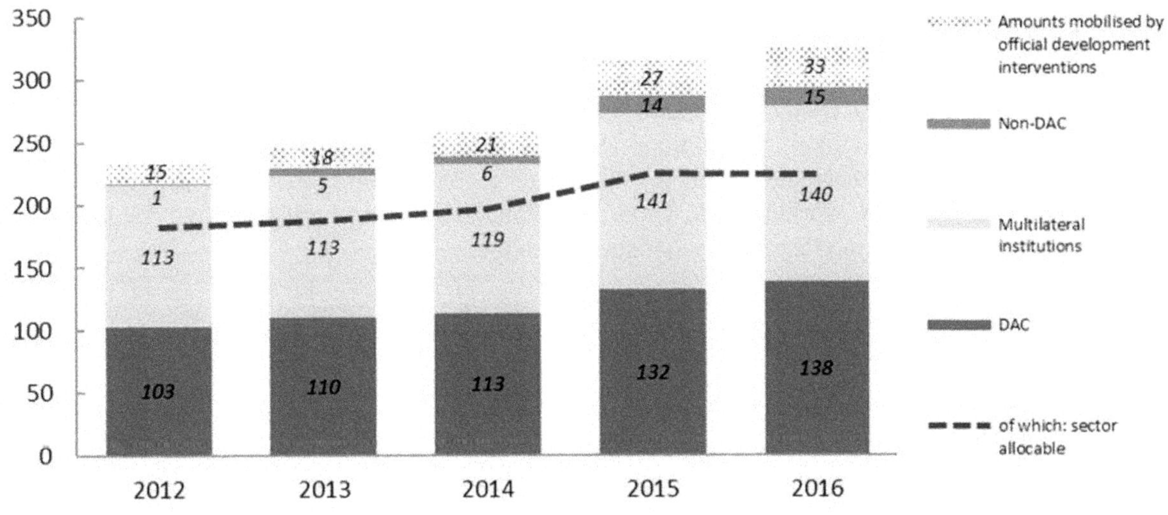

Note: DAC are countries members of the Development Assistance Committee of the Organisation for Economic Co-operation and Development (OECD). European Union (EU) Institutions are also a DAC member, but are part of the multilateral institutions group in this publication.
Source: (OECD, 2018[2]), "International development statistics (database)", http://www.oecd.org/dac/financing-sustainable-development/development-finance-data/idsonline.htm and (OECD, 2016[3]), "OECD DAC survey on amounts mobilised from the private sector by official development finance interventions 2012-2015", http://www.oecd.org/development/stats/mobilisation.htm. Amounts of private finance mobilised are estimated for 2016.

StatLink https://doi.org/10.1787/888933855371

There has also been a slight trend towards bilateralism in recent years. While the breakdown between bilateral and multilateral providers was slightly in favour of multilateral institutions five years ago (with a 52%-48% split), the breakdown is now the exact opposite with bilateral providers representing 52% of ODF in 2016.

Non-DAC providers are taking a growing place, though still modest according to OECD statistics, in the global concert of development finance

As highlighted in Chapter 2, while the DAC already covers funding by a large number of providers of development finance, there are still significant data gaps in the available information on ODF by sector, particularly from major Asian providers.

However, the number of providers that do publish official information on development finance, including by sector, keeps increasing. For example, the number of providers who are not members of the DAC, reporting to the OECD Creditor Reporting System, has increased from two in 2012 to twenty in 2016 – a substantial increase. In total, they provided an estimated USD 15 billion to developing countries in 2016. The overall evolution in ODF during the period 2012-16 reveals an increase in developmental flows coming from providers beyond the DAC community and particularly from Arab countries. This is a result, in part, of a better coverage of information reported by this group of providers (Figure 3.1). In 2016, 89% of ODF coming from non-DAC providers actually came from just three countries:

- the United Arab Emirates, which was ranked as the first provider of official development assistance (ODA) per capita in 2016[4]
- Kuwait, which would feature in 2016 as the 14th biggest provider to the DAC – in sector-allocable terms – if it had been a full member of the Committee
- Turkey, which was the second biggest provider of humanitarian aid in 2016, mainly providing assistance to the Syrian Arab Republic.

The trend of having more and more Arab countries providing information on development finance is likely to continue (See Section 3.2.1), which may also have a significant impact on the sector financing landscape in the coming years. For example, the OECD is currently working with Qatar and Saudi Arabia to include activity-level development co-operation flows in its statistical system.

Recent investments in the refugee crisis reduce the share of ODA allocated to sectors in developing countries

The share of aid that can be allocated by sector in OECD statistics is called sector-allocable aid (See Box 3.1). Overall sector-allocable aid is following a similar positive trend as ODF (Figure 3.1), showing sustained efforts by the provider community to report well by sector on its development finance. However, the share of sector-allocable aid against overall ODF has been showing signs of a decline over the last five years (Table 3.1). This is a result of the increase in humanitarian- and refugee-related costs, which are, by definition, not sector allocable. In 2016, in-donor[5] refugee costs represented 8% of ODA while in 2012 it represented 2.5%. The increase of in-donor refugee costs reduces the share of development finance that can be analysed by sector. Preliminary estimates for 2017 for DAC countries, show an improving picture. ODA spent by donor countries on hosting refugees fell by 13.6% to USD 14.2 billion as refugee arrivals, mainly in Europe, decreased. In-donor refugee costs were 9.7% of total net

ODA, down from 11% in 2016. Stripping out in-donor refugee costs, net ODA was up 1.1% from 2016 in real terms (OECD, 2018[4]).

Box 3.1. Sector allocable and non-sector allocable finance

In DAC statistics, while most contributions can be directly allocated to a given sector (e.g. education and infrastructure), some contributions are not susceptible to allocation by sector and are, therefore, reported as "non-sector allocable". These are:

- commodity aid and general programme assistance (e.g. general budget support and general food aid)
- actions related to debt (e.g. debt forgiveness and debt rescheduling)
- humanitarian aid (e.g. emergency response)
- in-donor costs (e.g. administrative costs and refugee costs)
- other unallocated costs (e.g. development awareness financing).

Source: (OECD, 2018[5]), "Converged statistical reporting directives for the CRS and the annual DAC questionnaire - Addendum 1 - Annexes - modules A, B, and C", https://one.oecd.org/document/ DCD/DAC/STAT(2018)9/ADD1/FINAL /en/pdf.

Table 3.1. Sector allocable ODA has decreased due to recent investments in refugee and humanitarian crises

	2012	2013	2014	2015	2016
Sector-allocable ODA as a proportion of total ODA (%)	78.7	76.3	76.8	72.2	67.7
Humanitarian assistance as a proportion of total ODA (%)	7.6	7.8	10.5	11.2	13.5
In-donor refugee costs as a proportion of total ODA (%)	2.5	2.6	3.6	6.3	8.0

Source: (OECD, 2018[2]), "International development statistics (database)", http://www.oecd.org/dac/financing-sustainable-development/development-finance-data/idsonline.htm.

StatLink https://doi.org/10.1787/888933855694

3.1.2. Providers' sector financing strategies are very stable over time with clear patterns between bilateral and multilateral providers

The breakdown of ODF across broad sector groupings (Figure 3.2) has not changed much in the last five years despite the recent growth in ODF. This reflects the high stability of sector allocation policies by official providers. ODF to broad sector groupings is broken down into three tiers, with "social sectors" and "infrastructure" representing two-thirds (34%, on average, over the period for each of the two groupings). The last third is broken down among the production sectors (14% of ODF on average), with "banking and business" and "multisector" activities representing approximately 9% of ODF over the period 2012-16 (Figure 3.3).

Figure 3.2. The growth in official development finance is benefitting all sector groupings

ODF by broad sector groupings in 2012-16, 2016 constant prices, USD billion commitments

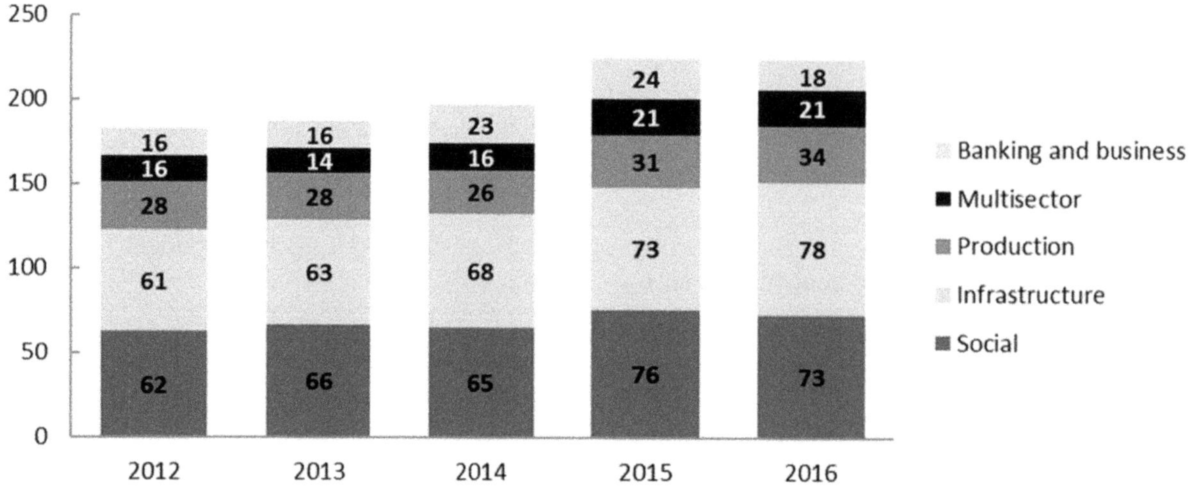

Source: (OECD, 2018[2]), "International development statistics (database)", http://www.oecd.org/dac/financing-sustainable-development/development-finance-data/idsonline.htm.

StatLink https://doi.org/10.1787/888933855390

Figure 3.3. The social and infrastructure sector groupings represent two thirds of sector-allocable official development finance

Share of ODF by sector groupings 2012-16, 2016 constant prices, USD billion commitments

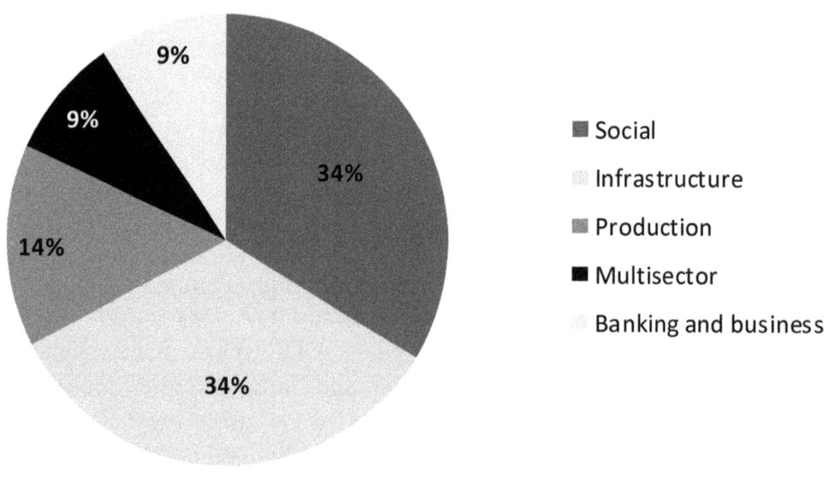

Source: (OECD, 2018[2]), "International development statistics (database)", http://www.oecd.org/dac/financing-sustainable-development/development-finance-data/idsonline.htm.

StatLink https://doi.org/10.1787/888933855409

Concessional flows concentrate on social sectors, but also fund sectors beyond these. Non-concessional financing is supporting "hard" sectors, such as infrastructure, but also "softer" ones, such as public financial management in middle-income countries.

Figure 3.4 provides an overview of the allocation by individual sectors of both concessional and non-concessional official flows for the period 2012-16.

Social sectors and services (i.e. health, education, governance and civil society, and other social infrastructure and services) are mainly financed using official concessional flows. ODA represents 81% of the financing to these sectors. A noticeable exception to this trend is the financing of the "government and civil society" sector which is also funded through OOF for an average of USD 5.3 billion a year. This support corresponds, almost in its entirety, to operations by the International Bank of Reconstruction and Development, the Inter-American Development Bank (IADB) and the Asian Development Bank (AsDB) in support of activities in the areas of public finance and public policy management. In addition, it supports decentralisation processes, mostly in middle-income economies in Asia (e.g. Indonesia and Philippines) and Latin America (e.g. Brazil, Colombia and Mexico). Social sectors and services are the main destinations of ODA flows. These flows, which are close to USD 55 billion a year, accounted for 42% of total ODA to sectors, on average, during the period 2012-16.

Figure 3.4. Concessional flows tend to focus on social sectors but not only

Concessional and non-concessional ODF by individual allocable sector and by type of official flow, average 2012-16 2016 constant prices, USD billion commitments

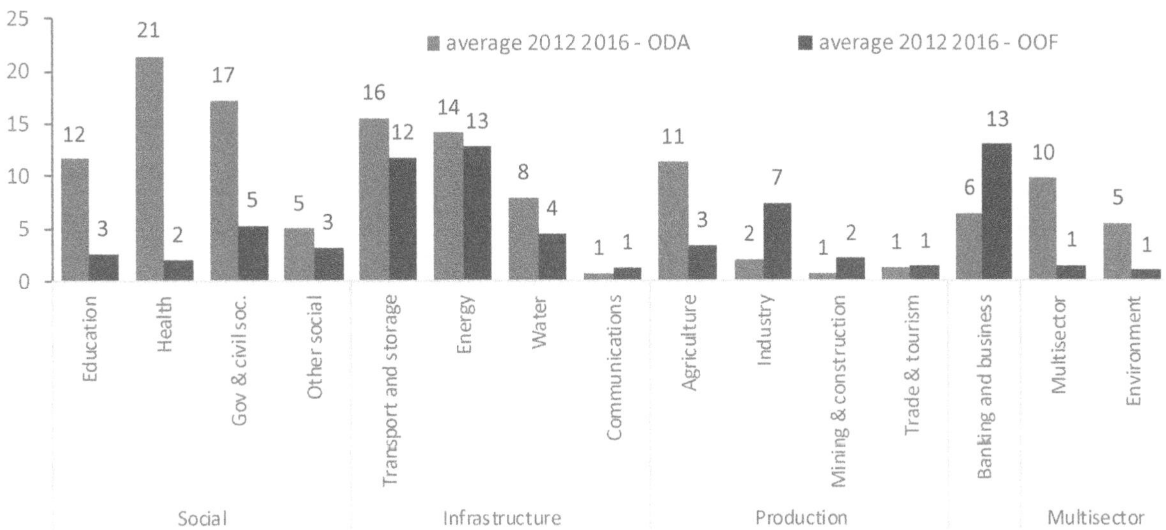

Source: (OECD, 2018[2]), "International development statistics (database)", http://www.oecd.org/dac/financing-sustainable-development/development-finance-data/idsonline.htm.

StatLink https://doi.org/10.1787/888933855428

Infrastructure sectors (including transport and storage, energy and water and communications) are funded more through concessional than non-concessional resources; ODA accounts for 56% of total ODF to these sectors. Infrastructure is the second main destination of ODA flows, representing 29% of total ODA to these sectors. However, infrastructure remains, with 42% of the total OOF to sectors, the main sector of destination of OOF flows.

Production sectors are almost equally funded by concessional and non-concessional flows, with ODA representing 52% of ODF to these sectors.

The banking and business sectors are largely funded through non-concessional resources, showing a good use of scarce ODA resources in sectors that tend to generate financial returns on investments and, therefore, do not always need concessional resources.

3.1.3. Private finance is mobilised in sectors where business is traditionally active, but there seems to be untapped potential for mobilisation in some sectors

Providers increasingly mobilise private finance for development. Since 2012, amounts mobilised by official development interventions are estimated to have more than doubled from 15 billion in 2012 to an estimated 33 billion in 2016 (Figure 3.1).

From a sector perspective, the mobilisation of private finance takes place in many different sectors, but, unsurprisingly, in much bigger volumes in sectors where prospects of financial returns for the private sector are high. On average, for the period 2012-16, more than 80% of the total private finance mobilised occurred in four sectors: "banking and business", "energy", "industry" and "mining and construction" (Figure 3.5).

Figure 3.5. Private finance is only mobilised in a handful of sectors

ODF and private finance mobilised through official development finance interventions by individual sectors, average 2012-16, 2016 constant prices, USD billion commitments

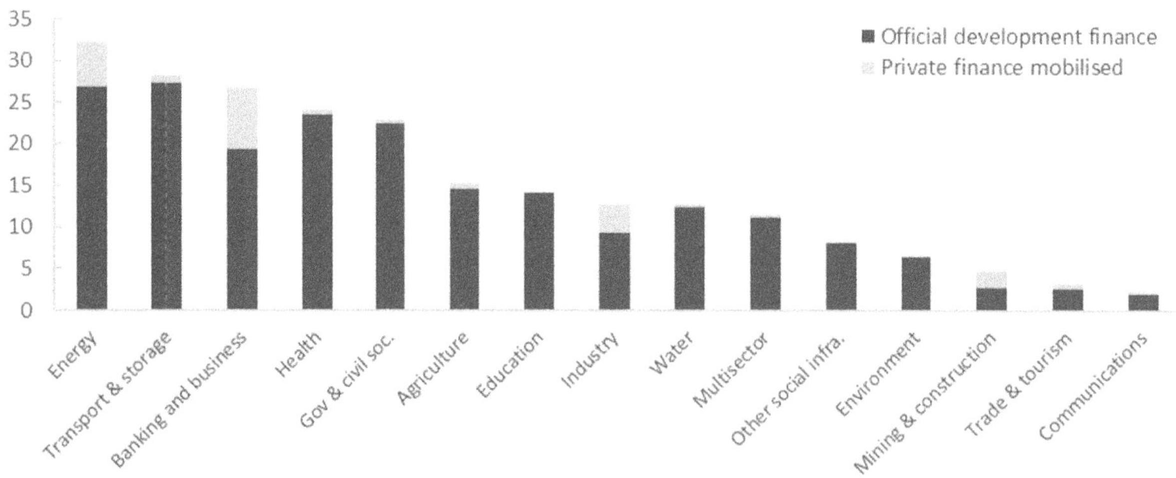

Source: (OECD, 2018[2]), "International development statistics (database)", http://www.oecd.org/dac/financing-sustainable-development/development-finance-data/idsonline.htm and (OECD, 2016[3]), "OECD DAC survey on amounts mobilised from the private sector by official development finance interventions 2012-2015", http://www.oecd.org/development/stats/mobilisation.htm.

StatLink https://doi.org/10.1787/888933855447

Very little private finance is mobilised in social sectors (e.g. health, education or government and civil society), even though these sectors do present some potential to attract the private sector. This has been shown, for example, in Ghana where private sector involvement came in response to unmet local demand for quality education (World Bank Group, $2017_{[6]}$). Other sectors, where the potential for mobilising resources could be considered as high given the traditional involvement of the private sector, do not show a high level of private finance mobilised by official providers. This is, for example, the case in "water", "agriculture" and the "transport and storage" sectors.

A first possible explanation for this potential lack of mobilisation in certain sectors may be related to the data currently available. The data collection on amounts mobilised from the private sector remains a fairly new exercise for providers, as it was only implemented in the DAC regular reporting in 2017[6]. It is, therefore, likely that as providers get more experience, the comprehensiveness and accuracy of the data will significantly improve in future years. This is increasingly likely as data collection on private finance mobilised is now fully integrated in the yearly data collection process of the DAC. Reporting on amounts mobilised in 2018 (on 2017 flows) has improved as it includes the majority of development finance institutions' and international finance institutions' operations designed to mobilise private finance for development. Also, as highlighted in Chapter 2, the lack of data from some of the major emerging economies (such as the People's Republic of China - hereafter "China" - and Brazil) also prevents drawing a comprehensive picture of the private finance mobilised for development purposes.

A second possible explanation is related to the fact that data collected on amounts mobilised only show the first sector of allocation. Therefore, funds allocated to the banking sector may well ultimately serve other sectors. This calls for a reflection on how to collect further information to improve sector analyses of the ultimate sector of financing. In that regard, "blockchain" technologies may be able to help in the future to track financial flows across sectors and institutions.

Another aspect is that the data in Figure 3.5 represent a baseline for future sector analyses. This is because providers have not yet had time to factor into their policies the AAAA, which is calling for the mobilisation of private resources. This only took place in 2015, towards the end of the period being studied in this publication. Data in future years should reflect the level of translation of political commitments taken in Addis into concrete increases in resource mobilisation.

Finally, from a policy perspective, the lack of resource mobilisation in certain sectors may indicate that providers need to step up their mobilisation efforts and systematically look into mobilising private finance in all sectors, including in the "transport and storage" or in the "water" sectors, as indicated above.

3.1.4. Providers indirectly contribute to sector financing by supporting domestic resource mobilisation, but data is missing on the magnitude of the amounts leveraged and the final destination of this financing in terms of sectors

Investing in domestic resource mobilisation is an excellent way to support sector financing. By helping to increase the tax base in developing countries, providers help them generate resources that can then be sovereignly allocated to priority sectors. This increases their autonomy and ownership over these funds. (See Box 3.2).

Box 3.2. The Addis Tax Initiative

The Addis Tax Initiative (ATI), started by the governments of Germany, Netherlands, United Kingdom, and United States, is a multi-stakeholder partnership of development partners and partner countries. It was launched at the 3rd Financing for Development Conference in Addis Ababa in 2015. It aims to catalyse significant increases in domestic revenue and improve the transparency, fairness, effectiveness and efficiency of tax systems in partner countries. Since its launch in 2015, membership has grown to include 41 countries and 13 supporting organisations – a mix of philanthropic, regional and international organisations. Members of the Initiative have agreed to three overarching commitments. First, the ATI development partners commit to collectively doubling technical co-operation in the area of domestic revenue mobilisation by 2020. The objective is to reach, collectively, USD 223.76 million in gross disbursements and USD 237.96 million in commitments. Second, the ATI partner countries commit to stepping up the mobilisation of domestic revenues in order to spur development. Third, all ATI signatories commit to promoting and ensuring policy coherence for development.

Note: See also https://www.addistaxinitiative.net and https://www.taxcompact.net/index.htm. *Source*: Case study collected through the OECD DAC Survey on other official flows carried out in 2017 and the ATI (Addis Tax Initiative, 2017[7])

In 2016, DAC members' disbursements in the area of domestic resource mobilisation represented about USD 348 million. These interventions can take many forms, including support to targeted policies or the improvement of local capacities in mobilising additional domestic resources.

In Paraguay for example, the rules on income tax and value added tax in the agricultural sector have been changed to encourage formalisation and increase tax collection in this sector. The introduction of the new agricultural income tax (IRAGRO) has been a success, recording in the first two and a half years (2014–2016) a tax-levy increase of 134.5% (Addis Tax Initiative, 2017[7])

Within a project on resource governance in West Africa, which has been implemented in Côte d'Ivoire, Guinea, Liberia, and Sierra Leone, the German Development Cooperation supported the installation of an inspection unit in Liberia's tax administration that specialises in the mining sector. A tax audit on an iron ore producer resulted in an additional charge of USD 10,743,561.

Finally, in Zambia and the United Republic of Tanzania (hereafter, "Tanzania"), over several years in the field of tax audit of multinational companies, the Norwegian Agency for Development Cooperation made key contributions to two major court rulings in 2016. These concerned transfer pricing arrangements in the mining sector. In Zambia, the result was a tax reassessment of an additional USD 47 million while in Tanzania the tax reassessment was an additional USD 120 million.[7]

3.2. The global division of labour on sector financing

This section examines key systemic dimensions of the sector landscape that shape the overall analysis across sectors. It first looks at the global division of labour between bilateral and multilateral providers and the evolving landscape of actors, with new, emerging providers starting to reshape this landscape. It then provides a stock-taking of the overall distribution of concessional and non-concessional flows to developing countries between bilateral and multilateral providers. Finally, it dives into the specific analysis of cross-cutting approaches and takes the example of gender equality as a fundamental dimension to consider when analysing sector financing.

3.2.1. The sector division of labour between bilateral and multilateral providers

A global division of labour: bilateral providers tend to focus on social sectors while multilaterals' portfolios target infrastructure as well as banking and business

Is there a global division of labour between bilateral and multilateral providers with regards to sectors? Considering that several bilateral providers (such as China, Brazil and India) do not, as yet, report data in a sufficiently granular way to enable analysis by sector, the current landscape provided in this section focuses on providers' reporting to the OECD Creditor Reporting System (OECD CRS) (OECD, 2018[8]).

Overall, even if both types of provider – bilateral and multilateral – support all sector groupings, multilateral institutions tend to focus their portfolios on infrastructure and the banking and business sectors[8], while bilateral providers rather favour social sectors (Figure 3.6).

During the period 2012-16, bilateral providers contributed, on average, USD 88 billion of sector-allocable ODF per year. Approximately 40% of their portfolios[9] has been focused on the social sectors compared with 29% for multilaterals. In these social sectors, bilateral providers also tend to provide slightly higher volumes of assistance than multilaterals (USD 35.2 billion versus USD 33 billion).

Multilateral institutions have been the most prominent actors in the infrastructure sector with an average USD 42.6 billion of ODF, compared to only USD 25.8 billion from bilateral providers. Overall, infrastructure represents a higher share of the multilaterals' portfolios (37%) versus the 29% share of the bilaterals' portfolios. In other sector groupings, the "banking and business" sector remains a grouping where multilaterals have a greater presence both in volume (almost three times that of bilaterals) and share (more than twice that of bilaterals).

Figure 3.6. Bilateral providers tend to focus on social sectors while multilaterals target infrastructure, as well as banking and business

Share of each sector in bilaterals' and multilateral providers' portfolios, average 2012-16, 2016 constant prices, USD commitments

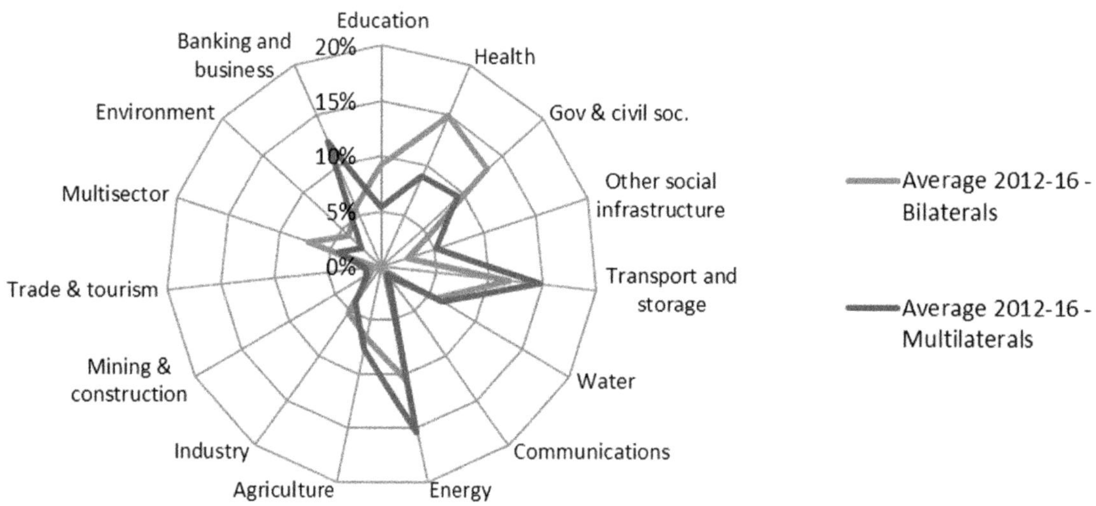

Source: (OECD, 2018[2]), "International development statistics (database)", http://www.oecd.org/dac/financing-sustainable-development/development-finance-data/idsonline.htm.

StatLink https://doi.org/10.1787/888933855466

High volumes of funding are provided by a limited number of providers in most sectors

Looking at the main players in each sector grouping, the landscape of bilateral and multilateral providers reveals that major volumes of sector financing are concentrated among a very limited number of providers (Figure 3.7).

For infrastructure, the most salient aspect is the critical role played by a small group of bilateral providers: the United States, Japan, Germany, France and Korea, and six of the largest multilateral development banks (MDBs)[10]. The contributions of these donors together represent more than 84% of the total ODF to this sector – on average, USD 57.5 billion per year for the period 2012-16.

In the social sectors, the concentration also remains relatively high, with the United States and the World Bank being the most prominent players. Their contributions are almost equivalent to those of the other 13 providers in the list of the top 15 providers (around USD 26 billion, on average, during the period 2012-16). Together, the United States and the World Bank provide close to 40% of all funding to the social sectors. The top 10 providers[11] contribute more than three-quarters (77%) of the total funding to these sectors.

In the banking and business sector, the World Bank Group is the biggest provider, representing 30% of all funding provided to this grouping. The six largest MDBs contribute 70% of all funding to this sector grouping.

Finally, the "production" sector grouping also reveals a high concentration of the number of partners. The top 10 providers[12] account for 79.4% of the total funding to this sector grouping. Korea is the second largest provider to this sector with a contribution of close to USD 4 billion.

Figure 3.7. Major volumes of sector financing are concentrated among a very limited number of providers

Top 15 bilateral and multilateral providers of ODF by broad sector, average 2012-16, 2016 constant prices, USD billion commitments

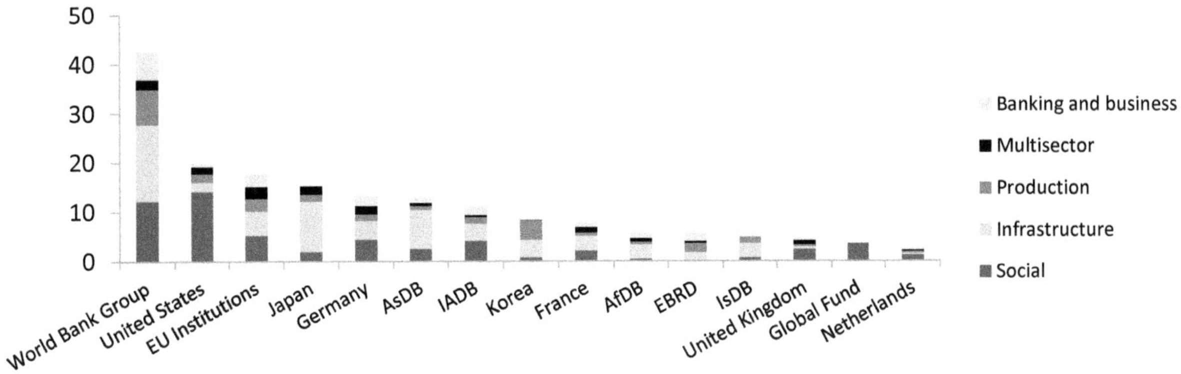

Note: AsDB includes ADB and the Asian Development Special Fund; IADB includes IADB, IADB Special funds and IDB Invest; and African Development Bank (AfDB) includes the AfDB and the African Development Fund.

Source: (OECD, 2018[2]), "International development statistics (database)", http://www.oecd.org/dac/financing-sustainable-development/development-finance-data/idsonline.htm.

StatLink https://doi.org/10.1787/888933855485

With sector information on major bilateral players beyond the DAC still missing, Arab providers position themselves as key sector actors

While information on the financial assistance provided by several key bilateral providers (e.g. China, India and Brazil) is still not disaggregated by sector, other providers have joined the OECD statistical system to report data by sector. By doing so, they make available their significant contributions across sectors.

For example, the United Arab Emirates is now one of the top ten bilateral providers in the production sectors and, together with Kuwait, is also among the top 10 providers for the infrastructure sector grouping. This trend of seeing Arab providers taking a stronger role in the bilateral sector landscape is likely to continue with new Arab providers gradually joining the OECD statistical system (see Table 3.2 and Box 3.3).

Table 3.2. Arab providers are taking a stronger role in the bilateral sector landscape

Top 10 ODF bilateral providers by sector grouping, 2012-16 average, 2016 constant prices, USD million

Social sectors	USD million	Multisector	USD million	Infrastructure	USD million
United States	14 137	Japan	1 683	Japan	10 165
Germany	4 401	Germany	1 674	Germany	3 860
United Kingdom	2 389	United States	1 380	Korea	3 562
France	2 112	France	1 125	France	2 999
Japan	1 955	United Kingdom	863	United States	1 903
Australia	1 257	Norway	597	United Kingdom	541
Netherlands	1 238	Australia	565	United Arab Emirates	443
Sweden	1 099	United Arab Emirates	383	Kuwait	375
Canada	1 095	Canada	329	Netherlands	313
Norway	1 079	Switzerland	293	Norway	256
Banking and business		**Production sectors**		**Total**	
Germany	1 992	Korea	3 945	United States	19 907
France	797	United States	1 733	Japan	15 308
United States	754	Japan	1 459	Germany	13 217
United Kingdom	346	Germany	1 290	Korea	8 407
Norway	310	France	663	France	7 695
Netherlands	293	Netherlands	409	United Kingdom	4 512
Sweden	112	United Kingdom	373	Netherlands	2 468
Switzerland	109	Canada	365	Norway	2 425
Denmark	98	United Arab Emirates	348	Australia	2 354
Canada	93	Switzerland	251	Canada	2 026

Source: (OECD, 2018[2]), "International development statistics (database)", http://www.oecd.org/dac/financing-sustainable-development/development-finance-data/idsonline.htm.

StatLink https://doi.org/10.1787/888933855713

The DAC is looking for new approaches in the context of its renewed mandate. It could continue engaging in substantive policy discussions with the Arab community in, for example, the infrastructure or the productive sectors to compare approaches. This would build on the recent collaboration on sector-related issues, as it recently did on water and sanitation, and energy through the Arab-DAC Dialogue on Development.[13]

More broadly, all providers can take the opportunity to use sector analyses as a platform for strengthened policy dialogue. This would build on the recognition that providers often face the same types of challenges when looking at their sector focus and allocations (e.g. in which sector to invest and with which instruments).

Box 3.3. Providers beyond the DAC increasingly contribute to a better picture on official development finance: The case of Saudi Arabia

Saudi Arabia is already reporting to the OECD on its development co-operation programme. It provides aggregate figures on development co-operation and humanitarian assistance by region, and multilateral aid and loan disbursements from, and repayments to the Saudi Fund for Development. Because Saudi Arabia reports at the aggregate level, its figures do not allow for a sector breakdown. Saudi Arabia started reporting at activity-level to the OECD in 2018 on 2016 and 2017 flows – the report was too late to include these data into the OECD annual publication of detailed data in December 2017. Saudi Arabia has, in the meantime, published its aid activities on the Saudi Aid Platform, a database which contains activity-level information on Saudi Arabia's aid contributions (which cannot strictly be considered as ODA). Currently, the platform records developmental, humanitarian and charity projects for the period 1996-2018, amounting to over USD 85 billion, on average USD 3.7 billion per year. A majority of these projects target developing countries along DAC definitions. Saudi Arabia is also working to extend its platform back to the 1970s. The platform is based on the OECD CRS statistical criteria, which will ensure easy transfer to the OECD systems once these data are available. Saudi Arabia's annual aid amounts, which are being reviewed by the OECD at the time of publishing this report, would position the country among the top 10 providers of the DAC membership on an ODF sector-allocable basis. Also, the country would feature in the top 10 in the broad sector grouping of "infrastructure" and "banking and business". Contributions by the country could help provide a better picture on those individual sectors where Saudi Arabia is most active – transport, banking and financial services, agriculture, water and sanitation, and education.

Source: (Saudi Arabia, 2018[91]) "Saudi Aid Platform" https://data.ksrelief.org/en/home.aspx, accessed on 04 September 2018.

Official providers may also want to join forces with actors beyond the official sphere that have specific experience in a given sector. In the health sector, providers could, for example, ensure a systematic exchange of experiences with the Bill & Melinda Gates Foundation (BMGF) or its local implementation partners. With USD 2.246 billion of funding to this sector, on average, for the period 2012-16, the BMGF is now the third largest provider to the health and reproductive health sectors. It is a custodian of in-depth experience in this area that can potentially benefit many bilateral and multilateral actors involved in this field (See also Chapter 2).

3.2.2. A very different use of concessional and non-concessional financing to sectors by bilateral and multilateral agencies

Bilateral agencies still very much use ODA as a source of financing for almost all sectors, but this may be because of a lack of reporting on other official flows. This calls for improved reporting on these types of flows.

Patterns of funding for bilateral providers (Figure 3.8) indicate that these still rely very much on ODA as a primary source of financing for almost all sectors. Multilateral agencies, in contrast, mostly use non-concessional lending (about 22% more than ODA flows), usefully complementing funding by bilateral providers.

The differences in patterns between bilateral and multilateral providers may be a consequence of the data currently available on other official flows for bilateral providers, which are still unevenly reported by this group (Ahmad and Nichols, 2017[10])). Another possibility is that bilateral providers refrain from using non-concessional lending in countries that are in potential debt distress (See Chapter 4). Finally, this difference in pattern may represent an opportunity for bilateral providers to further investigate the possibilities of providing non-concessional financing in certain countries. This could be, for example, in social sectors, where current data shows that multilateral agencies provide significant amounts of non-concessional financing (Figure 3.9).

Figure 3.8. Bilateral agencies still very much use ODA as a source of financing for almost all sectors, but this may be because of a lack of reporting on other official flows

ODA and OOF by individual allocable sector from bilateral providers, average 2012-16, 2016 constant prices, USD billion commitments

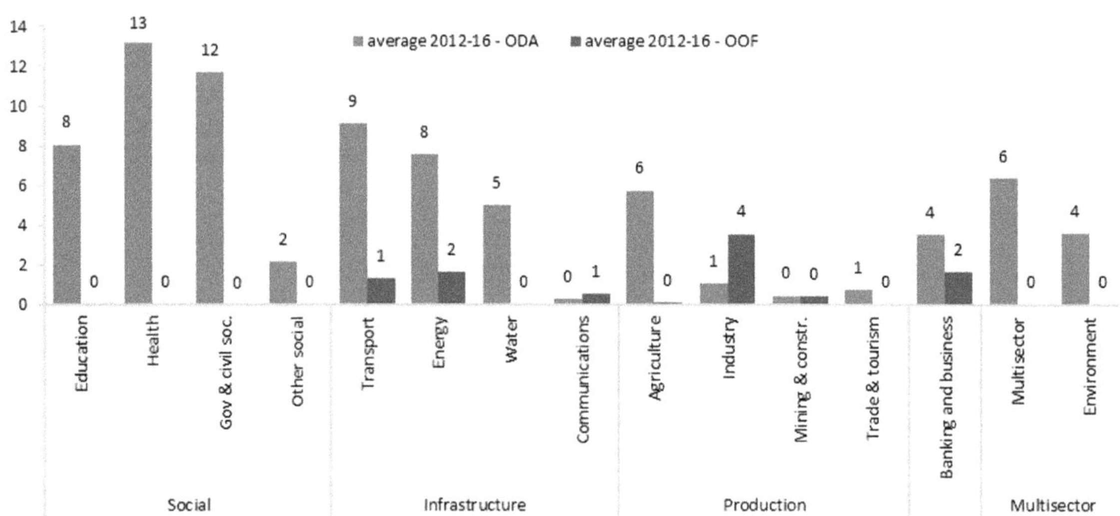

Source: (OECD, 2018[2]), "International development statistics (database)", http://www.oecd.org/dac/financing-sustainable-development/development-finance-data/idsonline.htm.

StatLink https://doi.org/10.1787/888933855504

Figure 3.9. Multilateral agencies also provide significant amounts of non-concessional financing to social sectors

ODA and OOF by individual allocable sector for multilateral providers, average 2012-16, 2016 constant prices, USD billion commitments

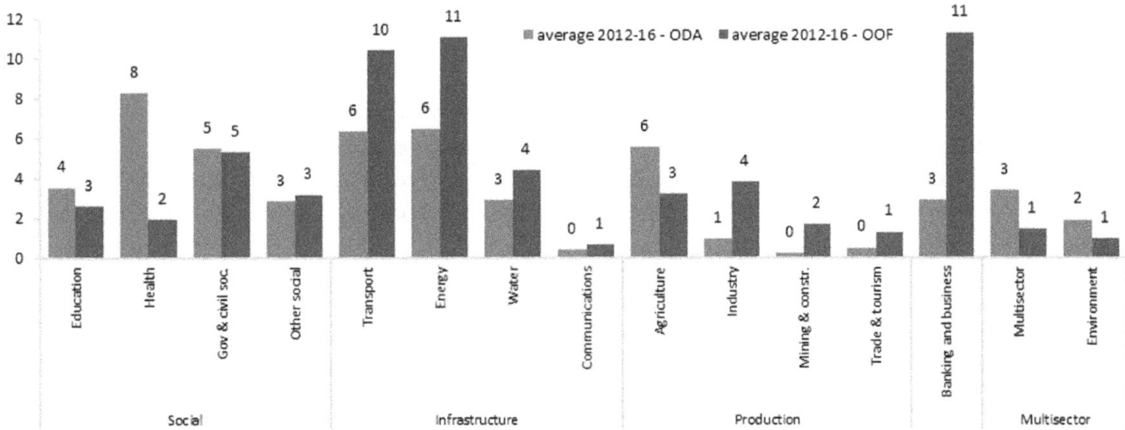

Source: (OECD, 2018[2]), "International development statistics (database)", http://www.oecd.org/dac/financing-sustainable-development/development-finance-data/idsonline.htm.

StatLink https://doi.org/10.1787/888933855523

3.2.3. Integration of cross-cutting approaches is still limited despite their importance in the new agenda

The section below focuses on gender equality as an example to illustrate how providers face challenges in integrating cross-cutting issues in their development agendas. Similar examples could be used with other cross-cutting issues, such as environmental sustainability.

Providers need to do much more to make their sector operations gender focused in most sectors

Gender equality is at the heart of sustainable development. The centrality of gender-related issues has been recognised in the 2030 Agenda through SDG 5 ("Achieve gender equality and empower all women and girls"). As such, it is both a standalone goal and an integral part of achieving other goals. Gender equality is also highlighted as a key dimension in the 3rd International Conference on Financing for Development[14]. A specific Addis Ababa Action Plan for Transformative Financing for Gender Equality and Women's Empowerment[15] was launched in July 2015.

Promoting gender equality is not just a moral imperative, it is an economic one, as there is wide evidence of a correlation between gender equality and economic performance (McKinsey Global Institute, 2015[11]) (World Economic Forum, 2014[12]). Gender equality, therefore, needs to be implemented as a key dimension across all economic and social sectors, including with targeted action and financing.

The OECD DAC, as part of its statistical reporting, has established a "marker system" that tracks the extent to which a given developmental activity responds to specific key policy objectives. The marker system facilitates monitoring and a comparison of members' activities in support of policy objectives related to environment, trade development, participatory development/good governance, reproductive health, as well as gender equality and women's empowerment (See Chapter 2). An activity is considered to be gender focused if the gender equality objective is marked as "principal" or "significant" (See Box 3.4).

Box 3.4. The Gender Equality Policy Marker

The OECD tracks aid in support of gender equality and women's empowerment using the DAC gender equality policy marker. This is a qualitative statistical tool to record aid activities that target gender equality as a policy objective. The gender equality policy marker is used by DAC members as part of the annual reporting of their aid activities to the DAC. It indicates for each aid activity whether it targets gender equality as a policy objective. The gender equality policy marker is based on a three-point scoring system:

- Principal (marked 2) means that gender equality is the main objective of the project/programme and is fundamental to its design and expected results. The project/programme would not have been undertaken without this objective.
- Significant (marked 1) means that gender equality is an important and deliberate objective, but not the principal reason for undertaking the project/programme.
- Not targeted (marked 0) means that the project/programme has been screened against the gender marker, but has not been found to target gender equality.

Data based on the marker provide a measure of aid that DAC members allocate in support of gender equality. In practice, the data allows derivation of key information related to gender equality financing. This includes a snapshot of:

- individual gender equality focused projects/programmes
- a global estimate of aid committed for gender equality
- the proportion of DAC members' aid focused on achieving gender equality and women's empowerment
- the sectors prioritised for gender equality focused aid
- the investments within the individual sectors
- the countries prioritised for gender equality focused aid.

Source: (DAC GENDERNET, December 2016[131]), "Handbook on the OECD DAC Gender Equality Policy Marker", www.oecd.org/dac/gender-development/Handbook-OECD-DAC-Gender-Equality-Policy-Marker.pdf and (OECD,(n.d.)[141]), "The DAC gender equality policy marker", http://www.oecd.org/dac/gender-development/dac-gender-equality-marker.htm (accessed on 5 September 2018).

While funding for programmes integrating gender equality as a significant objective has increased over time, aid with gender equality as a principal objective lags behind

During the period 2012-16, on average, USD 30.4 billion per year was targeted for gender equality as either a significant or principal objective. This represented 36% of bilateral allocable aid. However, only 4.9% of aid targeted gender equality as a principal objective. As such, while funding for programmes integrating gender equality as a significant objective has increased over time, aid with gender equality as a principal objective lags behind. The DAC Network on Gender Equality (GENDERNET) recommends that donors increase their support for dedicated programmes supporting gender equality and women's empowerment as a principal objective. This would respond to their commitments in the Agenda 2030 for Sustainable Development (DAC GENDERNET, 2018[15]).

In terms of sector distribution (Figure 3.10), there is a wide disparity across sectors in terms of the gender focus of activities, but social sectors are those where the volumes of financing for gender activities are generally the highest. Gender-focused funding in social sectors, such as education, health and government, represented USD 16.8 billion of the USD 30.4 billion (55% of the total) per year in 2012-16. The shares of gender volumes also confirm that social sectors (education, health, government and civil society, and other social infrastructure and services) have generally more gender-equality focused aid than other sectors (Figure 3.11). On average, 46% of the aid is gender equality focused for those activities that are screened against the gender marker in the social sectors.

Figure 3.10. There is a wide disparity across sectors in terms of the gender focus of activities

Gender equality focus by sector, average 2012-16, 2016 constant prices, USD billion commitments

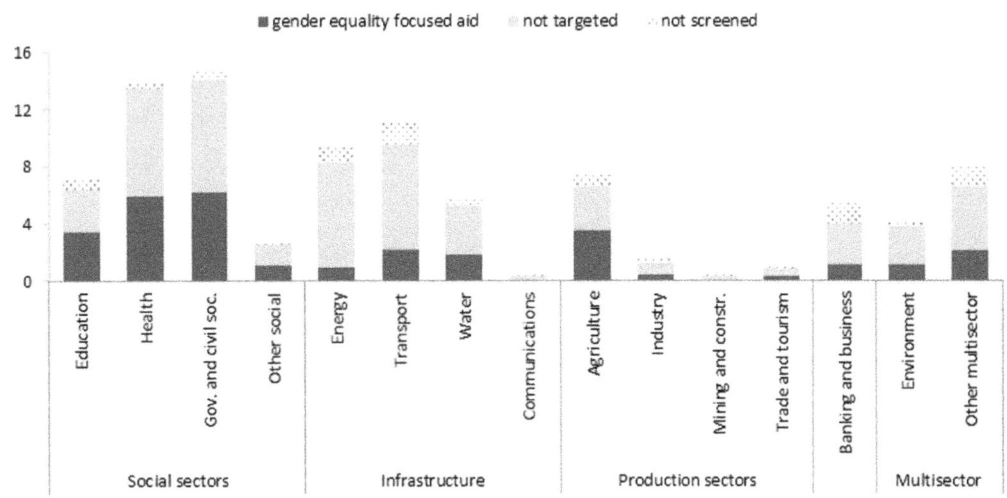

Note: Gender equality focused aid comprises projects marked as 1 or 2 by donors in the DAC statistical system.
Source: (OECD, 2018[2]), "International development statistics (database)", http://www.oecd.org/dac/financing-sustainable-development/development-finance-data/idsonline.htm.

StatLink https://doi.org/10.1787/888933855542

It is critical that women's participation is supported in programmes in the productive sectors. While agriculture seems to largely consider gender inequality (with 53% of screened activities having a gender equality focus in 2012-16), other productive sectors do not have a strong focus on gender equality. This shows the important work that still needs to be done to allow women to fully participate in all sectors of the economy.

Several sectors do not take into account gender inequality well enough. Only 21 % of aid allocated to the infrastructure sector grouping and 27% of aid to the banking and business sector are gender equality focused. The banking and business sector seems a particular area for progress, where a large amount of aid (25%) is not even screened for gender equality.[16]

Figure 3.11. Several sectors do not take into account gender equality well enough

Share of gender equality focused aid by sector, average 2012-16, USD commitments

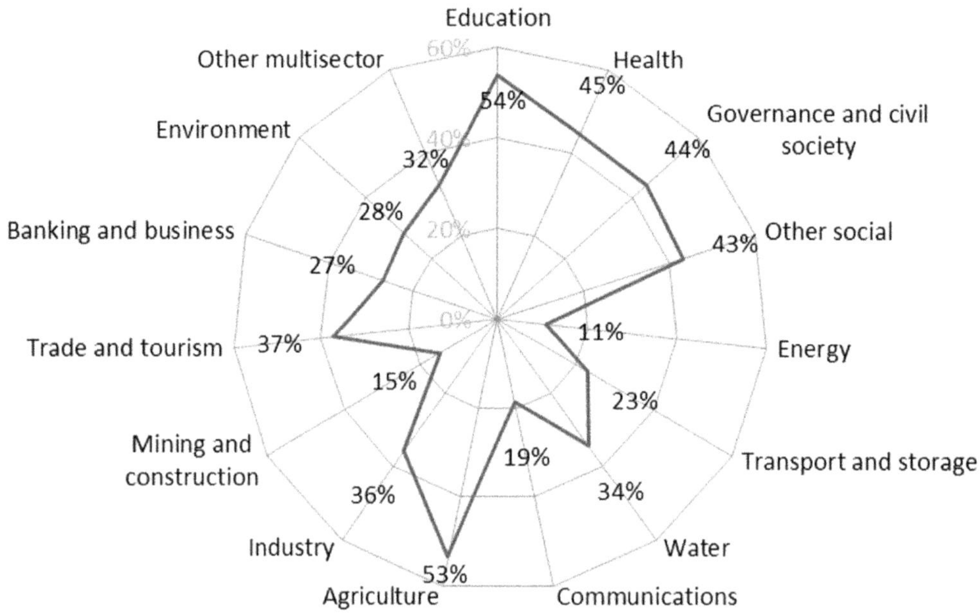

Source: (OECD, 2018[2]), "International development statistics (database)", http://www.oecd.org/dac/financing-sustainable-development/development-finance-data/idsonline.htm.

StatLink https://doi.org/10.1787/888933855561

3.3. The sector implications of an integrated and global development agenda

Following the presentation of the overall picture of ODF by sector in this chapter, the analysis in this section concentrates on the sector implications of the current development agenda. It provides some recommendations on strategic approaches for development co-operation providers to align sector strategies with the SDGs.

3.3.1. An integrated and global development agenda calls into question siloed sector approaches

The SDGs create an integrated and complex development framework that goes beyond sectors. SDG integration into providers' development co-operation strategies requires increased attention from them to policy coherence across sectors. Moreover, with this new agenda, addressing systemic issues is becoming increasingly important, presenting both challenges and opportunities for development progress in many sectors, particularly in countries most in need.

The 2030 Agenda points to the importance of policy coherence across sectors and can be a powerful driver towards more sustainable production and consumption models

The SDGs provide a highly integrated and interconnected framework, integrating the three dimensions of economic, social and environmental development. The interconnection of social, environmental and economic dimensions is reflected in the list of SDG targets, which creates a dense web of 'nexuses' across goals (see Figure 3.12). Nexuses are *"clusters of issues that are linked in such a way that interventions focusing on one issue are highly likely to have positive or negative impacts on other issues within the nexus"* (Jungcurt, 2016[16]). Given the networked configuration of the SDGs, the achievement of one goal can be consistent, reinforced or constrained by the achievement of other goals (Nilsson, Griggs and Visbek, 2016[17]). For instance, increasing electricity access (SDG 7) reinforces irrigation for food production (SDG 2). However, energy options are constrained by the need to provide clean energy, which is embedded in SDG 7 itself. Also, it is a requirement for achieving SDG 12 on responsible production and consumption and SDG 13 on climate change. Despite some goals being more related to one of these three dimensions, they are often all embedded within each goal, making the framework deeply interconnected. For instance, while the main aim of SDG 8 may seem to pursue primarily an economic objective as it aims to promote employment and economic growth, social and environmental dimensions are embedded within this goal as several targets explicitly integrate social dimensions (e.g. gender equality and decent work) or sustainability (e.g. energy efficiency).

The analysis of the network of SDG targets reveals that cross-cutting and thematic SDGs with economic dimensions, such as sustainable production and consumption (SDG 12), inequality (SDG 10), poverty (SDG 1) and growth and employment (SDG 8), are those with more links with other SDGs (Le Blanc, 2015[18]). This finding is not surprising given the wide scope of these goals and the widely recognised impact of economic growth on enabling or constraining development. It shows the importance of looking at the linkages between sectors in order to reduce trade-offs and harness synergies.

Achieving policy coherence across sectors and goals with economic dimensions offers the opportunity to redesign economic, environmental and social systems in a way that is sustainable, inclusive and prosperous. In particular, advancements in science, technology and innovation (STI) can boost development progress across sectors if designed in a way that promotes sustainability and inclusion, especially in banking, production and infrastructure. For instance, technological progress can be a powerful driver for green transformation as it increases the viability of low-carbon infrastructure, energy efficiency, value chain optimisation and sustainable agriculture [(Altenburg and Assmann, 2017[19]); (OECD, 2016[3]; OECD, 2016[3])]. Similarly, mobile technologies offer the opportunity to promote financial inclusion by offering poor people financial services previously inaccessible. This is shown by the development of mobile money transfer systems that are helping many poor people, including women, escape poverty and graduate from subsistence agriculture to small business (Suri and Jack, 2016[20]). These examples show that the development impact for various SDGs can be boosted by leveraging on development enablers (e.g. STI and finance) and by mainstreaming cross-cutting issues in specific sectors (e.g. gender and environment).

Figure 3.12. The Sustainable Development Goals as a complex network of targets

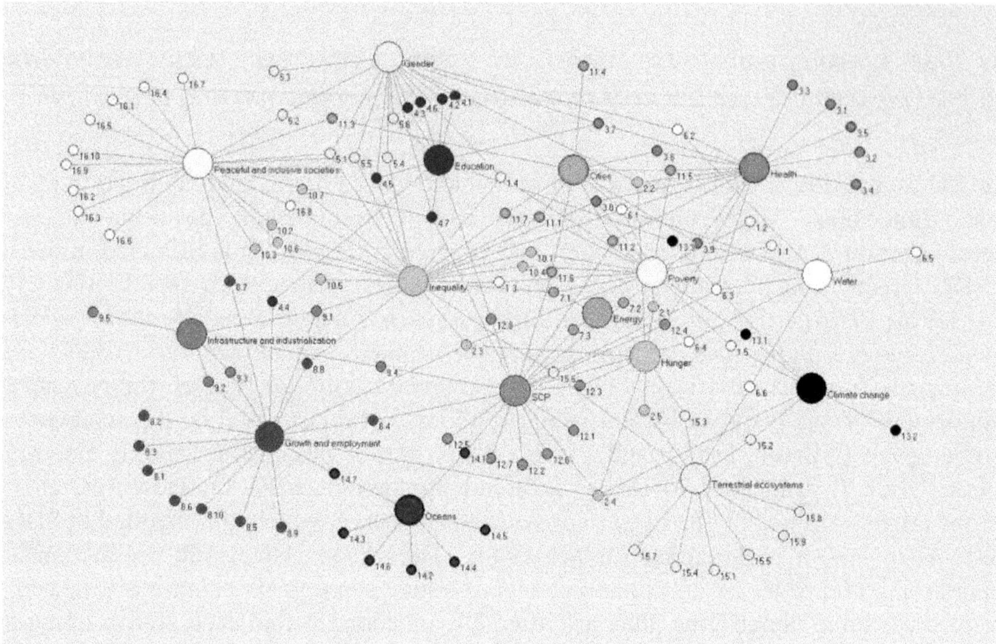

Source: (Le Blanc, 2015[18]), "Towards integration at last? The sustainable development goals as a network of targets", http://www.un.org/esa/desa/papers/2015/wp141_2015.pdf.

A number of global trends and challenges affect all countries, particularly the least developed and most fragile contexts across many sectors

A number of major global trends are significantly affecting the capacity of developing countries to achieve the SDGs across sectors. Resource-intensive growth, waste and climate warming are affecting, for example, SDG 12 on responsible production and consumption, SDG 15 on preserving natural ecosystems. They are hindering efforts towards achieving SDG 2 on food security and SDG 6 on water security, or SDG 1 on poverty eradication and SDG 3 on health. Demographic growth and urbanisation are also making urban planning and migration flows more difficult to manage [(United Nations, 2015[21]); (UN-Habitat, 2016[22])], thwarting, for example, efforts towards SDG 8 on full employment and decent work or SDG 11 on inclusive, safe and sustainable cities. Similarly, progress made in robotics and automation presents unprecedented opportunities, but also major social risks, such as job insecurity for low-skilled workers and labour polarisation [(UNCTAD, 2016[23]); (World Bank, 2016[24])] This progress also affects SDG 8 on full employment and decent work and SDG 10 on reduced inequality.

While global trends can compromise development achievements everywhere, they are more compelling in developing countries, given their higher vulnerability to shocks, crises and disasters. Global challenges, such as conflicts, pandemics, environmental disasters and knock-on shocks from price changes, trade and monetary policies or financial crises occurring outside developing countries [(UNHCR, 2017[25]); (ILO and UNDP, 2017[26]); (Kreft, Eckstein and Melchior, 2016[27])] tend to affect developing countries more than advanced economies.

Systemic adversity has a stronger effect in the most fragile contexts. It is becoming increasingly evident that in countries with weak institutions and higher exposure to risk, poverty is more entrenched – for both low- and middle-income countries – societies are more violent, and the effects of shocks and disasters of any kind are more severe (OECD, 2016[28]). For instance, environmental shocks and disasters more frequently and severely affect least developed countries (LDCs) and small island developing states (SIDS), which are more constrained in anticipating and responding to these events, putting 26 million people into poverty every year [(IMF, 2017[29]); (Hallegatte et al., 2017[30])]. Another example is the volatility of global food prices, which increased after 2010 and put an additional 44 million people in extreme poverty – as poorer people spend a high proportion of their incomes on food (UNCTAD, 2017[31]). Vulnerability to systemic issues can partly explain why, despite the remarkable development progress overall in developing countries, development progress is stagnant in sub-Saharan Africa, where two-thirds of fragile contexts are located (OECD, 2018[32]). Two-thirds of the extreme poor live in fragile contexts and this share could increase to more than 80% by 2035 (see Figure 3.13). This will be a consequence of the high rate of demographic growth among poor people in sub-Saharan Africa, particularly Nigeria, Democratic Republic of the Congo, Tanzania and Madagascar (OECD, 2018[32]).

Figure 3.13. Two-thirds of the extreme poor currently live in fragile contexts and this share could increase to more than 80 % in 2035

Number of poor people in the world (actual and estimated), 2015-35

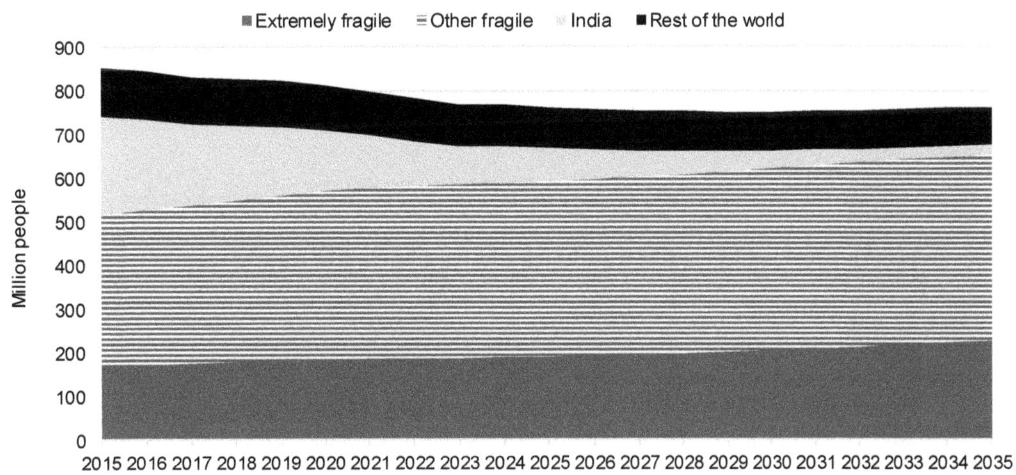

Note: Calculation by the authors using the list of fragile contexts from (OECD, 2018[32]). Fragile contexts include both low- and middle-income countries.
Source: (International Futures, n.d.[33]), Projections from the International Futures' database, www.ifs.du.edu/ifs/frm_MainMenu.asp.

StatLink https://doi.org/10.1787/888933855580

Other than monetary poverty, about 1.6 billion people in the world still experience multidimensional deprivations, including lack of access to energy, education, healthcare or safe drinking water. This is particularly so for women, children, rural inhabitants and farmers (ILO and UNDP, 2017[26]). Again, LDCs and fragile contexts, particularly in sub-Saharan Africa, are those with lower socio-economic conditions (see Figure 3.14). Given the above, ensuring that no countries are left behind will require not only supporting specific sectors, but also increasing resilience against adverse systemic issues in the most vulnerable contexts by reinforcing institutions and addressing the root causes of fragility.

Figure 3.14. LDCs and fragile contexts are those with lower socio-economic conditions

Human Development Index by developing country grouping, average for 2015

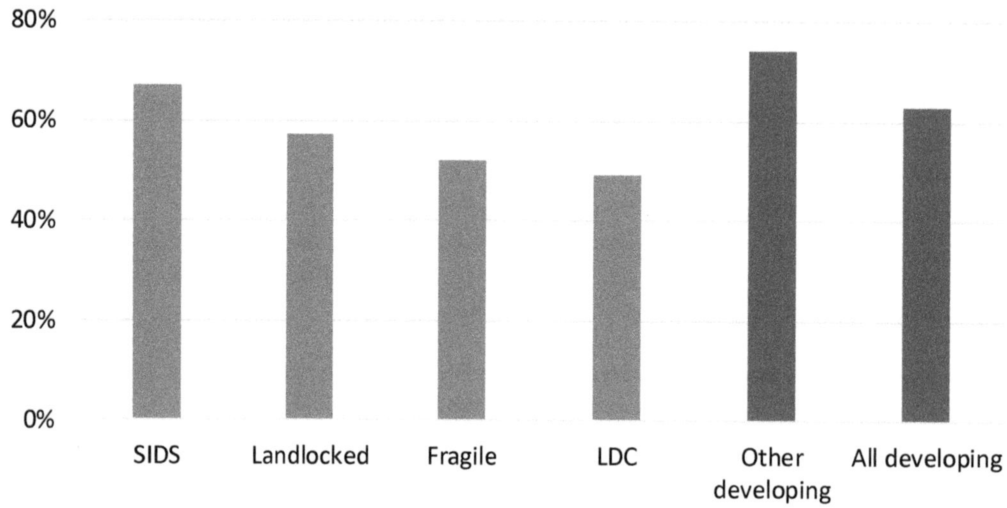

Note: 0% is the lowest score for human development and 100% the highest. Data analysis is based on 2015 data.

Source: Calculated by the authors using NDP's Human Development Index data (2015), http://hdr.undp.org/sites/default/files/2015_human_development_report.pdf.

StatLink https://doi.org/10.1787/888933855599

3.3.2. Holistic approaches are needed to achieve an integrated development agenda

The new multifaceted agenda of the SDGs, the increasing importance of policy coherence and the many systemic issues across sectors that developing countries are facing call for holistic approaches. However, designing such approaches may be challenging for development co-operation providers, which traditionally have looked at their interventions using sectors or specific policy areas as a way to structure their development interventions. Recognising that a perfect match between SDGs and sectors is difficult to achieve, the alignment of development partners' interventions with the SDG agenda requires aligning the intended results of their strategies, programmes and interventions with the SDG targets, and then monitoring and evaluating their contribution to these.

There is no 'one-size-fits-all' policy configuration to match SDGs and sectors

As highlighted in Chapter 2, it is extremely challenging to find a perfect match between sectors and SDGs. The majority of SDGs are very broad and cross-cutting (e.g. SDG 1 on poverty and SDG 10 on reducing inequality) as well as densely interlinked (see Figure 3.12). Thus, it would be unrealistic to design a one-size-fits-all policy or sector configurations to achieve all goals. This absence of a straightforward correspondence between sectors and SDGs makes programme design more challenging for policy makers and development partners. This is especially so as they have traditionally designed their interventions around sectors or policy areas rather than results. In fact, a recent survey carried out by the DAC secretariat of DAC members and some multilateral agencies shows that the programmatic complexity of the SDGs is a major challenge to aligning development co-operation portfolios with the 2030 Agenda.

Aiming for a one-size-fits-all framework for designing sector financing strategies would also go somewhat against the spirit of the 2030 agenda. While the SDGs are rather prescriptive in terms of the necessity to pay special attention to prioritising some groups of countries (e.g. LDCs) or groups of people (e.g. women and children), large discretion is left to policy makers as to how to achieve the goals. For instance, a contribution to SDG 4 on education could be supported through direct investment in education (e.g. building schools and training teachers). Or it could be supported by increasing access to electricity in rural areas (SDG 7) to enable children to study during the evening.

Supporting traditional sectors is one among several approaches to achieving the SDGs

Support for traditional sectors is only one among several strategies and approaches for development partners to carry out development co-operation. In particular, development partners can contribute to the development agenda by supporting global public goods (GPGs). At the country level, development partners can complement their country sector approaches with other strategies using themes rather than sectors (e.g. private sector development) or by supporting cross-cutting approaches (e.g. gender equality) (Figure 3.15).

Figure 3.15. Examples of strategies and programmes supported by development partners

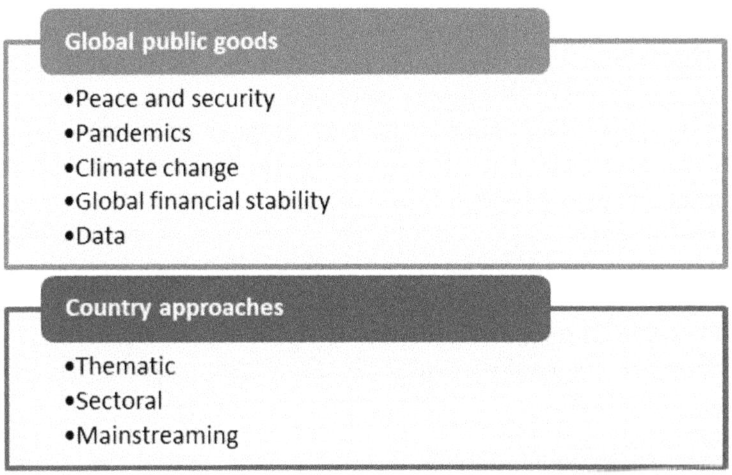

Source: Authors

GPGs are institutions, mechanisms and outcomes that provide quasi-universal benefits, covering more than one group of countries and several population groups (Kaul, Grunberg and Stern, 1999[34]). While bilateral providers contribute a lot to GPGs by setting up global programmes, initiatives and funds as part of their bilateral co-operation programmes, the provision of GPGs is more often associated with the work of multilateral organisations, civil society organisations (CSOs) and research institutes. Such institutions facilitate programme implementation, global standard-setting, monitoring of international agreements, data provision and research on areas such as peace and security, global financial stability, climate change and global pandemics.

Country programmes, in contrast, are designed to promote social, environmental and economic development in one country through sector, thematic or mainstreaming approaches:

- **Sector programmes** are provided to enhance the availability and the quality of social services, infrastructure and production systems. Sector programmes include policy and institutional development, the development of hard infrastructure, the provision of financial resources, and technical assistance to people and companies in various sectors and policy areas. This support includes, for instance, providing a loan to build a power plant, supporting a policy reform in the health sector or building the capacity of small-holder farmers.
- **Thematic programmes** use multiple sectors or policy areas to achieve economic and human development. For instance, private sector development (PSD) strategies and programmes, seek to improve the investment climate and productive capacity of developing countries in view of achieving economic growth and poverty reduction (Miyamoto and Chiofalo, 2017[35]). PSD strategies include supporting a variety of traditional sectors, including infrastructure, public governance, banking, and services and manufacturing. Similarly, broad thematic strategies, such as social protection and urban and rural development, also need interventions across a variety of sectors.
- **Mainstreaming** involves integrating cross-cutting issues, such as environment, gender equality, food security, human rights and social protection, into traditional sector projects or other thematic projects thus achieving multiple objectives simultaneously. Such projects are illustrated by the PSD work of the Department of Foreign Affairs and Trade in Pakistan, the Department for International Development (DFID) in Nigeria and the EU in Liberia. Such PSD projects specifically target poor people, women or food security thus mainstreaming poverty, gender equality and food security into PSD programming. Another way of mainstreaming is by adopting social and environmental safeguards. These are measures and guidelines preventing the occurrence of environmental and social damage in donor-funded projects.

Aligning development finance with the SDGs requires harmonising the objectives of sector and thematic programmes with the SDG targets prioritised by partner countries

The flexible and cross-cutting nature of development goals, the variety of country contexts and the different capacities and comparative advantages of development partners, call for differentiated approaches in SDG implementation. This requires moving from portfolio-based programmes to result-based approaches where sector and thematic programmes are organically designed, monitored and evaluated with the objective to fill SDG gaps in developing countries. For this reason, *ex-ante* analysis is needed to design strategies and programmes that contribute to the achievement of SDG targets as prioritised by partner countries, and to develop monitoring and evaluation systems to track progress and learn from experience.

In practice, strategic and programmatic design and implementation requires:

- prioritising areas that align with developing countries' needs and priorities
- developing sector and thematic country programmes that align the objectives and results expected with SDG targets
- monitoring and evaluating results using frameworks that are aligned with the SDGs (see Figure 3.16).

Figure 3.16. How can donors align sector financing strategies with the Sustainable Development Goals?

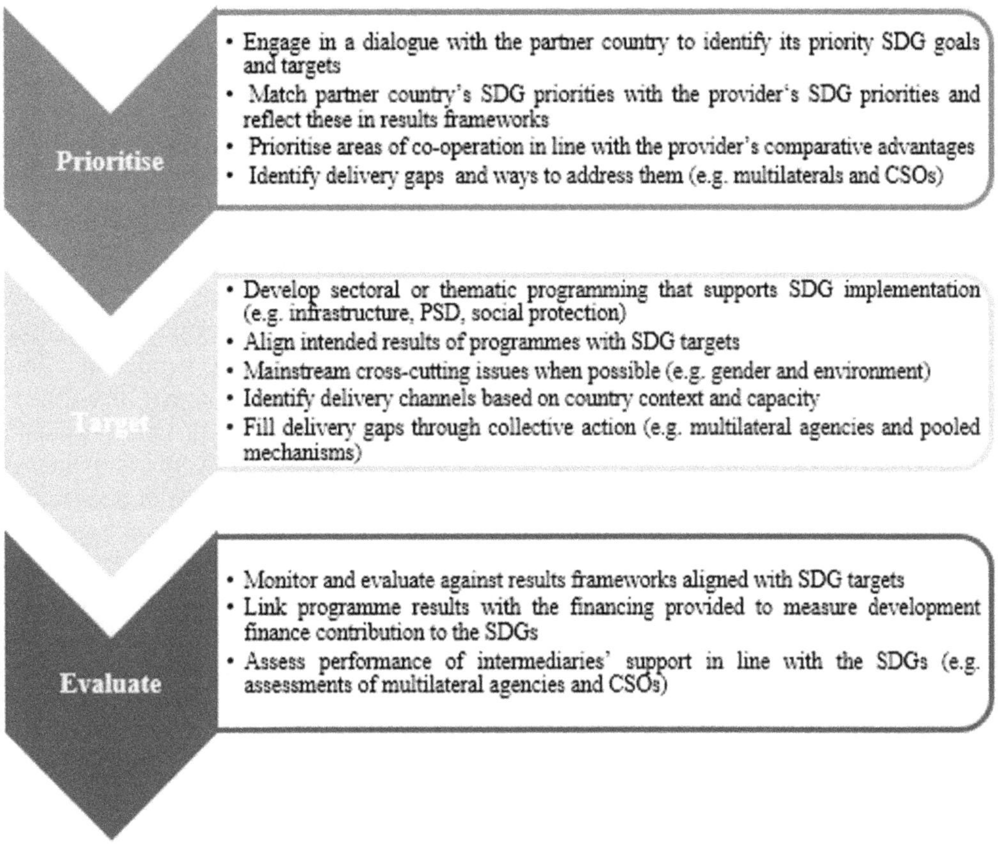

Source: Authors

OECD research shows that building on SDG-linked results frameworks to inform strategic and programmatic design and implementation can promote effective development co-operation in terms of: accountability, communication, strategic direction and learning for providers, recipients and the whole development co-operation community (Engberg-Pedersen and Zwart, 2018$_{[36]}$).

While the need to promote results-based design and implementation of development co-operation is more important now than ever, efforts among development partners to align strategies, programmes and portfolios with the SDGs are still anecdotal and at an early stage. Overall, bilateral and multilateral development partners are trying to support the 2030 Agenda by:

- aligning their policies and operational strategies with the SDGs

- designing and implementing programmes and projects that mainstream cross-cutting development issues
- creating indicators and monitoring tools to track their alignment with the SDGs
- carrying out research and analysis to monitor the state of advancement on the 2030 Agenda.

In terms of strategies, multilateral organisations are in the lead. In particular, the United Nations Development System (UNDS) is carrying out a 'whole-of-group' repositioning reform to better deliver on the 2030 Agenda. The World Bank Group has aligned its institutional structure by creating 'global practices' that are closely linked with some SDGs. Moreover, both the UNDS and the World Bank are carrying out research on SDG-relevant issues and are increasing co-operation to build on their respective comparative advantages, especially in fragile contexts. For bilateral development partners, Canada has, for example, recently adopted a development co-operation policy that puts gender equality at the centre of all Canada's efforts, although the implementation of the policy is still in the early stages of implementation.

In terms of mainstreaming cross-cutting issues in programmes and projects, both bilateral and multilateral development partners are contributing to these efforts – although much remains to be done. For example, while bilateral and multilateral development partners have increased resources for sector programmes/projects integrating gender or climate objectives, the volumes of financing represent, on average, small shares (10%-20%) of their total contributions [see e.g. (OECD, 2018[37]); (OECD, 2017[38])]. One explanation for this trend is that policy integration of cross-cutting issues in sector and thematic interventions/programmers is hard to design and implement. Evidence from peer reviews of DAC members shows that cross-cutting and integrated approaches need appropriate financing, policy commitment and technical capacity to be successful (OECD, 2014[39]). A review of the most recent DAC peer reviews shows that DAC members' effectiveness in integrating cross-cutting issues into their strategy and programmes is mixed. Some donors lack the capacity and resources to translate cross-cutting strategies into programmes [(OECD, 2015[40]); (OECD, 2015[41])] or do not provide appropriate funding or guidance to achieve these objectives [(OECD, 2018[42]); (OECD, 2017[43]); (OECD, 2017[44]); (OECD, 2017[45])]. Other donors, generally of larger size, seem to address cross-cutting issues, thematically or across projects, more robustly [(OECD, 2016[46]); (OECD, 2016[47]); (OECD, 2015[48]); (OECD, 2014[49])]. As an example, Denmark uses the human rights-based approach to mainstream poverty both at the strategic level and at the project level, through human rights assessments that put poverty at the centre of programming (OECD, 2016[50]).

Finally, in terms of results measurement, development partners are already using indicators that closely match the SDG indicators for those SDGs that relate to specific areas. More efforts are needed for SDGs that are broad and cross-cutting. For example, a comparative analysis by (Engberg-Pedersen and Zwart, 2018[36]) shows that there is already a strong link between the standard indicators used by eight major bilateral and multilateral development partners[17] and the related SDG targets and indicators. This strong link however occurs in "traditional" human development areas (i.e. SDGs 2, 3 and 6) and energy (SDG 7) more than in the broad cross-cutting areas such as gender equality (SDG 5), decent work and economic growth (SDG 8), and inequality (SDG 10). Ensuring that SDG-aligned results are communicated properly through appropriate narratives will be essential for learning and for generating political support for development co-operation (Engberg-Pedersen and Zwart, 2018[36]).

3.3.3. A cross-cutting and mostly unfunded development agenda points to the importance of both quantity and quality of financing

A cross-cutting and mostly unfunded development agenda points to the importance of both the quantity and quality of financing. In particular, financing needs depend not only on the volumes required to achieve specific development objectives, but also on the individual capacity of a country to mobilise resources and the potential of each sector to attract additional resources. Moreover, sufficient resources need to be provided for both output-based and system-wide approaches across sectors.

Financing volumes required to achieve the SDGs are only one dimension to take into account if the international community wishes to leave no one behind across sectors

Getting financing strategies right will be indispensable to meeting the integrated SDG financing needs in developing countries. The amounts involved are between USD 3 and 4 trillion a year, and are mostly unfunded (UNCTAD, 2014[51]). This comprehensive, integrated and mostly unfunded development agenda points to the importance of both the quantity of financing and the appropriate targeting of this financing. This means:

- mobilising sufficient financing volumes
- ensuring a balanced targeting of resources (sector/thematic areas, country allocation, types of beneficiaries, types of instrument and concessionality levels, channel of implementation, etc.)
- focusing on impact (short- and long-term results, public and private mobilisation effects, alignment with local needs, integration of cross-cutting issues, etc.).

Moreover, beyond filling gaps amounting to USD trillion, the SDGs call for leaving no one behind. This suggests that while the international community has a common development agenda, countries and people have different capacities to mobilise the necessary human and financial resources to this end. For example, compared to infrastructure and productive sectors, it is more difficult to mobilise private finance in social sectors. This requires rethinking the way financing needs and priorities are measured and communicated, going beyond business-as-usual support for economic growth as the main proxy.

In this respect, focusing too much on the financing needs shifts the attention towards sectors and countries that have more opportunities to be financed (such as infrastructure and production sectors in large and more advanced middle-income countries) given that the volume of financing needs is linked to the size of gross domestic product (GDP) and growth rates. However, large or more industrialised economies have more financing opportunities beyond the mobilisation of funds from development partners. They can more easily tap into capital markets for example. They also usually benefit from better investment climates, which increase opportunities for domestic and foreign investment in any sector [(OECD, 2015[52]); (Inderst and Stewart, 2014[53]); (Sagasti and Prada, 2012[54])].

For example, high-levels of GDP (including because of a large population size), sustained economic growth and a high level of industrialisation can explain why China and India make up the biggest share of financing needs for infrastructure, in volume terms, in developing countries (see Figure 3.17). Conversely, African countries, especially sub-Saharan ones, which are generally smaller economies and are less industrialised, account for a very small share. However, China and India have by far the best quality of infrastructure among developing countries, whereas sub-Saharan countries have the lowest, which suggests that the latter need infrastructure more than the former (Donaubauer, Meyer and Nunnenkamp, 2014[55]). Moreover, China and India also have various alternatives through which to finance their infrastructure beyond development partners. This makes the case of supporting sub-Saharan countries more compelling.

Achieving an integrated development agenda will also require transformational development in the more advanced economies, particularly to foster positive spill-overs from the richest to the poorest countries. For instance, while, overall, large emerging countries have more opportunities to finance infrastructure and production sectors on their own, development finance will still be needed to promote the green transition in these countries, as more advanced developing economies are among the largest contributors to climate change, which affects significantly the poorest countries. Therefore, bilateral and multilateral development partners should continue supporting infrastructure in these economies. But they need to do so by promoting low-carbon and climate-resilient technologies. This requires a major shift in the structure of bilateral and multilateral development partners' portfolios as green finance constitutes a small portion of their total support for infrastructure [see (OECD, 2017[56]); (Miyamoto and Chiofalo, 2015[57])].

Figure 3.17. China and India make up the biggest share of financing needs for infrastructure, in volume terms, in developing countries

Financing needs in infrastructure in developing countries by region (2017-2035)

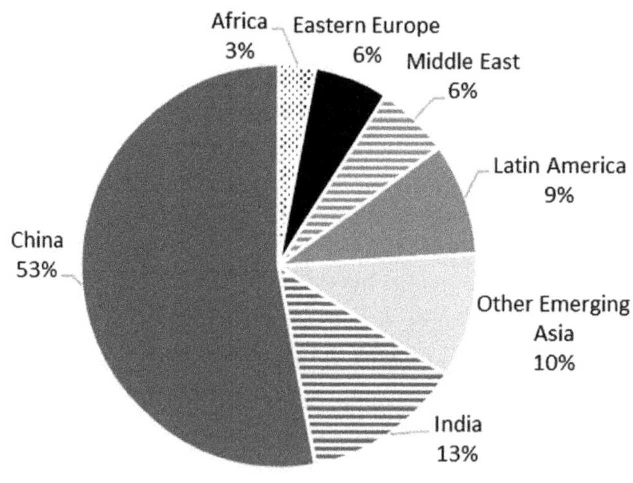

Source: Estimates based on (McKinsey, 2017[58]), "Bridging Infrastructure Gaps: Has the World Made Progress?" https://www.mckinsey.com/industries/capital-projects-and-infrastructure/our-insights/bridging-infrastructure-gaps-has-the-world-made-progress.

StatLink https://doi.org/10.1787/888933855618

Finally, recognising that opportunities to mobilise private resources for development vary greatly across sectors, development partners need to co-ordinate to ensure a balanced distribution of resources across sectors to achieve all the SDGs. As shown in Figure 3.18, sectors presenting clear business opportunities (e.g. information and communications technology, energy and agriculture) attract more private investment than those traditionally serviced by the public sector (e.g. health and education). This despite there being clear business opportunities also in these sectors where private provision of services is common. Moreover, while financing gaps in sectors with more reduced commercial opportunities are lower, in terms of volumes, the share of the financing gap is generally the highest. This shows that small amounts can be more difficult to mobilise in these areas than in those with the largest commercial opportunities. Beyond commercial opportunities, the decision of public and private service delivery across sectors is affected by national policy approaches. These are influenced by the cultural, economic and social characteristics of each country. This shows that bilateral and multilateral development partners need to ensure that sufficient resources are provided both for sectors that present business opportunities and those that support non-commercial initiatives, such as public sector and/or CSO projects, particularly in social sectors.

Figure 3.18. Sectors presenting clear business opportunities attract more private investment than those traditionally serviced by the public sector

Annual expenditures (left axis) and share of SDG financing gap (right axis) in key sectors in development countries, average 2015-30

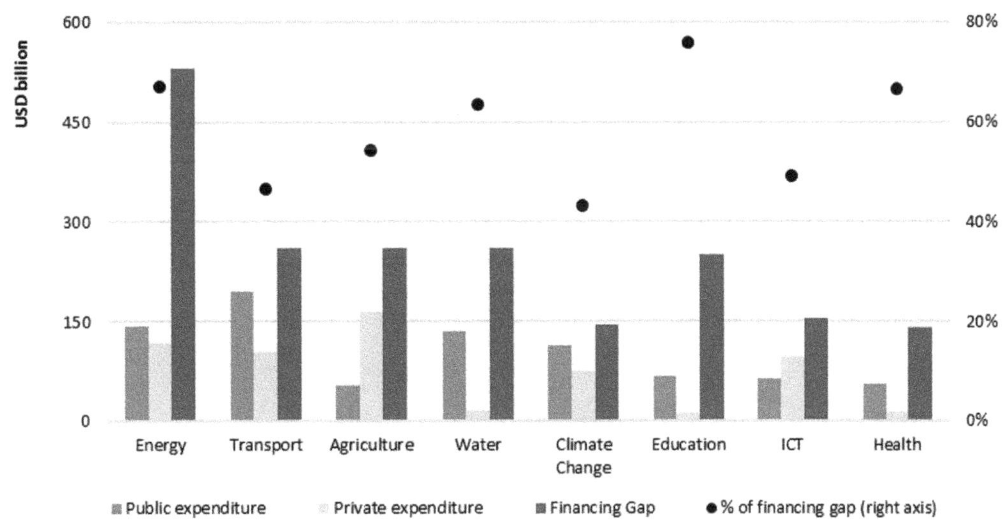

Note: Health and education needs include investment in infrastructure only. Climate change includes both mitigation and adaptation.

Source: Authors' calculations based on (UNCTAD, 2014[51]), "World Investment Report 2014: Investing in the SDGs, an Action Plan", http://unctad.org/en/PublicationsLibrary/wir2014_en.pdf.

StatLink https://doi.org/10.1787/888933855637

There is a need to balance support between institutional development and output-based projects

Despite the importance of addressing systemic issues and institutions, as explained above, development finance for policy and institutional development is declining. As shown in Figure 3.19, concessional support for these types of operations declined from almost a third of the total concessional finance from bilateral and multilateral development partners in 2009 to less than a quarter in 2016. Concessional support for these types of projects shows the increasing preference of donors for projects that deliver tangible outputs in specific sectors, e.g. power plants, vaccines and cash transfers, rather than long-term and system-wide approaches, such as policy and institutional development. This can be explained by the fact that as ODA providers are increasingly called to justify their ODA expenditures, there is an incentive to support programmes that:

- deliver tangible results in the short term
- ensure control of resources
- have performance, outputs and immediate outcomes that can easily be measured.

Conversely, system-wide approaches are less attractive for development finance providers because of the:

- mixed performance of public financial management in some partner countries
- reduced control of resources
- intrinsic difficulty of measuring the development results of capacity building and technical assistance.

Figure 3.19. Development finance for policy and institutional development is declining

Concessional support for policy and institutional development (left axis) and share of ODA for policies and institutions in 2007-16, 2016 constant prices, USD billion commitments

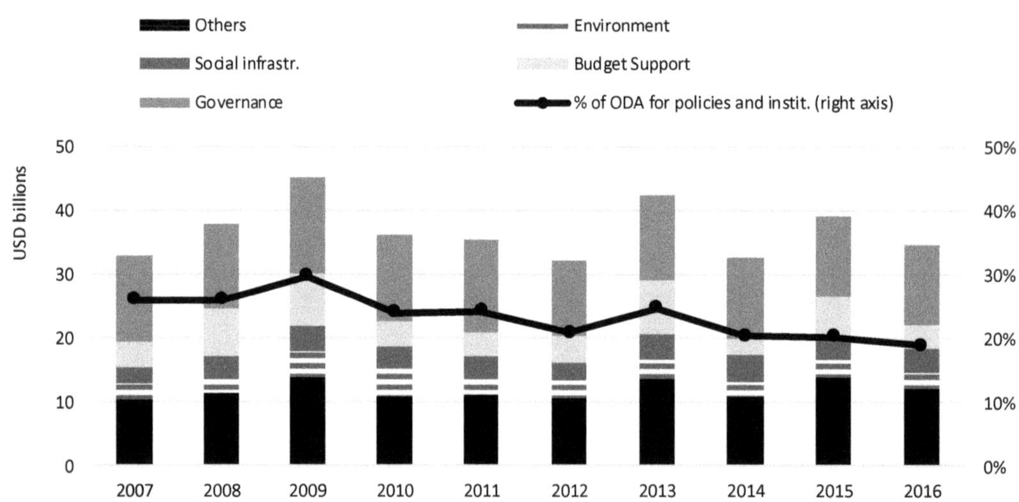

Note: Only codes related to policy and institutional development have been selected. See Annex for a full list of codes selected.
Source: (OECD, 2018[21]), "International development statistics (database)", http://www.oecd.org/dac/financing-sustainable-development/development-finance-data/idsonline.htm.

StatLink https://doi.org/10.1787/888933855656

Nevertheless, achieving a systemic development agenda will require balancing the support between these two types of programmes. As noted, development challenges are becoming increasingly entrenched in countries with lower institutional capacity and high vulnerability to shocks, conflicts and disasters. Supporting country-led frameworks that promote long-lasting development pathways in both the creation of domestic economic growth and the provision of social services, such as health and education, will be essential (see Chapter 5). Given the reduced business case for policy and institutional support, concessional finance needs to be preserved for these types of interventions. In particular countries need help to build institutional resilience against the adverse effects of systemic issues through domestic revenue mobilisation, disaster risk reduction and debt management. In addition, they need to promote technological, institutional and policy innovation across sectors.

With expenditures for humanitarian purposes increasing significantly, using ODA to address the root causes of fragility in the most vulnerable countries represents a strategic investment

Addressing the root causes of fragility will be crucial for both developing countries and donors. Expenses for humanitarian crises are increasing significantly and are shifting resources that otherwise could be used for development purposes. Specifically, bilateral and multilateral support for humanitarian assistance, both in developing countries and in donor countries, doubled from USD 14 billion in 2012 to USD 35 billion in 2016 (see Figure 3.20). In 2016, a fifth of concessional resources from bilateral and multilateral partners reporting to the DAC were used for humanitarian purposes, up from a tenth in 2012. Comparatively, the share of ODA for sector-allocable projects decreased in the same period from 79% to 68%, showing that a growing portion of ODA is financing emergency crises rather than development projects. Geopolitical tensions and conflicts are rising and affecting the most vulnerable countries. There are also growing populations in sub-Saharan Africa, where most of the countries in fragile contexts are located. Therefore, there is a need to increase support in developing countries for promoting peaceful, inclusive and sustainable development, including by building the resilience of country governments and promoting local development that reduces the needs for humanitarian support.

Figure 3.20. Bilateral and multilateral support for humanitarian assistance doubled from 2012 to 2016

ODA from bilateral and multilateral development partners to address humanitarian crises in 2012-16 and share of ODA for humanitarian an in-donor refugee costs, 2016 constant prices, USD billion commitments

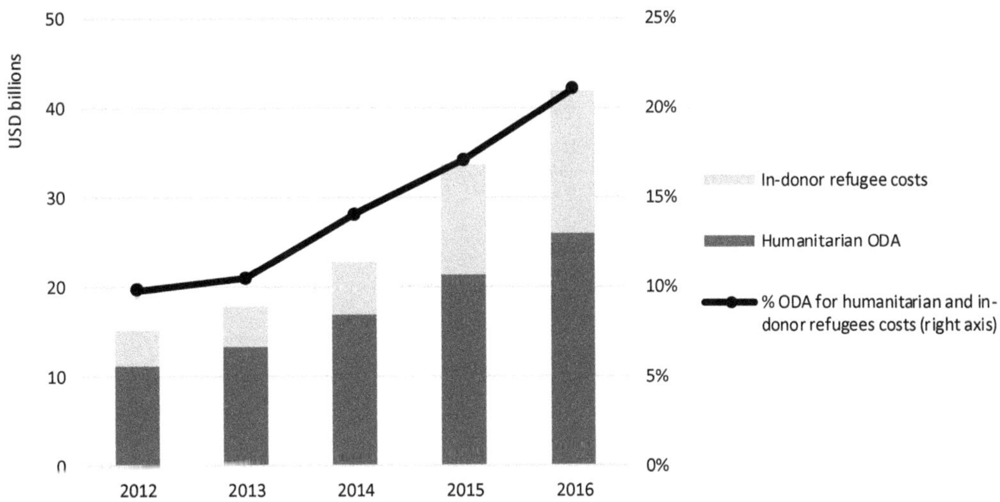

Source: (OECD, 2018[2]), "International development statistics (database)", http://www.oecd.org/dac/financing-sustainable-development/development-finance-data/idsonline.htm.

StatLink https://doi.org/10.1787/888933855675

A cross-sector and transformative development agenda requires financial resources to be balanced between country programmes and GPGs

In an increasingly globalised and interconnected society, in-country development progress is more and more dependent on the existence of an enabling environment for development. This means ensuring the provision of GPGs, such as global financial stability or peace and security. Despite the lack of definition of what constitutes GPGs, estimates of concessional financing for these activities are between USD 12 billion and USD 14 billion per year. This is mainly for peacekeeping and peace-building operations; data and research; and selected normative functions [(Birdsall and Diofasi, 2015[59]); (Development Initiatives, 2016[60])]. This figure does not include country financing for sectoral and thematic programmes with global spillovers, such as climate and health programmes. UN normative functions have been estimated at USD 5-6 billion a year, although the number is contested (Jenks and Topping, 2017[61]).

Funding to GPGs represents relatively small amounts compared to broader ODF (see Figure 3.1 in Section 3.1.1), probably because of a resistance to finance activities that have a universal benefit rather than a specific scope (Birdsall and Diofasi, 2015[59]). In a world comprising sovereign states, no single country can fully recover the benefit of its own spending for GPGs, which means low political returns on financing and incentives for inaction [(Kaul, 2012[62]); (Birdsall and Diofasi, 2015[59])]. Moreover, since GPGs are mainly funded through the multilateral system and since multilateral finance is increasingly earmarked, funding of GPGs faces important issues of lack of continuity and high transaction costs (Morris and Atansah, 2017[63]).

The inherent tendency to underfund GPGs by single sovereign states calls for collective action through the multilateral system. Going forward, it is necessary to ensure a clear division of labour based on the respective expertise of multilateral organisations in providing GPGs. Moreover, it will be necessary to find mechanisms that pool resources from a variety of actors (public and private, national and international) to raise funding for these functions that is adequate in volumes, predictability and flexibility. The current reform of the UN system offers the opportunity to reinforce its normative functions. Another example is the proposal to harness the World Bank's international development agency' reflows by setting apart a USD 10 billion window for GPG-related support (Morris and Atansah, 2017[63]). This would include support for grant finance and subsidies for GPG-related loans. Finally, current efforts by the international community to develop the total official support for sustainable development (TOSSD) framework (See Chapter 2) will also shed light on and, hopefully, provide incentives for increased funding to GPGs in the coming years.

Notes

[1] The statistical data for Israel are supplied by and under the responsibility of the relevant Israeli authorities. The use of such data by the OECD is without prejudice to the status of the Golan Heights, East Jerusalem and Israeli settlements in the West Bank under the terms of international law.

[2] For more information on becoming a DAC participant, please see: http://www.oecd.org/dac/dac-global-relations/Becoming_a_Participant_in_the_DAC.pdf.

[3] In the context of this publication, officially supported flows include both official flows to developing countries and private finance mobilised through official development interventions. In the context of the development of the new framework of TOSSD, a specific definition of the term "officially supported" flows is being developed (see in that regard the work of the International TOSSD Task Force at http://www.oecd.org/dac/financing-sustainable-development/development-finance-standards/tossd-task-force.htm).

[4] See the 2017 ODA press release at: http://www.oecd.org/dac/development-aid-rises-again-in-2016-but-flows-to-poorest-countries-dip.htm.

[5] In-donor expenditures are not cross-border flows, but are taken into account in DAC statistics in certain circumstances. They include for example some administrative and refugee costs incurred in the donor country. For more information, see (OECD, 2016[69]).

[6] Data in previous years were collected through ad hoc surveys, see more at http://www.oecd.org/dac/financing-sustainable-development/development-finance-standards/mobilisation.htm.

[7] The country examples have been extracted from (Addis Tax Initiative, 2017[7]).

[8] It is important here to note that the financing profiles of multilateral institutions vary greatly between lending institutions (multilateral development banks and regional development banks) and other multilateral institutions. The term multilateral here encompasses all UN agencies, funds and programmes – several of which fund social sectors exclusively.

[9] While this is the case for DAC providers as a group, the few non-DAC providers reporting to the OECD CRS tend to focus on infrastructure, like the multilateral institutions, but with amounts that are far smaller than the DAC countries.

[10] This group is comprised of the African Development Bank (AfDB), the Asian Development Bank (AsDB), the European Bank for Reconstruction and Development (EBRD), the European Investment Bank (EIB) as part of the EU Institutions, the Inter-American Development Bank (IDB), the World Bank (WB) and the International Finance Corporation (IFC, included in the WB Group).

[11] Including the United States, World Bank Group, EU Institutions, Germany, IADB, Global Fund, United Kingdom, AsDB, France and Japan.

[12] The World Bank Group, Korea, EU Institutions, EBRD, United States, Japan, IADB, Germany, IsDB, IFAD.

[13] In the area of education in fragile contexts, see for example the Co-Chair's summary of the Arab-DAC Dialogue that took place in Bern, Switzerland on 27 March 2017. For more information on the Arab-DAC dialogue, see also: http://www.oecd.org/dac/dac-global-relations/arab-dac-dialogue.htm

[14] See for example paragraph 6 in (United Nations, 2015[1]).

[15] This Action Plan, developed by the DAC GENDERNET, UN Women, and UN Member States, outlined the transformative policy and financing actions required to implement the Addis Ababa Action Agenda in support of achieving gender equality and empowering all women and girls. For more information see: http://www.oecd.org/dac/gender-development/Action%20Plan%20on%20Financing%20Gender%20Equality.pdf.

[16] For further analysis of aid to gender equality in the economic and productive sectors, see (DAC GENDERNET, 2018[84]).

[17] European Commission, Finland, Netherlands, New Zealand, Switzerland (Swiss Agency for Development and Cooperation), United Kingdom (DFID), the World Bank, and the Asian Development Bank.

References

Addis Tax Initiative (2017), *"ATI Monitoring Report 2015"*, International Tac Compact, Bonn, Germany, http://www.addistaxinitiative.net/documents/Addis-Tax-Initiative_Monitoring-Report_2015_EN.pdf. [7]

Ahmad, Y. and A. Nichols (2017), *"CRS reporting issues in 2016"*, OECD, Paris, http://www.oecd.org/officialdocuments/publicdisplaydocumentpdf/?cote=DCD/DAC/STAT(2017)15&docLanguage=En. [10]

AIIB et al. (2017), *"Joint MDB Statement of Ambitions for Crowding in Private Finance"*, https://www.bundesfinanzministerium.de/Content/DE/Downloads/G20-Dokumente/Hamburg_Genannte_Berichte/Joint-MDB-Statement-of-Ambitions.pdf?__blob=publicationFile&v=1. [74]

Altenburg, T. and C. Assmann (2017), *"Green Industrial Policy. Concept, Policies, Country Experiences"*, UN Environment; German Development Institute / Deutsches Institut für Entwicklungspolitk (DIE), http://wedocs.unep.org/bitstream/handle/20.500.11822/22277/Green_industrial_policy.pdf?sequence=1&isAllowed=y. [19]

Birdsall, N. and A. Diofasi (2015), *"Global Public Goods for Development: How Much and What For"*, https://www.cgdev.org/sites/default/files/CGD-Note-Birdsall-Diofasi-Global-Public-Goods-How-Much.pdf. [59]

DAC GENDERNET (2018), *"Aid to gender equality and women's empowerment: An Overview"*, OECD, Paris, https://www.oecd.org/dac/gender-development/Aid-to-gender-overview-2018.pdf. [15]

DAC GENDERNET (2018), *"How Does Aid Support Women's Economic Empowerment?"*, OECD, Paris, http://www.oecd.org/dac/gender-development/How-Does-Aid-Support-Womens-Economic-Empowerment.pdf. [84]

DAC GENDERNET (December 2016), *"Handbook on the OECD DAC Gender Equality Policy Marker"*, OECD, Paris, http://www.oecd.org/dac/gender-development/Handbook-OECD-DAC-Gender-Equality-Policy-Marker.pdf. [13]

Delalande, G. and V. Gaveau (2018), *"Senegal's perspective on TOSSD", OECD Development Working Papers, No 43*, OECD Publishing, Paris. [66]

Development Initiatives (2016), *"Measuring Aid to Global Public Goods (GPGs): An approach to estimating funding for GPGs from providers of official development assistance"*, http://devinit.org/wp-content/uploads/2016/07/Measuring-aid-to-global-public-goods-GPGs-Discussion-paper-July-2016.pdf. [60]

Donaubauer, J., B. Meyer and P. Nunnenkamp (2014), *"A New Global Index of Infrastructure: Construction, Rankings and Applications"*, https://www.ifw-members.ifw-kiel.de/publications/a-new-global-index-of-infrastructure-construction-rankings-and-applications/KWP_1929.pdf. [55]

EDFI (2016), *"Investing to Create Jobs, Boost Growth and Fight Poverty"*, https://www.deginvest.de/DEG-Documents-in-English/Download-Center/EDFI-Flagship-Report-2016.pdf. [75]

Engberg-Pedersen, P. and R. Zwart (2018), "The 2030 Agenda and Development Co-operation Results", *OECD Development Policy Papers*, No. 9, OECD Publishing, Paris, http://dx.doi.org/10.1787/2f391534-en. [36]

G20 (2017), *"Principles of MDBs' strategy for crowding-in Private Sector Finance for growth and sustainable development"*, http://www.bundesfinanzministerium.de/Content/DE/Downloads/G20-Dokumente/principles-on-crowding-in-private-sector-finance-april-20.pdf?__blob=publicationFile&v=2. [76]

Hallegatte, S. et al. (2017), *"Unbreakable : Building the Resilience of the Poor in the Face of Natural Disasters"*, World Bank, https://openknowledge.worldbank.org/handle/10986/25335. [30]

IADB (2017), *"Comparative Study of Equity Investing in Development Finance Institutions"*, Inter-American Development Bank, https://publications.iadb.org/bitstream/handle/11319/8207/Comparative-Study-of-Equity-Investing-in-Development-Finance-Institutions.pdf?sequence=8. [77]

ILO and UNDP (2017), *"2017 HLPF Thematic Review of SDG 1: End Poverty in All its Forms Everywhere"*, ILO, Geneva and UNDP, New York, NY., https://sustainabledevelopment.un.org/content/documents/14379SDG1format-final_OD.pdf. [26]

IMF (2018), *"Macroeconomic Development and Prospects in Low-Income Developing Countries (2018)"*, International Monetary Fund, http://www.imf.org/en/Publications/Policy-Papers/Issues/2018/03/22/pp021518macroeconomic-developments-and-prospects-in-lidcs. [83]

IMF (2017), *"World Economic Outlook: Seeking Sustainable Growth"*, IMF, Washington, DC, USA, http://www.imf.org/en/Publications/WEO/Issues/2017/09/19/world-economic-outlook-october-2017#Chapter%203. [29]

IMF/World Bank (2012), *"Revisiting the Debt Sustainability Framework for Low-Income Countries"*, International Monetary Fund and World Bank, Washington, DC, USA, http://www.imf.org/external/np/pp/eng/2012/011212.pdf. [79]

Inderst, G. and F. Stewart (2014), *"Institutional investment in infrastructure in emerging markets and developing countries"*, World, Bank, Washington, DC, USA., http://documents.worldbank.org/curated/en/238121468325297049/pdf/WPS6780.pdf. [53]

International Futures (n.d.), *IFs Modelling System, Version 7.31*, University of Denver, Denver, CO, USA, http://www.ifs.du.edu/ifs/frm_MainMenu.aspx (accessed on 11 September 2018). [33]

Jenks, B. and J. Topping (2017), *Financing the UN Development System*, Dag Hammarskjold Foundation, Upsala, Sweden, http://www.daghammarskjold.se/wp-content/uploads/2017/09/Financing-Report-2017_Interactive.pdf. [61]

Julks, A. and H. Kawamura (2017), *"Global context for achieving the 2030 Agenda for Sustainable Development: International financial flows and external debt"*, United Nations Department of Economic and Social Affairs, https://www.un.org/development/desa/dpad/wp-content/uploads/sites/45/publication/dsp_policy_10.pdf. [82]

Jungcurt, S. (2016), *"Towards Integrated Implementation: Tools for Understanding Linkages and Developing Strategies for Policy Coherence"*, International Institute for Sustainable Development, Winnipeg, Canada, http://sdg.iisd.org/commentary/policy-briefs/towards-integrated-implementation-tools-for-understanding-linkages-and-developing-strategies-for-policy-coherence/ (accessed on 26 April 2018). [16]

Kaul, I. (2012), "Global Public Goods: Explaining their Underprovision", *Journal of International Economic Law*, Vol. 15/3, pp. 729–750, https://doi.org/10.1093/jiel/jgs034. [62]

Kaul, I., I. Grunberg and M. Stern (1999), *"Global Public Goods"*, Oxford University Press, Oxford, UK. [34]

Kreft, S., D. Eckstein and L. Melchior (2016), *"Global Climate Risk Index 2017: Who Suffers Most From Extreme Weather Events? Weather-related Loss Events in 2015 and 1996 to 2015"*, United Nations Office for the Coordination of Humanitarian Affairs, New York, NY, USA and Geneva, Switzerland, https://reliefweb.int/sites/reliefweb.int/files/resources/16411.pdf. [27]

Le Blanc, D. (2015), *Towards integration at last? The sustainable development goals as a network of targets*, United Nations Department of Social and Economic Affairs, New York, NY, USA, http://www.un.org/esa/desa/papers/2015/wp141_2015.pdf. [18]

McKinsey (2017), *"Bridging Infrastructure Gaps: Has The World Made Progress?"*, McKinsey and Company, Washington, DC, USA, https://www.mckinsey.com/industries/capital-projects-and-infrastructure/our-insights/bridging-infrastructure-gaps-has-the-world-made-progres. [58]

McKinsey Global Institute (2015), *"The Power of Parity: how advancing women's equality can add $12 trillion to global growth"*, https://www.mckinsey.com/featured-insights/employment-and-growth/how-advancing-womens-equality-can-add-12-trillion-to-global-growth. [11]

Miyamoto, K. and E. Chiofalo (2017), "Development Co-operation for Private Sector Development: Analytical Framework and Measuring Official Development Finance", *OECD Development Co-operation Working Papers*, No. 32, OECD Publishing, Paris, http://dx.doi.org/10.1787/ded2028f-en. [35]

Miyamoto, K. and E. Chiofalo (2015), "Official Development Finance for Infrastructure: Support by Multilateral and Bilateral Development Partners", *OECD Development Co-operation Working Papers*, No. 25, OECD Publishing, Paris, http://dx.doi.org/10.1787/5jrs3sbcrvzx-en. [57]

Mooney, H. and C. de Soyres (2017), *Debt Sustainability Analyses for Low-Income Countries: An Assessment of Projection Performance*, International Monetary Fund, Whashington, DC, USA, http://www.imf.org/~/media/Files/Publications/WP/2017/wp17220.ashx. [67]

Morris, S. and P. Atansah (2017), *"Multilateral development banking for 21st century challenges: Addressing global public goods"*, Dag Hammarskjold Foundation, Upsala, Sweden, http://www.daghammarskjold.se/wp-content/uploads/2017/09/Financing-Report-2017_Interactive.pdf. [63]

Nilsson, M., D. Griggs and M. Visbek (2016), *Policy: Map the interactions between Sustainable Development Goals*, Vol. 534, Nature Publishing Group, London, pp.320-322, http://dx.doi.org/10.1038/534320a. [17]

OECD (2018), *"Aid to gender equality and women's empowerment"*, OECD, Paris, http://www.oecd.org/dac/gender-development/Aid-to-gender-overview-2018.pdf. [37]

OECD (2018), *"Converged statistical reporting directives for the CRS and the annual DAC questionnaire - Addendum 1 - Annexes - modules A, B, and C"*, OECD, Paris, https://one.oecd.org/document/DCD/DAC/STAT(2018)9/ADD1/FINAL/en/pdf. [5]

OECD (2018), *"International development statistics (database)"*, OECD, Paris, http://www.oecd.org/dac/financing-sustainable-development/development-finance-data/idsonline.htm. [2]

OECD (2018), *"Creditor Reporting System"*, OECD, Paris, https://stats.oecd.org/Index.aspx?DataSetCode=crs1. [8]

OECD (2018), *Making Blended Finance Work for the Sustainable Development Goals*, OECD Publishing, Paris, http://dx.doi.org/10.1787/9789264288768-en. [4]

OECD (2018), *OECD Development Co-operation Peer Reviews: Korea 2018*, OECD Development Co-operation Peer Reviews, OECD Publishing, Paris, http://dx.doi.org/10.1787/9789264288829-en. [42]

OECD (2018), *States of Fragility 2018*, OECD Publishing, Paris, http://dx.doi.org/10.1787/9789264302075-en. [32]

OECD (2017), *"2017 Report on the DAC Untying Recommendation"*, https://one.oecd.org/document/DCD/DAC(2017)6/FINAL/en/pdf. [81]

OECD (2017), *"Climate-related development finance 2016"*, OECD, Paris, https://www.oecd.org/dac/financing-sustainable-development/development-finance-topics/Climate-related-development-finance-in-2016.pdf. [38]

OECD (2017), *"Development Co-operation Report 2017: Data for Development"*, OECD Publishing, Paris, http://dx.doi.org/10.1787/dcr-2017-en. [68]

OECD (2017), *DAC High Level Communiqué: 31 October 2017*, https://www.oecd.org/dac/DAC-HLM-2017-Communique.pdf. [64]

OECD (2017), *Investing in Climate, Investing in Growth*, OECD Publishing, Paris, http://dx.doi.org/10.1787/9789264273528-en. [56]

OECD (2017), *OECD Development Co-operation Peer Reviews: Finland 2017*, OECD Development Co-operation Peer Reviews, OECD Publishing, Paris, http://dx.doi.org/10.1787/9789264287235-en. [43]

OECD (2017), *OECD Development Co-operation Peer Reviews: Luxembourg 2017*, OECD Development Co-operation Peer Reviews, OECD Publishing, Paris, http://dx.doi.org/10.1787/9789264284364-en. [45]

OECD (2017), *OECD Development Co-operation Peer Reviews: The Netherlands 2017*, OECD Development Co-operation Peer Reviews, OECD Publishing, Paris, http://dx.doi.org/10.1787/9789264278363-en. [44]

OECD (2016), *"OECD DAC survey on amounts mobilised from the private sector by official development finance interventions 2012-2015"*, http://www.oecd.org/development/stats/mobilisation.htm. [3]

OECD (2016), *"OECD Development Co-operation Peer Reviews: Denmark 2016"*, OECD Development Co-operation Peer Reviews, OECD Publishing, Paris, http://dx.doi.org/10.1787/9789264259362-en. [50]

OECD (2016), *"OECD Development Co-operation Peer Reviews: Denmark 2016"*, OECD Development Co-operation Peer Reviews, OECD Publishing, Paris, http://dx.doi.org/10.1787/9789264259362-en. [70]

OECD (2016), *"Converged statistical reporting directives for the Creditor Reporting System (CRS) and the annual DAC questionnaire" - DCD/DAC(2016)3/FINAL*, OECD, Paris, http://www.oecd.org/dac/financing-sustainable-development/development-finance-standards/DCDDAC(2016)3FINAL.pdf. [69]

OECD (2016), *OECD Development Co-operation Peer Reviews: Denmark 2016*, OECD Development Co-operation Peer Reviews, OECD Publishing, Paris, http://dx.doi.org/10.1787/9789264259362-en. [65]

OECD (2016), *OECD Development Co-operation Peer Reviews: Denmark 2016*, OECD Development Co-operation Peer Reviews, OECD Publishing, Paris, http://dx.doi.org/10.1787/9789264259362-en. [47]

OECD (2016), *OECD Development Co-operation Peer Reviews: United States 2016*, OECD Development Co-operation Peer Reviews, OECD Publishing, Paris, http://dx.doi.org/10.1787/9789264266971-en. [46]

OECD (2016), *Private Sector Engagement for Sustainable Development: Lessons from the DAC*, OECD Publishing, Paris, http://dx.doi.org/10.1787/9789264266889-en. [85]

OECD (2016), *States of Fragility 2016: Understanding Violence*, OECD Publishing, Paris, http://dx.doi.org/10.1787/9789264267213-en. [28]

OECD (2015), *Mapping Channels to Mobilise Institutional Investment in Sustainable Energy*, Green Finance and Investment, OECD Publishing, Paris, http://dx.doi.org/10.1787/9789264224582-en. [52]

OECD (2015), *Multilateral Aid 2015: Better Partnerships for a Post-2015 World*, OECD Publishing, Paris, http://dx.doi.org/10.1787/9789264235212-en. [86]

OECD (2015), *OECD Development Co-operation Peer Reviews: Belgium 2015*, OECD Development Co-operation Peer Reviews, OECD Publishing, Paris, http://dx.doi.org/10.1787/9789264239906-en. [41]

OECD (2015), *OECD Development Co-operation Peer Reviews: Germany 2015*, OECD Development Co-operation Peer Reviews, OECD Publishing, Paris, http://dx.doi.org/10.1787/9789264246133-en. [48]

OECD (2015), *OECD Development Co-operation Peer Reviews: Portugal 2016*, OECD Development Co-operation Peer Reviews, OECD Publishing, Paris, http://dx.doi.org/10.1787/9789264248571-en. [40]

OECD (2014), *"Mainstreaming cross-cutting issues: 7 Lessons from DAC Peer Reviews"*, OECD, Paris, http://www.oecd.org/dac/peer-reviews/Final%20publication%20version%20of%20the%207%20Lessons%20mainstreaming%20cross%20cutting%20issues.pdf. [39]

OECD (2014), *OECD Development Co-operation Peer Reviews: United Kingdom 2014*, OECD Development Co-operation Peer Reviews, OECD Publishing, Paris, http://dx.doi.org/10.1787/9789264226579-en. [49]

OECD((n.d.)), *"The DAC gender equality policy marker"*, http://www.oecd.org/dac/gender-development/dac-gender-equality-marker.htm (accessed on 02 October 2018). [14]

Sachs, J. and G. Schmidt-Traub (2017), *"Global Fund lessons for Sustainable Development Goals"*, Vol. 356/6333, American Academy for the Advancement of Science, Washington, DC, pp. 32-33, http://dx.doi.org/10.1126/science.aai9380. [80]

Alonso, J. and J. Ocampo (eds.) (2012), *The New Face of Development Co-operation: The Role of South-South Co-operation and Corporate Social Responsibility*, Columbia University Press, New York, NY. [54]

Saudi Arabia (2018), *"Saudi Aid Platform"*, Saudi Arabia, Riyadh, https://data.ksrelief.org/en/home.aspx. [9]

Suri, T. and W. Jack (2016), *"The long-run poverty and gender impacts of mobile money"*, Vol. 354/6317, American Academy for the Advancement of Science, Washington, DC, http://dx.doi.org/10.1126/science.aah5309. [20]

UNCTAD (2017), *"Commodity dependence and the Sustainable Development Goals"*, United Nations Conference on Trade and Development, Geneva, http://unctad.org/meetings/en/SessionalDocuments/cimem2d37_en.pdf. [31]

UNCTAD (2016), *"Robots and Industrialization in Developing Countries"*, United Nations Conference on Trade and Development, Geneva, http://unctad.org/en/PublicationsLibrary/presspb2016d6_en.pdf. [23]

UNCTAD (2016), *"World Investment Report 2016 - Investor Nationality: Policy Challenges"*, United Nations Conference on Trade and Development, Geneva, http://unctad.org/en/PublicationsLibrary/wir2016_en.pdf. [71]

UNCTAD (2014), *"World Investment Report 2014: Investing in the SDGs, an Action Plan"*, United Nations Conference on Trade and Development, Geneva, http://unctad.org/en/PublicationsLibrary/wir2014_en.pdf. [51]

UN-Habitat (2016), *"Urbanization and Development: Emerging Futures"*, United Nations Human Settlements Programme, Nairobi, https://unhabitat.org/wp-content/uploads/2014/03/WCR-%20Full-Report-2016.pdf. [22]

UNHCR (2017), *"Global Trends: Forced Displacement in 2016"*, United Nations Commissioner for Refugees, FilippoGrandi, http://www.unhcr.org/5943e8a34.pdf. [25]

United Nations (2015), *"Addis Ababa Action Agenda of the Third International Conference on Financing for Development"*, UN, New York, NY, http://www.un.org/esa/ffd/wp-content/uploads/2015/08/AAAA_Outcome.pdf. [1]

United Nations (2015), *"Transforming our world: the 2030 Agenda for Sustainable Development"*, UN, New York, NY, http://www.un.org/ga/search/view_doc.asp?symbol=A/RES/70/1&Lang=E. [72]

United Nations (2015), *"World Population Prospects: The 2015 Revision, Key Findings and Advance Tables"*, UN, New York, NY, https://esa.un.org/unpd/wpp/publications/files/key_findings_wpp_2015.pdf. [21]

World Bank (2018), *"Global Economic Prospects: Broad-Based Upturn, but for How Long?"*, http://www.worldbank.org/en/publication/global-economic-prospects. [78]

World Bank (2016), *World Development Report 2016: Digital Dividends*, World Bank, Washington, DC, http://documents.worldbank.org/curated/en/896971468194972881/pdf/102725-PUB-Replacement-PUBLIC.pdf. [24]

World Bank Group (2017), *"Creating Markets in Ghana - Country Private Sector Diagnostic"*, World Bank, Washington, DC, https://www.ifc.org/wps/wcm/connect/ac42c20a-c82c-48b7-8432-221c0e066e2a/CPSD-Creating-Markets-in-Ghana-Nov-2017_v1.pdf?MOD=AJPERES. [6]

World Bank Group (2015), *"Catalogue of the MDBs and the IMF Financing Solutions"*, http://www5.worldbank.org/mdgs/documents/MDBs-IMF-DevFin-Solutions-11-3-15.pdf. [73]

World Economic Forum (2014), *"The Global Gender Gap Index 2014: the case for Gender Equality"*, http://reports.weforum.org/global-gender-gap-report-2014/part-1/the-case-for-gender-equality/. [12]

Chapter 4. Linking sector strategies to national contexts

This chapter provides an overview of donors' sector allocations of official development finance (ODF) to different country groups. It focuses in particular on the dynamics and trade-offs between various types of flows reaching developing countries. In doing so it takes into account the scarcity of official development assistance (ODA) resources, their declining trend as countries develop and the compensatory role played by other official flows (OOF) when countries embark on a transition path. The analysis of these trade-offs is a first step towards informing the international development community about patterns emerging in financing for development (FfD) flows to sectors. It aims to contribute to the 2015 Addis Ababa Action Agenda, which called for "scaled-up and more effective international support, including both concessional and non-concessional financing". The first section of this chapter provides an overview of financing and a more detailed sub-sectoral analysis of ODF flows for three different income categories (low income countries, lower middle-income countries and upper middle-income countries).[1] The second section provides a similar overview for countries most in need (least developed countries, landlocked developing countries, small island developing states and countries in fragile contexts). The chapter concludes by looking at the main policy messages that can be derived from these analyses.

Key messages

Key messages to providers of development co-operation emerging from this chapter include:

- **Allocations of other official flows (OOF) to the education and health sectors in lower middle-income countries (LMICs) appear to be much lower than in the other social sectors.** The share of OOF in LMICs amounts to only 6% in health and 12% in education, as opposed to 28% in government and civil society and 34 % in other social sectors. Making more resources available for education and health can boost economic productivity by tackling the root causes of the middle-income trap.
- **Agriculture faces considerable challenges in attracting OOF compared to other productive sectors.** This applies across all developing country income categories. Only 6% of official development finance (ODF) to low-income countries (LICs) is in the form of OOF. As countries develop, this proportion remains far below that in the other productive sectors. The share of OOF in agriculture reaches 57% in upper middle-income countries (UMICs), when other productive sectors receive around 90%.
- **Least developed countries (LDCs) receive most grants.** Despite higher risk perceptions, evidence exists that LDCs can offer opportunities for providers to support the development of the private sector, including through blended finance packages.
- **In landlocked developing countries (LLDCs), providers do not prioritise infrastructure.** The share of infrastructure in ODF is 33% in LLDCs, almost the same as in other developing countries (ODCs) – 34%. In principle, it should be higher, especially in transport and ICTs, to compensate for the challenges of being landlocked.
- **In small island developing states (SIDS), non-concessional finance is lower than in ODCs, for almost all sectors and in any income category.** For example, in the water sector, the share of OOF represents only 1% in LMIC-SIDS as against 30% in other LMICs.
- **Adopting a smart, sector approach to transition finance is essential, but demands new research.** This publication takes an initial look at the benefits of analysing transition finance gaps from a sector perspective. For example, it can help to identify when providers should target specific sectors as countries climb the income per capita ladder.
- **For countries in fragile contexts (FCs), providers of development co-operation use guarantee instruments much more than in ODCs.** Of the amounts mobilised by official development interventions in FCs, 65% are mobilised using guarantee instruments as against only 38% in non-FCs.

4.1. Official development finance by income groupings

From the donor community perspective, the key consideration when a country develops is to ensure a long-lasting impact of its development finance efforts. This implies a progressive mobilisation of domestic and private resources in a sound macroeconomic context (e.g. debt sustainability) towards independence from ODA while avoiding economic and development setbacks. Financing for development is about using the right instruments at the right time for the right projects towards greater development, gradually building capacity for a fast and smooth transition towards less reliance on ODA (See Box 4.1).

This section of the chapter provides an overview of ODF patterns – i.e. ODA and OOF – in different sectors and different country contexts to better understand interlinkages and trade-offs between these two types of flow.[2] This overview highlights the transition of countries as they attract more OOF, a type of flow traditionally focused on productive investment that can raise productivity, incentivise job creation and develop human capital. In general, developing countries perceive the transition from ODA to OOF positively: the resources become more investment oriented and provide them with more tools to develop on their own.[3] (Cordella and Ulku, 2007[1]) (Moss, Pettersson and Van de Walle, 2006[2]) (Gupta et al., 2004[3]) (Benedek et al., 2014[4]), (Bulow and Rogoff, 2005[5]).

4.1.1. An overview of official finance by income groupings

As for the rest of this report, the following overview is based on five main sector groupings: social, infrastructure, production, banking and business, and multisector over the period 2012-16.[4] This section will focus on how ODA and OOF are allocated across sectors and income groups. The aim is to improve the understanding of behaviours and recommend reallocations of resources by providers to accelerate development processes or/and correct paths to facilitate sustainable FfD.

As described in Box 4.1, when countries pursue their development pathways, the relative weights of the different financing resources change. A snapshot for specific income groupings is shown in Figure 4.2 below.

Sector-allocable official finance to the poorest countries mostly consists of ODA, while OOF becomes more prominent when countries develop

Thus, ODA represent 93% of flows to LICs, where OOF represent the remaining 7%. The ODA portion falls to 64% in LMICs, OOF then accounting for 36% in this income grouping. In UMICs, the breakdown between ODA and OOF is almost the opposite of that in LMICs, with ODA being 34% of total ODF and OOFs being 66%.

Box 4.1. What is transition finance?

The study of transition finance consists of understanding the dynamics of external flows (concessional, non-concessional, private flows at market terms, philanthropy and remittances) - as well as domestic resources - to developing countries as they move along the development continuum. The ultimate objective is to combine the right policy and financing mixes to ensure the long-term effects and contribution of development finance to the Sustainable Development Goals (SDGs) (Cattaneo and Piemonte, 2018[61]). The OECD *Global Outlook on Financing for Sustainable Development* (OECD, 2018[7]) provides a holistic framework for navigating the global development finance architecture, supporting better policies for better finance and promoting inclusive and sustainable development. As shown in Figure 4.1, as countries pursue their development pathways, the relative weights of the different financing flows change: ODA resources decline; OOF, private and domestic resource mobilisation (DRM) resources grow with different patterns; and remittances show a parabolic trend. Observations made in this chapter should be seen in the overall context of this wider set of flows.

Figure 4.1. The mix of external flows changes as countries move along the development continuum

Average 2012-16, 2016 constant prices, USD billion disbursements

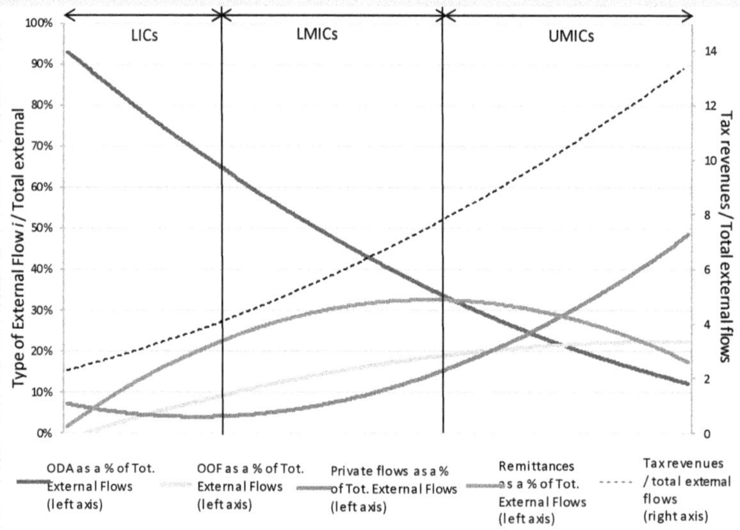

Sources: (OECD, 2018[8]) *"International development statistics (database)"*, http://www.oecd.org/dac/financing-sustainable-development/development-finance-data/idsonline.htm *(ODA, OOF); Development Assistance Committee (DAC) database (private flows); World Bank database (remittances); United Nations University World Institute for Development Economics Research (UNU-WIDER) database (tax revenues).*

StatLink https://doi.org/10.1787/888933855732

Figure 4.2. Concessionality of ODF decreases as countries develop economically

Share of ODA and OOF in total ODF by income and sector groupings, average 2012-16, 2016 constant prices, USD billion commitments

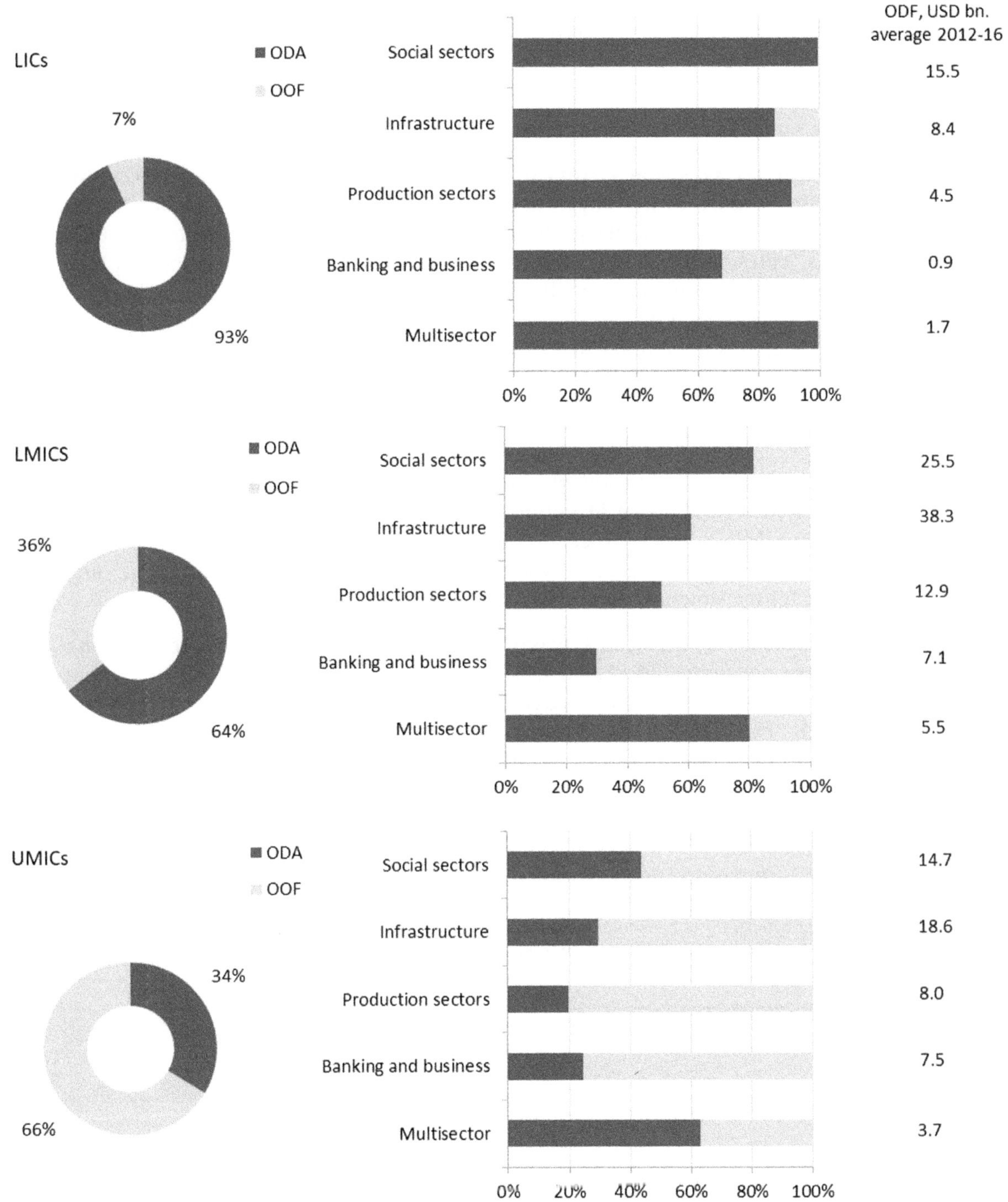

Source: (OECD, 2018[8]) "International development statistics (database)", http://www.oecd.org/dac/financing-sustainable-development/development-finance-data/idsonline.htm.

StatLink https://doi.org/10.1787/888933855751

The overall transition from ODA to OOF is homogeneous across sector categories

All sector categories are largely ODA funded in LICs. LMICs still attract a large volume of ODA for the social sectors and infrastructure, but the banking and business and production sectors are becoming less dependent on concessional flows and can instead turn to non-concessional flows. In UMICs, every sector grouping is able to attract more OOF than ODA.[5]

Comparing the same sector in different income groupings reveals the following:

- **In volume terms, social sectors in LICS receive less ODF than LMICS, but three times more in per capita terms** (see the right column in Figure 4.2 and columns 5, 6 and 7 in Table 4.2 further below for data in per capita terms). ODF to LICs represented USD 15.5 billion on average per year in the period 2012-16; nevertheless, this amount is smaller than in LMICs (USD 25.5 billion). However, in per capita terms ODF for social sectors to LICs (USD 24.1 on average per capita) is almost three times that of LMICs (USD 8.5 per capita). UMICs receive the smallest amount of ODF to social sectors among the three income groupings, both globally (USD 14.7 billion on average per year in the period 2012-16) and in per capita terms (USD 6.2).
- **While social sectors are not able to attract non-concessional flows in LICs, they are in second place in volume terms in UMICs,** attracting 24% of total OOF to UMICs, even exceeding the production sectors (19%) (Table 4.1). UMICS use non-concessional resources in social sectors to engage in large projects for the structural reform of their economies (Box 4.2).
- **Infrastructure is the sector grouping where most of the non-concessional flows are concentrated** (Table 4.1) with 61% of OOF going to LICs targeting infrastructure, while this percentage reaches 47% of OOF in LMICs and 38% in UMICs). This reflects the finding that investment in infrastructure can be financially and economically viable. This is especially true in energy and transport, where investments are concentrated (Herrera, 2005[9]) (Henckel, 2010[10]), (Estache, 2012[11]).

Table 4.1. Non-concessional flows are mostly concentrated in infrastructure

Volumes of other official flows by income group and shares by sector groupings, average 2012-16, 2016 constant prices, USD billion commitment

	LICs	LMICs	UMICs
Total OOF to:	2.0	31.8	34.8
Social sectors	4%	14%	24%
Infrastructure	**61%**	**47%**	**38%**
Production sectors	21%	20%	19%
Banking & business	14%	16%	16%
Multisector	0%	3%	3%

Source: (OECD, 2018[8]) "International development statistics (database)", http://www.oecd.org/dac/financing-sustainable-development/development-finance-data/idsonline.htm.

StatLink https://doi.org/10.1787/888933855922

Box 4.2. Upper middle-income countries' use of other official flows

Looking at other official flows (OOF) to upper middle-income countries in social sectors, Brazil receives the most (22% of total), followed by Mexico (14%) and Colombia (11%). These three Latin American countries concentrate their OOF finance in the governance sector. They use it to fund big macroeconomic stability programmes, mainly through Inter-American Development Bank (IADB) resources. For example, Brazil engaged in a fiscal stability consolidation programme for the development of the State of Bahia for USD 0.5 billion in 2012. Mexico received USD 0.7 billion in 2014 to support the development and implementation of alternatives for the strengthening and modernisation of its tax system. Colombia obtained a loan for USD 0.4 billion in 2014 to deepen its fiscal reform. These three examples show that these UMIC countries are able to undertake large structural reform programmes using non-concessional resources with the eventual aim of mobilising domestic resources.

Overall, providers seem to respond to countries' financing needs as they move up the income ladder

LICs with little or no access to domestic or international financial markets are highly ODA dependent. Indeed, in cases of extreme poverty, external aid to social sectors, for example, may meet the most basic human needs, so donors are essentially fulfilling their role of solidarity. LMICs are already better able to access these markets and thus require fewer concessional resources. The donor community is responding by offering non-concessional loans to finance investment in the more profitable sectors, such as infrastructure. And finally, when countries reach the UMIC status, developing countries are able to benefit from (and are receiving) increasing levels of debt to sustain even more growth. They do this by diversifying their non-concessional finance to other sectors, such as production and structural reform programmes. Thus, at a macro level the international community is doing what seems most appropriate.

However, it is necessary to examine subsector resource allocations to better analyse some of the transition dynamics, such as the "middle-income trap" (see Box 4.3). This affects more than two-thirds of the recipient countries on the Development Assistance Committee (DAC) List of ODA recipients.[6] It is important to remember that this analysis only covers ODF flows. Other flows such as private investments, DRM and remittances are not considered in this publication, but will be the subject of additional research within the OECD DAC. Obstacles to the progressive transition from ODF to non-ODF flows could better explain the traps or setbacks in the development path of a given country. Any FfD strategy should not limit itself to ODF, and the understanding of ODA versus OOF interactions should only be seen as a first step in the design of financial policies for development.[7] (Ghatak, 2014[12]) (Kaldewei, 2015[13]) (Ratha, 2010[14]) (Sahay, 2015[15]) (Samargandi, 2013[16])

Box 4.3. What is the middle-income trap?

This concept was first suggested by the World Bank in 2005, and quickly gained popularity among economists. It refers to the fact that the majority of the countries that left the low-income country category to reach middle-income status in the 1960s and 1970s have remained there ever since. These economies showed sharp decelerations in growth and in increases in the pace of productivity, remaining "trapped" in the middle-income status and unable to become high-income economies.

Source: Authors based on (Agénor, 2017[17]), (Agénor, 2012[18]), (Aiyar, 2013[19]) (Gill, 2015[20])

4.1.2. Sub-sector and regional observations

Sub-sector allocations reveal more differentiated dynamics than those observed at sector grouping levels

Table 4.2 provides a snapshot (in columns 1, 2 and 3) of the distribution of ODF flows by subsector and income category. For example, column 2 indicates that LMICs attract more ODF resources than LICs and UMICs, for all the sectors. It then provides information on the average ODF volumes by sector (column 4). For example, health received USD 18.2 billion of ODF on average in the period 2012-16. Columns 5, 6 and 7 indicate the amount of ODF per capita for each income grouping. The table gives more dynamic information in columns 8, 9 and 10, showing how and when non-concessional loans take the lead (or not) in the composition of ODF by sector and income grouping. This demonstrates when countries engage in a virtuous cycle of being able to attract more OOF and becoming less ODA dependent.

Table 4.2. Sub-sector allocations reveal more differentiated dynamics than those observed at sector grouping levels

ODF by sector and income grouping, USD per capita, and shares of OOF by income grouping, average 2012-16, 2016 constant prices, USD billion commitment

	ODF to LICs	ODF to LMICs	ODF to UMICs	Total ODF (USD billion, average 2012-16)	USD per capita LICs	USD per capita LMICs	USD per capita UMICs	Share of OOF in LICs	Share of OOF in LMICs	Share of OOF in UMICs
	(1)	(2)	(3)	(4)	(5)	(6)	(7)	(8)	(9)	(10)
Social sectors					24.1	8.5	6.2			
Education	20%	49%	31%	12.2	3.8	2.0	1.6	2%	12%	48%
Health	40%	45%	16%	18.2	7.3	2.7	1.2	0%	6%	49%
Gov. & civil soc.	26%	44%	30%	17.9	11.2	2.6	2.3	0%	28%	58%
Other social	16%	48%	36%	7.4	1.8	1.2	1.1	0%	34%	74%
Infrastructure					13.0	12.5	7.7			
Water	15%	56%	28%	11.6	2.8	2.2	1.4	6%	29%	70%
Energy	12%	63%	25%	25.2	4.5	5.1	2.5	16%	47%	68%
Transport & storage	13%	56%	31%	26.7	5.5	4.9	3.5	18%	33%	72%
Communications	8%	51%	41%	1.7	0.2	0.3	0.3	42%	64%	72%
Production sectors					7.0	4.4	3.5			
Agriculture	29%	52%	19%	12.5	5.7	2.2	1.0	6%	23%	57%
Industry	5%	50%	46%	8.5	0.6	1.4	1.7	31%	79%	91%
Mining & construction	7%	61%	31%	2.6	0.3	0.6	0.4	39%	76%	83%
Trade & tourism	14%	35%	50%	1.9	0.4	0.2	0.4	7%	39%	91%
Banking & business	6%	46%	48%	15.4	1.4	2.5	3.4	32%	70%	75%
Multisector	16%	50%	34%	10.9	2.7	1.8	1.6	1%	20%	37%
Total				172.7	48.2	29.7	22.4			

Note: For every line, columns 1, 2 and 3 add up to 100%, reflecting sector by sector how ODF is distributed in every income category; column 4 refers to total ODF by sector; columns 5, 6 and 7 show ODF per capita by income groupings and by sector; columns 8, 9 and 10 do not add up to 100% as they show how much OOF is directed to every sector in every income category (for example 2% of ODF flows in LICs are directed to education – so 98% of ODF to education in LICs are ODA flows).
Source: (OECD, 2018[8]) "International development statistics (database)", http://www.oecd.org/dac/financing-sustainable-development/development-finance-data/idsonline.htm.

StatLink https://doi.org/10.1787/888933855941

The main findings from Table 4.2 are as follows:

- **All sectors in LICs are mainly ODA financed, as shown by the share of non-concessional flows in total ODF**. The proportion of OOF grows gradually as countries develop (columns 8, 9 and 10).[8]
- **In per capita terms, LICs receive more support than LMICs and UMICs in all social sectors** (education, health, governance, and civil society, and other social, individually), **the water sector, transport and storage, agriculture and multisector** (see column 5). Only some infrastructure sectors (energy and communications), production sectors (industry, mining and construction), and banking and business receive more financing in LMICs and/or UMICs (see columns 6 and 7).

- **While most subsectors show fairly linear transition patterns from concessional to non-concessional financing, this is not the case for education and health.** OOF financing could be triggered sooner in the development continuum, as it reaches only 6% of ODF in health and 12% in education in the LMIC category (28% in governance and 34% in other social sectors). Also, these proportions reach 49% in health and 48% in education in UMICs (so between 6 and 12%, and 49 and 48% the margin could be filled more progressively). Making more resources available in education and health is especially important as investing in these sectors can boost productivity improvements for long-term growth, precisely tackling major handicaps in the so-called middle-income trap.
- **Agriculture faces considerable challenges in attracting OOF compared to other productive sectors, across all developing country income categories.** Among LICs only 6% of ODF is in the form of OOF, and while countries develop, the level remains well below the other sectors of the grouping. Agriculture is able to deliver high private and social profits, so a higher level of OOF would be desirable. This presumes taking into consideration the macroeconomic situation of each recipient country, its rate of debt in relation to its gross national income (GNI), capacity to respond to new obligations, etc.
- **The water sector in LICs seems to attract less non-concessional finance than other infrastructure sub-sectors.** OOF to water in LICs are relatively small (6%) compared to the other sub-sectors of this grouping, but grow quickly, reaching 29% of non-concessional flows in LMICs and 70% in UMICs.
- **What is the ideal mix of external financial flows at each level of development? Can the donor community help engineer a virtuous transition pattern earlier in the development continuum?** Is it possible to expect, for example, that in sectors such as health and education OOF (or other non-ODA flows) could shoulder a greater burden than ODA investments, prior to the UMIC stage of development? (See column 10, where non-concessional flows represent almost 50% of the total ODF reaching UMICs).[9] If an LMIC has a healthy macroeconomic environment, helping it to accelerate reforms and invest in capacity building at this stage of development would improve its business environment and attract new and more capital to finance development. (Brown, 2001[21]) Could the donor community consider alternative financing for these sectors in LMICs if the macro environment of a country allows it?[10] More considerations along these lines will be explored in forthcoming OECD work (OECD, 2018, forthcoming[22]).

Looking at ODF by income categories and regions (see Figure 4.3), the most striking aspects are:

- **Asia attracts the largest share of non-concessional flows in the LMIC and UMIC income categories.**
- **America and Asia are able to trigger higher levels of OOF in the UMIC category, especially compared to Africa and Oceania.**

Thus, there could be room for UMIC countries in Africa and Oceania to accelerate their transition from ODA to OOF.

Figure 4.3. Regions attract different levels of non-concessional flows across income groups

Share of ODA and OOF by income categories and regions, average 2012-16, 2016 constant prices, USD commitments

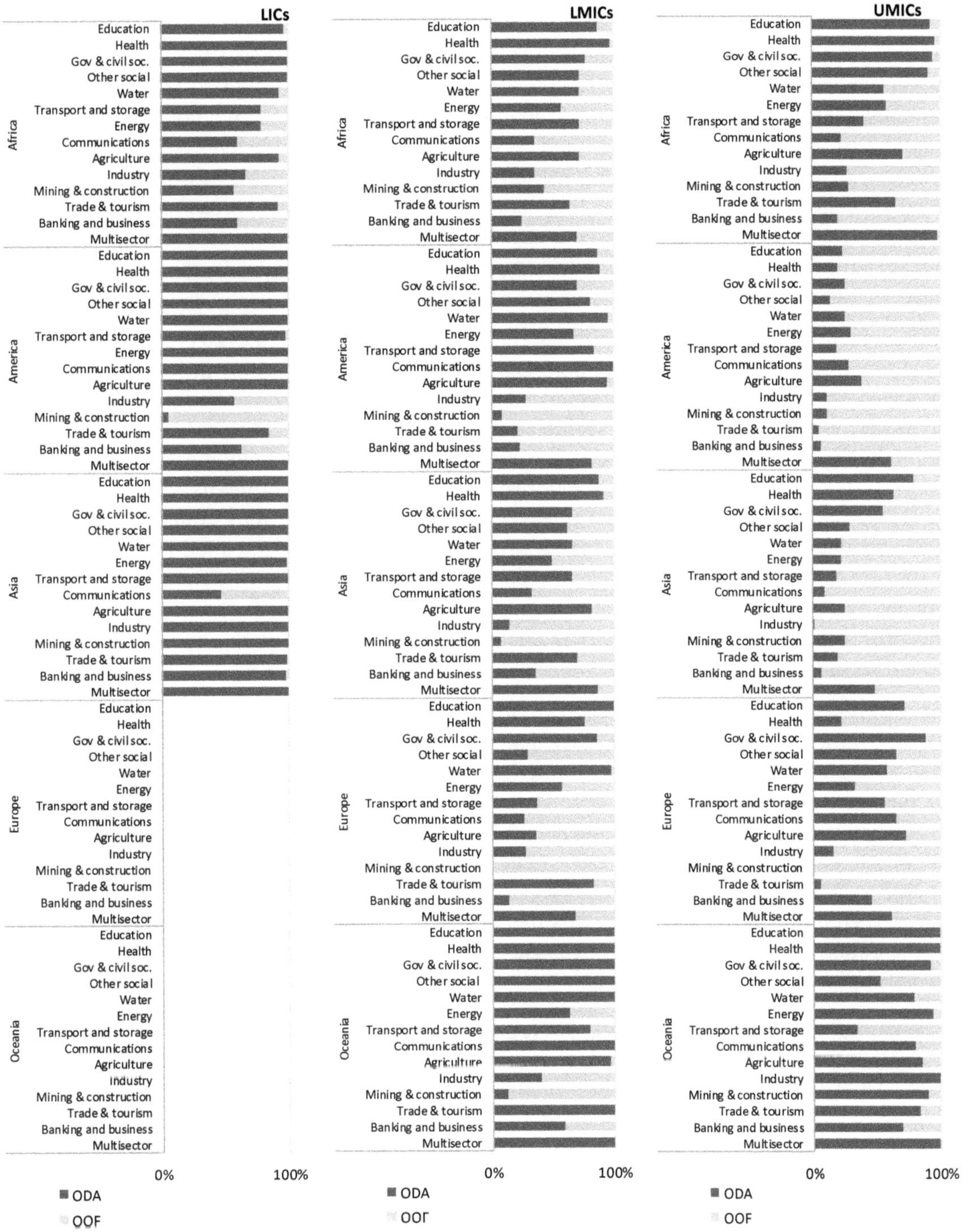

Note: there are no LICs in Europe or Oceania.

Source: (OECD, 2018[8]) "International development statistics (database)", http://www.oecd.org/dac/financing-sustainable-development/development-finance-data/idsonline.htm.

StatLink https://doi.org/10.1787/888933855770

4.2. Official development finance to countries most in need

In recent years, the OECD DAC has been working to develop co-operation approaches and tools tailored to respond to a wide variety of country contexts, with a special focus on countries most in need (LDCs, LICs, LLDCs, SIDS and FCs).

At the 2014 DAC High-Level Meeting (HLM), ministers recognised the need to better target concessional finance and agreed to "allocate more of total ODA to 'countries most in need', including least developed countries (LDCs), low-income countries, SIDS, landlocked developing countries and fragile and conflict-affected states" (OECD, 2014[23]). The DAC reaffirmed this commitment at its 2016 HLM, acknowledging the need to better tailor development co-operation instruments and approaches to different country circumstances and needs (OECD, 2016[24]). In its May 2017 meeting, the DAC discussed the issue of transition finance in general and how it relates to countries most in need, in particular.

More recently, the 2017 DAC High Level Communiqué (OECD, 2017[25]) called for "analytical work to help identify where ODA is most needed (such as in least developed countries, low-income countries, small island developing states, landlocked developing countries, and fragile and conflict-affected contexts) and where additional actions may be required" (para. 19). It recognised "the need to ensure that development co-operation approaches and tools can effectively respond to the new complexity of sustainable development by providing appropriate support to countries as they transition through different phases of development" (para. 20). The Communiqué also called for review and reflection "on the evidence base that documents the consequences of different graduation processes on access to development finance from all sources, and (…) policy analysis on the different patterns of co-operation, including financing, channels, and objectives in countries in transition" (para. 20).

The following section will therefore provide analysis based on official finance targeting each of these groups of countries individually, over the period 2012-16.[11] The differences and commonalities of the ODA/OOF interlinkages will be examined especially in relation to the sectors' specific patterns followed by these flows. When relevant, the country groupings are compared with "Other developing countries" (ODCs), which include all countries on the DAC List of ODA Recipients minus the countries included in the country grouping under study (LDCs, LLDCs, SIDS or FCs). Comparing these four country groupings to ODCs highlights the extent to which development finance patterns in the country groupings differ from those in the rest of the developing countries outside this grouping.

4.2.1. Least developed countries (LDCs)

The LDC category contains 47 developing countries,[12] representing 13% of the world's population and 38% of the world's extreme poor (see Box 4.4). These 47 countries are categorised as having long-term structural handicaps measured by three indicators, recorded simultaneously. A country can be included in the LDC category if:

- at the moment of its examination: its GNI per capita (Atlas method, World Bank) is lower than USD 1 025
- it has a human asset index (HAI) lower than 60
- it has an economic vulnerability index (EVI) above 36.

Countries should also have a population size of less than 75 million for inclusion in this category (United Nations, 2008[26]), (United Nations, 2018[27]).

Today, the LDCs grouping is not composed exclusively of LICs, but also of 17 LMICs and even three UMICs due to the asymmetry in the inclusion and graduation criteria. From its creation in 1971, and despite several improvements to the definition criteria, to date only five countries have graduated from the LDC category: Botswana in 1994, Cabo Verde in 2007, Maldives in 2011, Samoa in 2014 and Equatorial Guinea in 2017. Vanuatu will be eligible for graduation in 2020 and Angola will be eligible in 2021.[13]

Figure 4.4 shows, for each of the LDC groupings, the composition of ODA and OOF received in 2012-16.

Figure 4.4. Least developed countries are highly funded by concessional finance

Share of ODA and OOF in total ODF (left hand chart) and share of ODA and OOF in total ODF by sector groupings (right hand chart) in LDCs, average 2012-16, 2016 constant prices, USD commitments

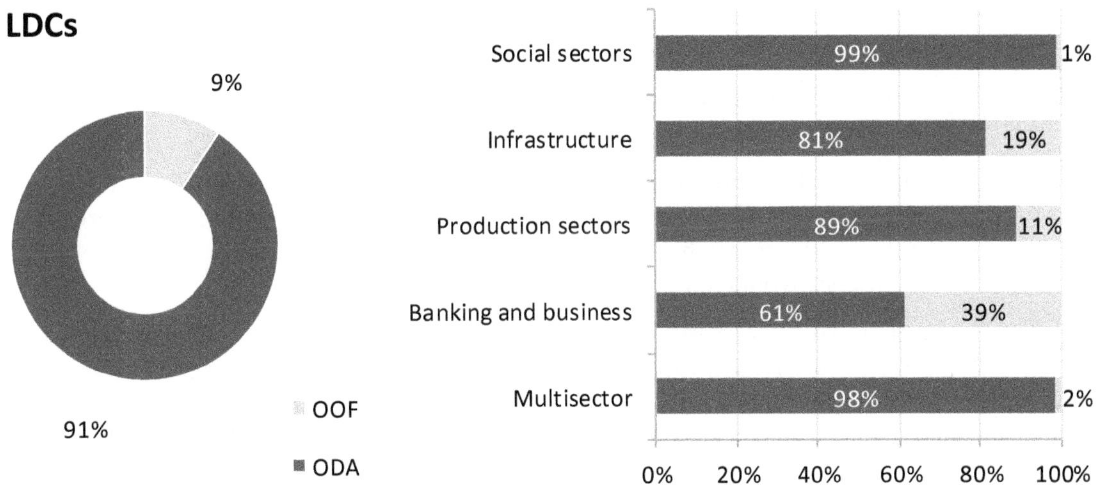

Source: (OECD, 2018[8]), "International development statistics (database)", http://www.oecd.org/dac/financing-sustainable-development/development-finance-data/idsonline.htm

StatLink https://doi.org/10.1787/888933855789

LDCs are highly funded by concessional finance, with most of the donor effort being concentrated in the social sectors and infrastructure

Total ODF to LDCs amounted to USD 45 billion during the period 2012-16, where concessional finance represented 91% or USD 40.8 billion (see Figure 4.4 and Table 4.3). Social sectors and infrastructure concentrated most of donor efforts (these two sectors represented 77% of total ODF to LDCs, mainly in the form of concessional flows). More granular sector allocation analysis reveals that health, followed by the government and civil society sectors, are by far the two social sectors most supported by providers of development co-operation. (Table 4.3).

Box 4.4. DAC members' special measures regarding least developed countries

LDCs were first recognised as a group of countries of special interest for the DAC community in 1978. According to their *Recommendation on the Terms and Conditions of Aid* that year, DAC members agreed that the average grant element in ODA to LDCs should be either 90% of a given donor's annual commitment to all LDCs, or at least 86% of the donors' commitments to each individual LDC.

Another action was undertaken in 1981. This was introduced during the first United Nations conference on LDCs, where DAC donors committed to providing between 0.15% and 0.20% of donor GNI in the form of ODA to LDCs. This target is now contained in the Istanbul Programme of Action (2011) and states, for 2011-20:

- that donor countries providing more than 0.20% of their GNI as ODA to least developed countries should continue to do so and maximise their efforts to further increase ODA to least developed countries;
- that other donor countries which have met the 0.15% target should undertake to reach 0.20% expeditiously; and
- that all other donor countries which have committed themselves to the 0.15% target have to reaffirm their commitment and undertake either to achieve the target by 2015 or to make their best efforts to accelerate their endeavours to reach the target.

Also, at their HLM in April 2001, DAC members declared their objective of untying ODA to LDCs to the greatest extent possible. They also stated their intention to promote and ensure adequate ODA flows, especially to LDCs. In January 2002, they specifically recommended the untying of LDCs in the following areas:

- balance of payments and structural adjustment support
- debt forgiveness
- sector and multisector programmes assistance
- investment project aid
- import and commodity support
- commercial services contracts and ODA to non-governmental organisations for procurement-related activities.

Finally, in December 2014, DAC members reached a new agreement to modernise reporting practices regarding ODA loans, thus creating incentives for providing highly subsidised loans to LDCs (OECD, 2015[28]).

Table 4.3. LDCs represent an opportunity for ODF providers to engage in non-ODA financing

DF volumes to LDCs and shares of OOF, average 2012-16, 2016 constant prices, USD billion commitments

	ODA	OOF	Total ODF	OOF/ODF
Social sectors				
Education	3.5	0.1	3.6	2%
Gov & civil soc.	6.0	0.1	6.1	2%
Health	8.9	0.0	8.9	0%
Other social infrastructure and services	1.7	0.0	1.7	1%
Infrastructure				
Water	2.6	0.2	2.8	8%
Energy	4.3	1.3	5.6	24%
Transport & storage	4.6	0.9	5.5	16%
Communications	0.2	0.2	0.4	49%
Production sectors				
Agriculture	4.6	0.3	4.8	5%
Industry	0.4	0.3	0.8	38%
Mining & construction	0.1	0.1	0.2	38%
Trade & tourism	0.3	0.0	0.3	13%
Banking & business	1.0	0.6	1.6	39%
Multisector	2.6	0.0	2.6	2%
Total	40.8	4.2	45.0	

Source: (OECD, 2018[8]) "International development statistics (database)", http://www.oecd.org/dac/financing-sustainable-development/development-finance-data/idsonline.htm.

StatLink https://doi.org/10.1787/888933855960

Some key questions on the financing of LDCs require specific attention by the development community

While this publication focuses on providing an overview of sector financing, the analysis carried out raised a number of questions related to LDC financing. These require further study. For example, is the low level of OOF explained by the specific needs of LDCs in terms of concessional finance? Or could it be that donors do not wish to carry out OOF operations because they first need to maximise their ODA levels to meet their ODA commitments? Are social and/or economic vulnerabilities (the other two factors, in addition to GNI per capita, that determine the LDC status (Alonso, 2014[29])) such that they justify low levels of OOF in certain sectors?[14] Or is it that LDCs' risk ratings are so high that it makes it simply prohibitive for them to borrow? Finally, could this situation reflect debt sustainability issues that prohibit borrowing from responsible lenders?

LDCs represent an opportunity for ODF providers to engage in non-ODA financing

Even if LDCs are often perceived as more risky, they also represent opportunities for providers to engage in non-ODA financing (UNCTAD, 2011[30]). This is in line with the call made in the Addis Ababa Action Agenda (AAAA) (United Nations, 2015[31]) to mobilise all resources for developing countries. The AAAA also recognises that funding sources additional to ODA are necessary to provide the financing needs for achieving the 2030 Agenda. Therefore non-ODA financing opportunities should also be explored in LDCs. Box 4.5 provides examples of such opportunities in the renewable energy sector.

Box 4.5. Examples of private investments in least developed countries

1. Cambodia solar power project

This project involved the construction and operation, using local resources, of a 10 MW solar power plant in Bavet City, Svay Rieng Province, Cambodia, on a build-own-operate basis. There was an acute energy shortage in Svay Rieng Province, which has special economic zones with growing industrial economic activity and consequently a rising demand for electricity. The province had been relying entirely on imported power from Viet Nam, whose supply was insufficient and unstable. The project represented the first utility-scale solar power plant and the first competitively tendered private-sector renewable energy project in the country. The project sells power to Électricité du Cambodge at a very competitive tariff, below the average supply cost, without any feed-in tariffs or subsidies. The project was ripe for blended finance, and the USD 13.6 million cost was funded by equity and USD 9.2 million of debt (including a long-term direct loan of USD 3.25 million from the Asian Development Bank). Construction started in September 2016, generation started in August 2017, and commercial operations were achieved in October 2017. This project demonstrated the benefits of increasing Cambodia's power supply through the involvement of the private sector. It also signalled to the market that infrastructure investments led by the private sector can be successfully undertaken in a transparent manner, at a competitive price and with a sound financing package. As such, the project will contribute to meeting the electricity demand, including a balanced electricity supply between dry and wet seasons. It will also enable full electrification of villages by 2020 and electrification of 70% of households via the national grid by 2030.

2. Mobisol in Kenya, Rwanda and the United Republic of Tanzania

Mobisol is a German private company that provides affordable stand-alone solar energy systems for households and small businesses in rural Kenya, Rwanda and United Republic of Tanzania ("Tanzania"). Mobisol's products are made affordable by a rent-to-own scheme that offers microfinance loans over a period of 48 months in small instalments that are payable via mobile money. Mobisol solar energy systems come with a full service package that includes customer service, free maintenance and remote monitoring technology. The systems can illuminate households; power laptops, radios, TVs, and fridges; and charge mobile phones.

Mobisol's first investor, a professional in the German solar industry, financed Mobisol's initial product development and its first employees. After successfully completing the pilot phase, the company was able to attract further investors and development finance institutions such as Germany's Deutsche Investitions- und Entwicklungsgesellschaft (DEG) and Finnfund. Blended finance from international donors was particularly relevant for project scaling and the early project development phases. In terms of results, over 120 000 households were electrified and over 12.1 MW solar capacity was installed. Over 580 000 indirect beneficiaries profited from electrification infrastructure substituting grid connection. Almost 700 full-time staff were employed and about 1 400 small entrepreneurs worked as contractors, over 95% of them in Rwanda and Tanzania.

Source: OECD Secretariat's survey carried out in preparation for this publication.

4.2.2. Landlocked developing countries

The Landlocked developing countries (LLDCs) category is a grouping of 32 developing countries[15] that face particular challenges related to their lack of direct access to the sea, which leads to geographical isolation from international markets. Imports and exports of goods and services need to transit through other countries. This generates higher trade costs, major logistical and infrastructure challenges (e.g. changes in transport modes, international road and rail connections with neighbours' networks, etc.). All of these impose serious constraints on their development.[16] Infrastructure is the main sector in which LLDCs need assistance in order to overcome their isolation and facilitate their path to development. Currently, high transport costs erode the competitiveness of LLDCs (most LLDCs are commodity exporters). They spend almost twice as much of their export earnings on transport and insurance services than the average for developing countries (and three times more than the average for developed economies).[17]

In 1965, the United Nations Convention on Transit Trade of Landlocked States addressed LLDCs' concerns for the first time. In 1970 the General Assembly, within the context of the Second United Nations Development Decade, included a section on special measures in favour of LLDCs. It called for "appropriate attention to the special needs of LLDCs in extending adequate financial and technical assistance to projects designed for the development and improvement of the transport and communications infrastructure needed by these countries". The situation of transit transport systems was reviewed again in 1995 (at the General Assembly) and in 2003 (at the United Nations global conference in Kazakhstan). A programme of action was adopted as a result, focusing on transport infrastructure and maintenance, transit policies and trade facilitation measures.

LLDCs have unrealised potential to attract non-ODA flows

As shown in Figure 4.5, only 23% of total official aid, USD 7.3 billion per year over 2012-16, was provided in the form of OOF to LLDCs, compared to 44% for ODCs.

Figure 4.5. LLDCs have unrealised potential to attract non-ODA flows

Share of OOF and ODA in LLDCs and ODCs, average 2012-16, 2016 constant prices, USD commitments

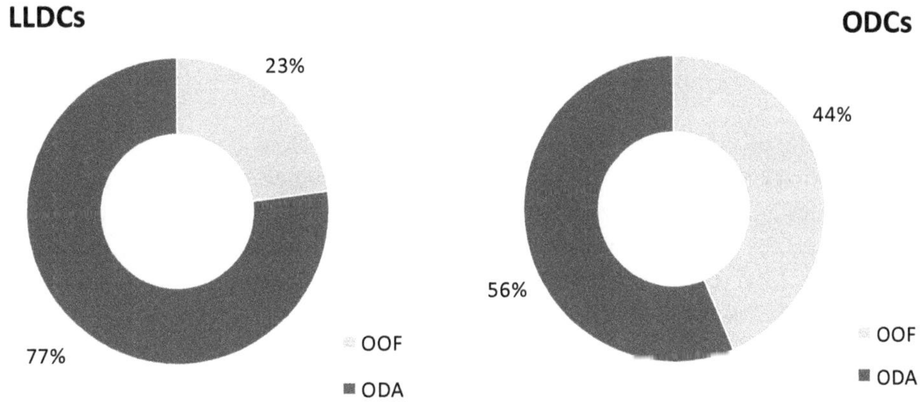

Source: (OECD, 2018[8]) "International development statistics (database)", http://www.oecd.org/dac/financing-sustainable-development/development-finance-data/idsonline.htm

StatLink https://doi.org/10.1787/888933855808

Providers need to redouble efforts towards infrastructure investments in LLDCs

Providers' support to LLDCs mainly focuses on social sectors – infrastructure is only the second most supported sector. Total ODF to social sectors was USD 13 billion over the period 2012-16 (41% of total ODF to LLDCs). Support to infrastructure amounted to USD 10.3 billion (33 % of total ODF to LLDCs) (Figure 4.6). Also, LLDCs get a similar share of their ODF going to key infrastructure sectors in comparison to ODCs (33% compared to 34% for ODCs). Providers should therefore carefully consider increasing their support on hard and soft infrastructure investment in LLDCs.

Figure 4.6. Providers need to redouble efforts towards infrastructure investments in landlocked developing countries

Share of ODA and OOF in LLDCs by sector groupings, and shares of ODF by sector groupings in LLDCs and ODCs, average 2012-16, 2016 constant prices, USD commitments

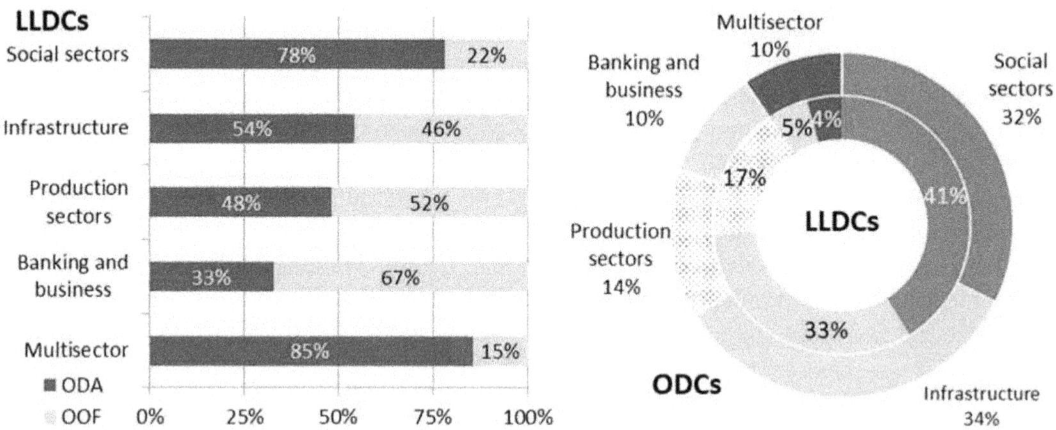

Note: the double pie chart on the right shows total ODF to LLDCs in the inner circle and total ODF to all ODCs in the outer circle.
Source: (OECD, 2018[8]) "International development statistics (database)", http://www.oecd.org/dac/financing-sustainable-development/development-finance-data/idsonline.htm.

StatLink https://doi.org/10.1787/888933855827

The lower levels of total ODF to infrastructure in LLDCs compared to ODCs are due to smaller provisions of non-concessional finance to the energy and water sectors

The lower levels of total ODF to infrastructure in LLDCs compared to ODCs are explained by smaller provisions of non-concessional finance to the energy and water sectors (35% versus 50% and 14% versus 40%, respectively). They are not explained, as could be expected, by transport and storage. In fact, LLDCs receive slightly more OOF as a percentage of total ODF than ODCs in transport and storage: 44% versus 43%, respectively. (Table 4.4 and Table 4.5).

Table 4.4. LLDCs receive a smaller share of OOF for energy and water than ODCs

Volumes of ODA, OOF and ODF and share of OOF by sector in LLDCs, average 2012-16, 2016 constant prices, USD commitments

	ODA	OOF	Total ODF	Share of OOF in total ODF to this sector
Social sectors				
Education	1.9	0.1	2.1	7%
Health	5.0	0.1	5.0	1%
Gov. & civil soc.	4.2	0.4	4.6	9%
Other social infrastructure and services	1.0	0.2	1.3	19%
Infrastructure				
Water	1.6	0.3	1.9	**14%**
Energy	2.4	1.3	3.7	**35%**
Transport & storage	2.6	2.0	4.6	44%
Communications	0.1	0.1	0.1	61%
Production sectors				
Agriculture	3.1	0.5	3.6	14%
Industry	0.3	0.4	0.7	59%
Mining & construction	0.1	0.7	0.8	92%
Trade & tourism	0.2	0.0	0.3	15%
Banking & business	0.6	1.0	1.6	62%
Multisector	1.3	0.1	1.4	5%

Source: (OECD, 2018[8]) "International development statistics (database)", http://www.oecd.org/dac/financing-sustainable-development/development-finance-data/idsonline.htm.

StatLink https://doi.org/10.1787/888933855979

Table 4.5. ODCs receive a larger share of OOF for energy and water than LLDCs

Volumes of ODA, OOF and ODF and share of OOF by sector in ODCs, average 2012-16, 2016 constant prices, USD commitments

	ODA	OOF	Total ODF	Share of OOF In total ODF to this sector
Social sectors				
Education	9.6	2.5	12.1	20%
Gov. & civil soc.	13.0	4.9	17.9	27%
Health	16.6	1.9	18.5	10%
Other social infrastructure and services	3.9	2.9	6.9	43%
Infrastructure				
Water	6.3	4.2	10.5	40%
Energy	11.7	11.5	23.2	50%
Transport & storage	12.9	9.7	22.6	43%
Communications	0.7	1.2	1.8	64%
Production sectors				
Agriculture	8.2	2.8	11.0	26%
Industry	1.8	7.0	8.7	80%
Mining & construction	0.6	1.3	2.0	69%
Trade & tourism	1.0	1.3	2.3	56%
Banking and business	5.8	12.0	17.8	67%
Multisector	13.8	2.4	16.2	15%

Source: (OECD, 2018[8]) "International development statistics (database)", http://www.oecd.org/dac/financing-sustainable-development/development-finance-data/idsonline.htm.

StatLink https://doi.org/10.1787/888933855998

4.2.3. Small island developing states (SIDS)

The OECD DAC identifies 35 countries[18] as SIDS, located across different geographic areas. SIDS share a number of structural challenges and geophysical constraints that result in disproportionately large economic, social and environmental challenges. These structural features have a major impact on SIDS' ability to access finance (OECD, 2018[32]) (OECD/The World Bank, 2016[33]). There are numerous commonalities among the countries in this group, such as small geographic and population sizes, remoteness and high exposure to environmental disasters. However, large differences also exist in terms of income level, population density, geographic spread and relative development progress. While most SIDS are UMICs (24 countries), 8 are LMICs and another 3 are LICs.

Concessional finance represents the bulk of ODF to SIDS

During 2012-16, SIDS received on average USD 4.3 billion in official concessional finance each year from bilateral and multilateral donors,[19] representing 75% of their total official flows, compared to 64% for ODCs (Figure 4.7).

Figure 4.7. Concessional finance represents the bulk of ODF to SIDS

Share of ODA and OOF to SIDS and ODCS, average 2012-16, 2016 constant prices, USD commitments

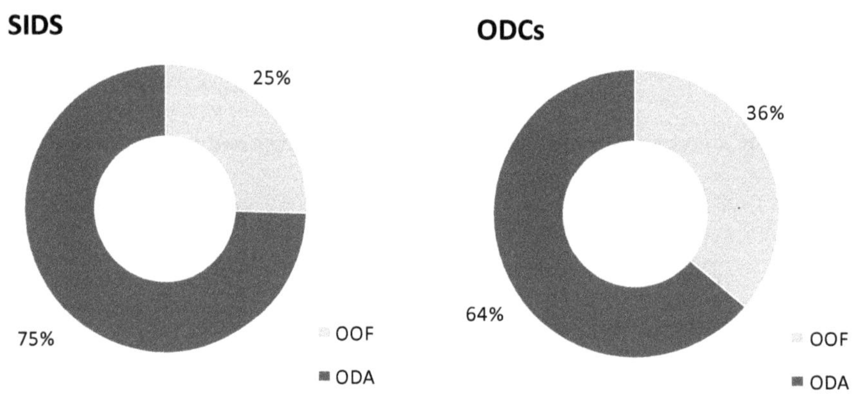

Source: (OECD, 2018[8]) "International development statistics (database)", http://www.oecd.org/dac/financing-sustainable-development/development-finance-data/idsonline.htm.

StatLink https://doi.org/10.1787/888933855846

High proportion of ODA in the ODF to SIDS in all income categories

The high proportion of ODA in the composition of ODF to SIDS is valid for all income categories. In LIC-SIDS ODA flows represented 97% of ODF versus 93% for other LICs, in LMIC-SIDS ODA represented 91% of total ODF and 63% for other LMICs, and even in UMIC-SIDS ODA was 52% of total ODF flows compared to 32% for other UMICs).

Figure 4.8 shows the allocation of official resources to SIDS by income group broken down by the main sector groupings. When analysing the underlying financing patterns of the different income groupings, it emerges that LIC-SIDS and Other LICs are very similar. However, this is not the case for the other two categories. LMIC-SIDS and UMIC-SIDS receive, in relative terms, less non-concessional flows than Other LMICs and Other UMICs in each of the sector groupings (except for banking and business in the UMIC category). This is even more evident in the production sectors (non-concessional flows in LMIC-SIDS represent 6% of total ODF but 82% in Other LMICs; compared to 34% in UMIC-SIDS and 82% in Other UMICs).

Figure 4.8. ODA represents the bulk of ODF to SIDS in all income and sector groupings

Share of ODA and OOF in ODF to SIDS by income and sector groupings, average 2012-16, 2016 constant prices, USD commitments

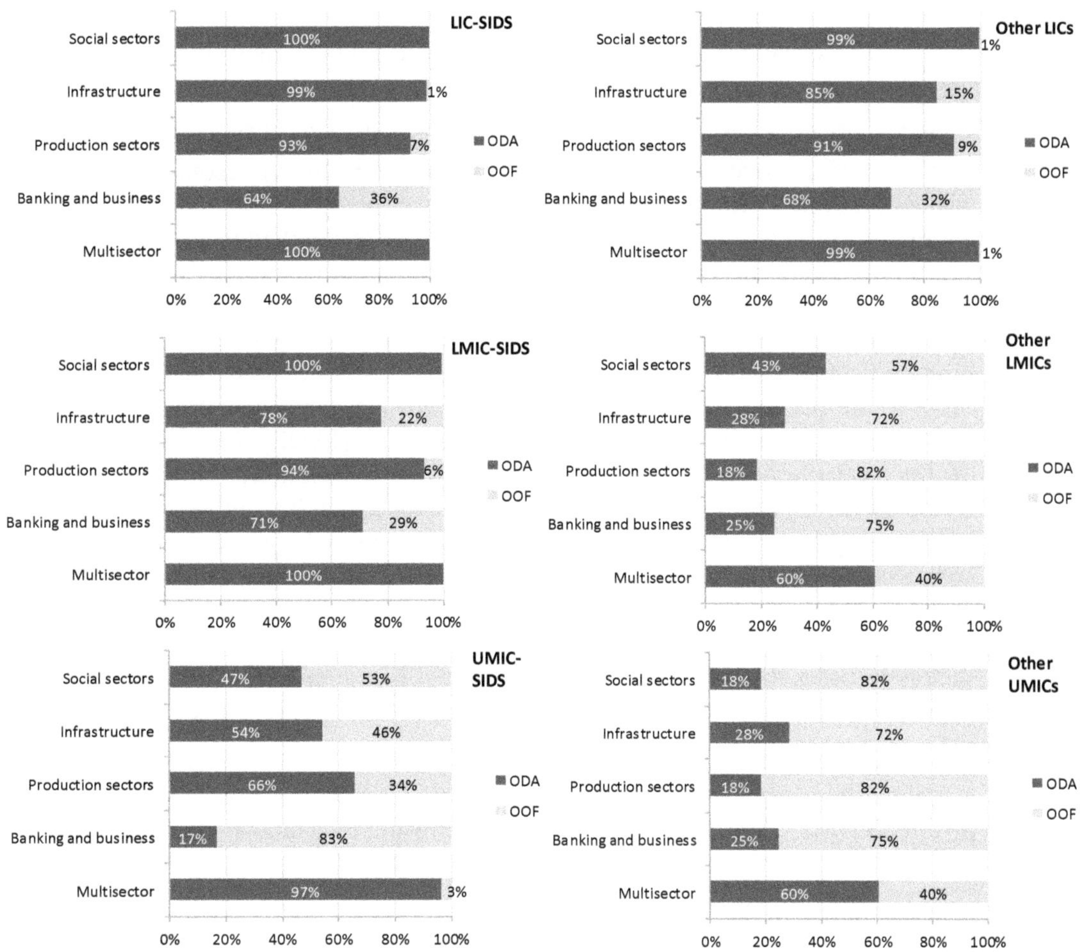

Source: (OECD, 2018[8]) "International development statistics (database)", http://www.oecd.org/dac/financing-sustainable-development/development-finance-data/idsonline.htm.

StatLink https://doi.org/10.1787/888933855865

In order to identify the underfinanced subsectors of the sector groupings just highlighted, Table 4.6 shows the sector component of each of the sector groupings compared with ODCs for LMIC-SIDS and UMIC-SIDS.[20]

SIDS find it difficult to follow a virtuous transition path towards more OOF, and remain highly ODA dependent for almost all sub-sectors

For almost all sub-sectors, non-concessional finance is lower for SIDS than for ODCs at any income category (see the "Share of OOF" column in Table 4.6).[21] This shows the difficulty that SIDS have in following the virtuous transition finance path shown at the beginning of this chapter (see Box 4.1) and achieving sustainable development (with ODA decreasing, OOF increasing, then private flows and DRM flows growing exponentially). It also suggests that the donor community should reflect on ways to make the most of ODF in preparation for transition in these countries.[22]

There are several possible reasons why OOF do not reach SIDS as they should in LMICs or UMICs:

- SIDS benefit from a "small island exception" from the World Bank. It permits the provision of International Development Association (IDA) resources to small island economies with a per capita income above the operational cut off for IDA eligibility. As a consequence, non-ODA resources are supplied at a higher income status, sustaining the countries' abilities to access concessional financing. This could create windfall effects and discourage financing sources other than ODA. For example, in the production sector, it appears that only the International Finance Corporation (IFC) and Korea provided non-concessional loans to LMIC-SIDS in the period 2012-16, and that there were just three new providers in the UMIC category (Inter-American Development Bank [IADB], International Bank of Reconstruction and Development [IBRD] and Belgium). However, SIDS would have been expected to have IBRD funds at LMIC status (in non-small island exception countries) as well, and, in general, a bigger diversity of non-concessional finance providers. It could be useful to analyse the possibility of changing the composition of ODF flows on a country-by-country basis. It could also be useful to evaluate the opportunities for reallocating ODA and OOF across sectors in order to face the transition gaps, mobilise non-ODF flows and trigger the transition patterns of foreign direct investments and DRM financing.
- In addition, the current average high levels of public debt facing some SIDS could explain difficulties with regards to prospective access to non-concessional or private finance. High levels of public debt result in a higher risk of default, limiting the provision of new debt and making it more expensive to borrow.
- Further factors could relate to the absorptive capacity and management of new projects (financed by new debt). The low rate of return of some projects could be added to these, especially in the infrastructure sector, because of diseconomies of scale resulting from the provision of public goods to small populations. An economy must be capable of attracting new (non-concessional) resources as a first step to reaching more and new financing to replace ODA finance, taking on the responsibility of its management and acquiring the capacities and skills for its long-term development. In order to do so, it is important to consider new and more risk-mitigating instruments (see Chapter 5). It is also important to convince donors that are traditionally ODA-only providers to consider diversifying their funding modalities.

Table 4.6. SIDS find it difficult to follow a virtuous transition path towards more OOF

Volumes of ODA, OOF and ODF and share of OOF by income and sectors, average 2012-16, 2016 constant prices, USD million commitments

LMIC-SIDS	ODA	OOF	Total ODF	Share of OOF	Other LMICs	ODA	OOF	Total ODF	Share of OOF
Social sectors					**Social sectors**				
Education	201.3	0.0	201.3	0%	Education	5 064.7	716.1	5780.7	12%
Health	218.1	0.0	218.1	0%	Health	7 439.1	471.1	7 910.2	29%
Gov. & civil soc.	333.1	3.3	336.4	1%	Gov. & civil soc.	5 290.4	2 204.3	7 494.7	6%
Other social	51.6	0.0	51.6	0%	Other social	2 313.6	1 209.7	3 523.3	34%
Infrastructure					**Infrastructure**				
Water	91.3	0.7	92.0	1%	Water	4 525.0	1 915.7	6 440.7	30%
Energy	77.9	36.2	114.1	32%	Energy	8 348.8	7 464.3	15 813.1	47%
Transport & storage	320.6	98.0	418.7	23%	Transport & storage	9 683.1	4 816.7	14 499.8	33%
Communications	15.3	7.7	23.0	34%	Communications	303.2	553.7	856.9	65%
Production					**Production**				
Agriculture	114.2	2.1	116.3	2%	Agriculture	4 871.7	1 459.1	6 330.8	23%
Industry	2.6	1.8	4.4	41%	Industry	874.9	3 343.5	4 218.4	79%
Mining & construction	1.1	5.0	6.1	81%	Mining & construction	378.9	1 229.8	1 608.8	76%
Trade & tourism	9.7	0.0	9.7	0%	Trade & tourism	390.9	261.4	652.3	40%
Banking & business	23.6	9.5	33.0	29%	**Banking & business**	2 085.0	4 959.3	7 044.4	70%
Multisector	164.3	0.0	164.3	0%	**Multisector**	4 229.4	1 076.4	5 305.8	20%
UMIC-SIDS	**ODA**	**OOF**	**Total ODF**	**Share of OOF**	**Other UMICs**	**ODA**	**OOF**	**Total ODF**	**Share of OOF**
Social sectors					**Social sectors**				
Education	149.5	101.0	250.4	40%	Education	1 810.4	1 674.1	3 484.4	48%
Health	126.0	156.0	282.0	55%	Health	1 347.2	1 268.8	2 616.0	49%
Gov. & civil soc.	162.6	166.2	328.8	51%	Gov. & civil soc.	2 082.7	2 924.6	5 077.3	58%
Other social	40.8	116.8	157.6	74%	Other social	645.4	1 858.0	2 503.3	74%
Infrastructure					**Infrastructure**				
Water	144.6	25.4	170.0	15%	Water	817.1	2 352.2	3 169.3	74%
Energy	145.7	121.0	266.7	45%	Energy	1 869	4 155	6 024	69%
Transport & storage	117.1	178.3	295.4	60%	Transport & storage	2 100.9	5 824.9	7 925.8	73%
Communications	25.8	26.3	52.1	51%	Communications	173.3	490.4	663.7	74%
Production					**Production**				
Agriculture	112.6	18.2	130.7	13%	Agriculture	897.5	1 327.9	2 225.4	60%
Industry	18.9	12.5	31.3	40%	Industry	322.9	3 543.3	3 866.2	92%
Mining & construction	2.1	12.3	14.4	86%	Mining & construction	127.1	706.7	833.8	85%
Trade & tourism	18.6	39.0	57.6	68%	Trade & tourism	66.8	822.7	889.5	92%
Banking & business	36.6	197.3	233.9	84%	**Banking & business**	1 782.3	5 809.9	7 592.2	77%
Multisector	244.0	9.1	253.1	4%	**Multisector**	2 056.8	1 351.8	3 408.6	40%

Source: (OECD, 2018[8]) "International development statistics (database)", http://www.oecd.org/dac/financing-sustainable-development/development-finance-data/idsonline.htm.

StatLink https://doi.org/10.1787/888933856017

4.2.4. Countries in fragile contexts (FCs)

The OECD DAC defines fragility[23] as the combination of exposure to risk and insufficient capacity of the state, system and/or communities to manage, absorb or mitigate those risks. The fragility framework (OECD, 2016[24]) is built around five dimensions: economic, environmental, political, societal and security. Using these, the 2018 OECD's *States of Fragility Report* (OECD, 2018[34]) identifies 58 FCs[24] (28 LICs, 26 LMICs and 4 UMICs), of which 15 are extreme FCs.

Because of the way that the FCs are defined and the many variables taken into account (see Box 4.6), the final list of FCs is very diverse. Therefore compiling sector statistics for this group of 58 FCs does not appear sufficiently robust.[25] For these reasons, the analysis in this subsection focuses on the overall picture of ODA and OOF rather than providing a detailed sector analysis, as for previous country groupings. As a way to advance the policy discussion on interventions in FCs, this subsection provides an overview on the use of various financial instruments, including risk-management instruments, recognising that FCs are often perceived as riskier areas by both public and private actors.

Box 4.6. The OECD's states of fragility: taking a multidimensional approach to fragility

The notion of sustainable development is profoundly multidimensional, and nowhere is this truer than in FCs. Therefore, analysing these FCs, designing the right programming, making allocation decisions and measuring results also requires taking a multidimensional approach to well-being rather than a sector approach.

The OECD has long recognised the multidimensionality of people's well-being and of the resources needed to sustain this over time. With this in mind, the OECD developed a multidimensional well-being framework – the Better Life Index – that can gauge whether people's lives are improving, and inform policy efforts toward this end at the same time. Starting in 2015, this concept has been applied to the states of fragility framework and to the approaches that OECD members are encouraged to take when working in FCs.

The OECD's multidimensional approach recognises five different dimensions of fragility, with extensive interlinkages between them:

- economic fragility: vulnerability to risks stemming from weaknesses in economic foundations and human capital
- environmental fragility: vulnerability to environmental, climatic and health risks that affect people's lives and livelihoods
- political fragility: vulnerability to risks inherent in political processes, events or decisions
- security fragility: vulnerability of overall security to violence and crime, including both political and social violence
- societal fragility: vulnerability to risks affecting social cohesion

that stem from both vertical and horizontal inequalities.

The approach measures each of these dimensions on a spectrum of intensity that links fragility with a combination of risks and coping capacities, and then synthesises the results (the multidimensional aspect). While previous approaches framed fragility as a matter of weak governance, the new fragility framework builds on the recognition that fragility influences states and societies in different ways. It affects all countries to some degree, not just developing countries. It is part of OECD's larger effort to move away from the "fragile states list" – a binary view of the world – towards a universal concept of fragility.

Source: (OECD, 2016[24]), "States of Fragility 2016: Understanding Violence", http://dx.doi.org/10.1787/9789264267213-en

Figure 4.9 shows the list of countries defined as FCs when applying the fragility framework.

Figure 4.9. The States of Fragility Framework, 2018

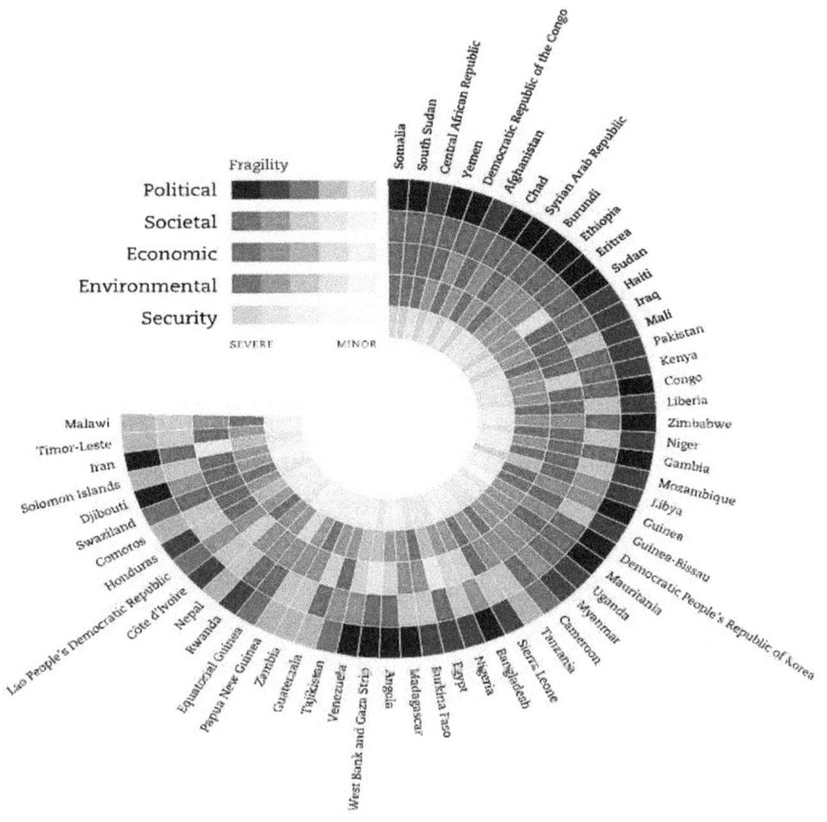

Note: The States of fragility framework was designed before the change of name of Swaziland - now called Kingdom of Eswatini.
Source : (OECD, 2018[35]), "States of Fragility Framework", http://www.oecd.org/dac/conflict-fragility-resilience/statesoffragilityframework2018.htm

ODA remains a critical source of finance for fragile contexts

Figure 4.10 gives a descriptive snapshot of the situation of these 58 fragile contexts in a sector ODF perspective. It shows that ODF (which represented USD 66.8 billion on average per year over the period 2012-16 on a commitment basis) in FCs comprises much more ODA (91%) than in ODCs (61%). This is in line with the 2030 Agenda, where ODA is called on to play a specialised role, targeting critical gaps where it adds the most value according to the context.

Figure 4.10. ODA remains a critical source of finance for fragile contexts

Share of ODA and OOF in ODF to FCs and ODCs, average 2012-16, 2016 constant prices, USD commitments

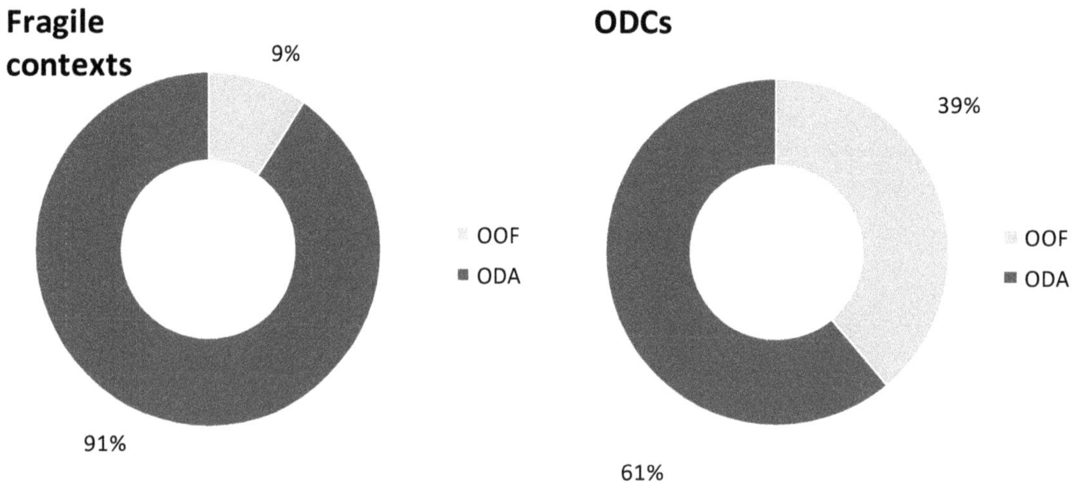

Source: (OECD, 2018[8]) "International development statistics (database)", http://www.oecd.org/dac/financing-sustainable-development/development-finance-data/idsonline.htm.

StatLink https://doi.org/10.1787/888933855884

Fragility and vulnerability are associated with risk in development. In order to mitigate these perceived risks, guarantees, insurances and blended finance facilities can be deployed to fragile contexts

For example, the International Finance Corporation–Multilateral Investment Guarantee Agency (IFC–MIGA) private sector window (PSW) (MIGA,(n.d.)[36]) was created under the IDA18 replenishment to expand private investment in the poorest countries and in particular those identified as fragile. Under four windows, PSW provides project-based guarantees without sovereign indemnity to source private investment for large infrastructure projects. The MIGA Guarantee Facility expands coverage of MIGA guarantees via reinsurance. The Local Currency Facility provides long-term local currency investments in countries where capital markets are not developed. The Blended Finance Facility blends support with IFC investments to help small and medium-sized enterprises. New instruments are also being created and especially adapted to FCs – parametric insurance, sovereign risk financing, catastrophe bonds and micro insurance (Poole, 2018[37]).

Official providers are using risk-mitigation instruments, such as guarantees, in FCs much more than in other contexts

As shown in Figure 4.11, 22% of all private finance mobilised by ODF interventions targets FCs. When looking at the composition of instruments used to mobilise this finance in FCs and non-FCs, it appears that providers make great use of guarantees in FCs. Of the amounts mobilised in FCs, 65% are done so using guarantee instruments, as against only 38% in non-FCs. This figure is encouraging as it shows that providers effectively consider the risk perceived by the private sector and use appropriate instruments, such as guarantees, to address it.

Figure 4.11. Official providers use higher proportions of guarantees in fragile contexts

Share of amounts mobilised from the private sector by ODF interventions and share of instruments used to mobilise private finance in FCs and non-FCs, average 2012-16, 2016 constant prices, USD commitments

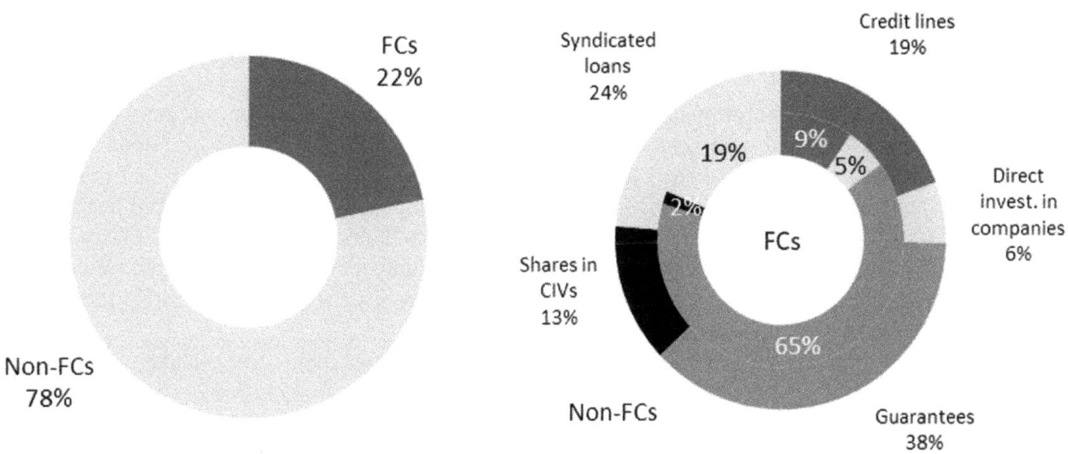

Note: the double pie chart on the right shows FCs in the inner circle and all ODCs in the outer circle.
Source: (OECD, 2018[8]) "International development statistics (database)", http://www.oecd.org/dac/financing-sustainable-development/development-finance-data/idsonline.htm and (OECD, 2016[38]), "OECD DAC survey on amounts mobilised from the private sector by official development finance interventions 2012-2015", http://www.oecd.org/dac/financing-sustainable-development/development-finance-standards/mobilisation.htm with estimates for 2016.

StatLink https://doi.org/10.1787/888933855903

Notes

[1] The World Bank income categories are: low income countries (LICs), lower middle-income countries (LMICs), upper middle-income countries (UMICs), and high-income countries (HICs). The World Bank classifies countries into these groups based on their GNI per capita using the Atlas method. The current thresholds are as follows: LICs: < USD 1 005 per capita; LMICs: USD 1 006-3 955; UMICs: USD 3 956-12 235 and HICs: > USD 12 236. The DAC defines countries most in need as: least developed countries (LDCs), landlocked developing countries (LLDCs), small island developing states (SIDS) and fragile and conflict-affected contexts (FCs).

[2] The statistical data for Israel are supplied by and under the responsibility of the relevant Israeli authorities. The use of such data by the OECD is without prejudice to the status of the Golan Heights, East Jerusalem and Israeli settlements in the West Bank under the terms of international law.

[3] Loans with greater concessionality may be prone to being over-borrowed and therefore less efficiently used than loans with less concessionality. This decreases the need for efficient investment (Odedokun, 2003[39]); (Moss, Pettersson and Van de Walle, 2006[2])Moss. Moreover, given the fact that loans need to be repaid, a higher level of loans in official assistance associated with higher interest rates would require higher mobilisation of fiscal revenues. It would also require investment in high-impact projects. In fact, a higher proportion of loans in official assistance was associated with larger domestic revenues (Gupta et al., 2004[3]); (Benedek et al., 2014[4]) (Cordella and Ulku, 2007[1]) found that "the level of loan concessionality that maximises growth: (i) is negatively correlated with the quality of a recipient country's policy and institutions, (ii) decreases with the level of initial income, (iii) and increases with the existing debt obligations." Other voices have called for increasing the number of grants distributed (Bulow and Rogoff, 2005[5]), so as to take into account the risk exposure of development banks rather than favouring the emergence of developing countries.

[4] See the Annex at the end of this report for more information, and in particular a list of the subsectors that make up these five sector categories.

[5] Except for the "multisector" grouping, which is not a sector grouping per se.

[6] Until the 1990s the neoclassical growth model (Solow) was largely accepted, as it provided a good explanation of what happened in the growth processes. The model basically suggests that differences in observed growth across countries stem from factor accumulation, especially capital investment. This model is still useful for LICs. However, with accelerating technological upgrading, it is no longer useful for middle-income countries.

[7] For example, any FfD strategy should include a plan to remove or reduce those obstacles through capacity building and investment in transformational change enablers.

[8] Combining all income categories (LICs, LMICs and UMICs) and excluding regional/unspecified flows, OOF represents 24% of total official flows in social sectors, 45% in infrastructure, 54% in production sectors and 72% in banking and business.

[9] As countries experience growth and transition through the development continuum (i.e. moving from low to higher levels of GNI per capita), it is possible to observe some distinctive patterns for each of the financial flows composing the global set of external flows they receive. Among other external flows, concessional flows (ODA) decrease and non-concessional flows (OOF) increase (Cattaneo, O. and Piemonte, C., 2018[7]).

[10] It is important to highlight these two sectors as they are key to removing inequalities in society and to combating poverty. Improvements in these two sectors can help countries to escape from the well-known middle-income trap.

[11] With the exception of LICs, analysed in the preceding section.

[12] LDCs: Afghanistan, Angola, Bangladesh, Benin, Bhutan, Burkina Faso, Burundi, Cambodia, Central African Republic, Chad, Comoros, Democratic Republic of the Congo (hereafter "DRC"), Djibouti, Eritrea, Ethiopia, Gambia, Guinea, Guinea-Bissau, Haiti, Kiribati, Lao People's Democratic Republic (hereafter "Lao PDR"), Lesotho, Liberia, Madagascar, Malawi, Mali, Mauritania, Mozambique, Myanmar, Nepal, Niger, Rwanda, São Tomé and Principe, Senegal, Sierra Leone, Solomon Islands, Somalia, South Sudan, Sudan, Timor-Leste, Togo, Tuvalu, Uganda, United Republic of Tanzania, Vanuatu, Yemen and Zambia.

[13] To avoid setbacks, the LDC graduation criteria states that a country eligible for graduation must cease to meet two of the three graduation thresholds, and that this eligibility must be observed over two consecutive triennial reviews. To ensure a smooth transition, the General Assembly recommended the extension and gradual phasing out of LDC-specific support for some time after graduation.

[14] Nevertheless, when looking at OOF loans, Bangladesh was able to benefit from considerable volumes from the Asian Development Bank in recent years: 20 loans delivered in the period 2012-16 for a total of USD 2.8 billion, mainly spent on energy and transport and storage.

[15] Afghanistan, Armenia, Azerbaijan, Bhutan, Plurinational State of Bolivia, Botswana, Burkina Faso, Burundi, Central African Republic, Chad, Kingdom of Eswatini, Ethiopia, the Former Yugoslav Republic of Macedonia, Kazakhstan, Kyrgyzstan, Lao PDR, Lesotho, Malawi, Mali, Republic of Moldova, Mongolia, Nepal, Niger, Paraguay, Rwanda, South Sudan, Tajikistan, Turkmenistan, Uganda, Uzbekistan, Zambia, Zimbabwe.

[16] Other areas that are major constraints to LLDCs' development include high dependency on commodities, lack of value addition to exports or limited industrialisation.

[17] These figures are based on the United Nations Conference on Trade and Development (UNCTAD) estimates derived from the International Monetary Fund (IMF) balance of payment statistics (UNCTAD, 2018[41]).

[18] As for other country groupings, there are several definitions of SIDS. The United Nations identify 52 countries or territories under this grouping. They first defined a SIDS grouping in 1992, then came others such as the European Union with ACP (Africa, Caribbean and Pacific), and the World Trade Organisation with the economic vulnerability index (Small Vulnerable Economies). The World Bank has been applying a small island exception in determining IDA eligibility since 1985.

[19] Including the regional groupings Oceania and West Indies.

[20] The analysis by subsector has not been included for LIC-SIDS versus other LICs, as the results are almost the same.

[21] Trade and tourism in both the LMIC-SIDS and UMIC-SIDS categories are OOF-neglected (0% in LMIC-SIDS versus 40% for Other LMICs and 68% for UMIC-SIDS versus 92% for Other UMICs). This means that major current investments in this sector are financed by foreign direct investment. It also means that there are no resources flowing directly to local investors for them to invest in this sector. Knowing the huge potential of tourism in SIDS, a study could be conducted into whether mixed investments could better fill the gap of capacity building for the local population and whether some incentives could be put in place to prepare SIDS to develop in the long run could also be analysed. It could be useful to explore some options involving quality investment.

[22] As discussed in previous OECD work on SIDS, while the broad nature of development needs in several SIDS can make prioritisation difficult, some areas and sectors that would seem vital to promoting sustainable development in SIDS receive relatively little support. For instance, high costs and limited access to energy constrain development in SIDS, yet the energy sector received less than 9% of total ODF to SIDS in 2012-16.

[23] There are several other definitions of fragility, such as those from the World Bank, the UK government's Department for International Development (DFID) and the Overseas Development Institute (ODI). The different lists of fragile countries differ by the theoretical background concepts and the use of different indicators, proxies and/or value judgments.

[24] From a total of 146 ODA-eligible countries.

[25] This is why the OECD takes a multidimensional approach to analysing ODA flows to FCs, rather than using traditional sectors. For example, the *States of Fragility Report* identifies ODA flows that seek to reduce economic fragility. It also analyses whether contexts that are economically fragile are receiving ODA targeted at the root causes of that form of fragility. The results are interesting: some of the extremely fragile contexts with respect to the long-term drivers of growth receive fairly high levels of ODA per capita (Liberia, Solomon Islands and South Sudan), but others do not (Burundi, Central African Republic, Chad and DRC). In some specific sectors, ODA per capita is even negatively correlated to fragility in the long-term drivers of growth. This is the case, for instance, for industry and mining and construction, which tends to prioritise non-FCs with relatively sound economic fundamentals (such as Mauritius, Serbia and Tunisia).

References

Agénor, P. (2017), "Caught in the Middle? The Economics of Middle-Income Traps", *Journal of Economic Surveys*, Vol. 31/3, pp. 771-791, https://onlinelibrary.wiley.com/doi/abs/10.1111/joes.12175. [17]

Agénor, P. (2012), *Avoiding Middle-Income Growth Traps*, World Bank Group, http://siteresources.worldbank.org/EXTPREMNET/Resources/EP98.pdf. [18]

Aiyar, S. (2013), *"Growth Slowdowns and the Middle-Income Trap"*, IMF, Washington, D.C., https://www.imf.org/external/pubs/ft/wp/2013/wp1371.pdf. [19]

Alonso, J. (2014), *LDC and Other Country Groupings: How useful are current approaches to classify countries in a more heterogenous developing world?*, UNDESA, Department of Economics and Social Affairs, http://www.un.org/en/development/desa/policy/cdp/cdp_background_papers/bp2014_21.pdf. [29]

Benedek et al. (2014), *"Foreign aid and revenue: Still a crowding-out effect?"*, IMF Working Papers, Washington, D.C., https://www.imf.org/en/Publications/WP/Issues/2016/12/31/Foreign-Aid-and-Revenue-Still-a-Crowding-Out-Effect-26085. [4]

Brown, L. (2001), *Measuring Capacity Building*, University of North Carolina at Chapel Hill, https://issat.dcaf.ch/download/29857/419317/664_guidelines%20on%20how%20to%20measure%20capacity%20building.pdf. [21]

Bulow, J. and K. Rogoff (2005), *Grants versus loans for development banks*, Harvard Community, pp. 393-397, https://dash.harvard.edu/bitstream/handle/1/11129181/Bulow_Rogoff_Grants_versus_Loans_AER2005.pdf. [5]

Cattaneo, O. and C. Piemonte (2018), *"Transition finance: update on ongoing discussions and work"*, OECD, Paris. [6]

Chudik, A. (2015), *"Is there a debt-threshold Effect on Output Growth?"*, IMF, Washington, D.C., https://www.imf.org/external/pubs/ft/wp/2015/wp15197.pdf. [40]

Cordella, T. and H. Ulku (2007), *"Grants vs. loans"*, IMF, Washington, D.C., pp. 139-162, http://citeseerx.ist.psu.edu/viewdoc/download?doi=10.1.1.551.4716&rep=rep1&type=pdf. [1]

Estache, A. (2012), *The impact of infrastructure on growth in developing countries*, IFC, https://www.ifc.org/wps/wcm/connect/054be8804db753a6843aa4ab7d7326c0/INR+Note+1+-+The+Impact+of+Infrastructure+on+Growth.pdf?MOD=AJPERES. [11]

Ghatak, M. (2014), *Theories of Poverty Traps and Anti-Poverty Policies*, London School of Economics, http://econ.lse.ac.uk/staff/mghatak/WBERPovTrap.pdf. [12]

Gill, I. (2015), *The Middle-Income Trap Turns Ten*, World Bank Group, http://documents.worldbank.org/curated/en/291521468179640202/The-middle-income-trap-turns-ten. [20]

Gupta et al. (2004), *The persistence of fiscal adjustments in developing countries*, pp. 209-212, https://www.tandfonline.com/doi/abs/10.1080/13504850410001674812. [3]

Henckel, T. (2010), *The economics of infrastructure in a globalised world: issues, lessons and future challenges*, Brookings, https://www.brookings.edu/wp-content/uploads/2016/06/0604_infrastructure_economics_mckibbin.pdf. [10]

Herrera, S. (2005), *The Economic Rate of Return of World Bank Projects*, World Bank, http://documents.worldbank.org/curated/en/642631468331806005/pdf/704270WP0P09810C00err0and0cba0in0WB.pdf. [9]

Kaldewei, C. (2015), *Las brechas estructurales en los países de renta media*, ECLAC, https://www.cepal.org/es/publicaciones/39705-brechas-estructurales-paises-renta-media-consideraciones-un-diagnostico-nivel. [13]

MIGA((n.d.)), *http://ida.worldbank.org/financing/ida18-ifc-miga-private-sector-window*. [36]

Moss, Pettersson and Van de Walle (2006), *"An aid-institutions paradox? A review essay on aid dependency and state building in sub-Saharan Africa"*, Center for Global Development, https://www.cgdev.org/publication/aid-institutions-paradox-review-essay-aid-dependency-and-state-building-sub-saharan. [2]

Odedokun, M. (2003), "No. 2003/04", in *"Economics and politics of official loans versus grants: Panoramic issues and empirical evidence"*, World Institute for Development Economics (UNU-WIDER), http://archive.unu.edu/hq/library/Collection/PDF_files/WIDER/WIDERdp2003.04.pdf. [39]

OECD (2018), *"International development statistics (database)"*, OECD, Paris, http://www.oecd.org/dac/financing-sustainable-development/development-finance-data/idsonline.htm. [8]

OECD (2018), *"States of Fragility Framework"*, OECD, Paris, http://www.oecd.org/dac/conflict-fragility-resilience/statesoffragilityframework2018.htm. [35]

OECD (2018), *"Creditor Reporting System"*, OECD, Paris, https://stats.oecd.org/Index.aspx?DataSetCode=crs1. [42]

OECD (2018), *Global Outlook on Financing for Sustainable Development 2019: Time to Face the Challenge*, OECD Publishing, Paris, http://dx.doi.org/10.1787/9789264307995-en. [7]

OECD (2018), *Making Development Co-operation Work for Small Island Developing States*, OECD Publishing, Paris, http://dx.doi.org/10.1787/9789264287648-en. [32]

OECD (2018), *States of Fragility 2018*, OECD Publishing, Paris, http://dx.doi.org/10.1787/9789264302075-en. [34]

OECD (2017), *HLM Communiqué*, OECD, Paris, https://www.oecd.org/dac/DAC-HLM-2017-Communique.pdf. [25]

OECD (2016), *"OECD DAC survey on amounts mobilised from the private sector by official development finance interventions 2012-2015"*, OECD, Paris, http://www.oecd.org/dac/financing-sustainable-development/development-finance-standards/mobilisation.htm. [38]

OECD (2016), *"States of Fragility 2016: Understanding Violence"*, OECD Publishing, Paris, http://dx.doi.org/10.1787/9789264267213-en. [24]

OECD (2015), *"Concessional loans before and after the HLM"*, OECD, Paris. [28]

OECD (2014), *"DAC High Level Meeting - Final Communiqué - 16 December 2014"*, http://www.oecd.org/dac/OECD%20DAC%20HLM%20Communique.pdf. [23]

OECD (2018, forthcoming), *Transition Finance: Methodology and main findings*. [22]

OECD/The World Bank (2016), *Climate and Disaster Resilience Financing in Small Island Developing States*, OECD Publishing, Paris, http://dx.doi.org/10.1787/9789264266919-en. [33]

Poole, L. (2018), *Financing for Stability in the Post-2015 Era*, OECD Publishing Paris, http://dx.doi.org/10.1787/c4193fef-en. [37]

Ratha, D. (2010), "Shadow Sovereign Ratings for Unrated Developing Countries", *World Development*, http://dx.doi.org/10.1016/j.worlddev.2010.08.006. [14]

Sahay, R. (2015), *"Rethinking Financial Deepening: Stability and Growth in Emerging Markets"*, IMF, Washington, D.C., https://www.imf.org/external/pubs/ft/sdn/2015/sdn1508.pdf. [15]

Samargandi, N. (2013), *Is the relationship between financial development and economic growth monotonic for middle income countries?*, pp. 66-81, https://www.sciencedirect.com/science/article/pii/S0305750X14003684. [16]

UNCTAD (2018), *http://unohrlls.org/about-lldcs/*. [41]

UNCTAD (2011), *Foreign Direct Investment in LDCs: lessons learned from the decade 2001-10 and the way forward*, http://unctad.org/en/docs/diaeia2011d1_en.pdf. [30]

United Nations (2018), *http://undocs.org/en/E/2018/33*. [27]

United Nations (2015), *"Addis Ababa Action Agenda of the Third International Conference on Financing for Development"*. [31]

United Nations (2008), *"Handbook on the Least Developed Country Category: Inclusion, Graduation and Special Support Measures"*, United Nations, New York, NY, http://www.un.org/en/development/desa/policy/cdp/cdp_publications/2008cdphandbook.pdf. [26]

Chapter 5. Designing effective sector financing instruments and approaches

This chapter provides a cross-sector analysis of official development finance by the financial instruments, approaches and channels of implementation used by development partners. The first section focuses on the use of various instruments across sectors, outlining the main trends and patterns in the use of concessional and non-concessional resources. The second section explores funding patterns across the different financing approaches and implementation channels used in development co-operation across sectors.

Key messages

Key messages to providers of development co-operation emerging from this chapter include:

- **The interest and resources to promote commercial solutions that can close important financing gaps in infrastructure, climate change and social services are growing.** For example, annual commitments from European Development Finance Institutions (EDFI) increased from USD 11 billion in 2005 to USD 36 billion in 2015, mainly driven by government replenishments and reinvested earnings. Recent political commitments to harness the potential of the private sector have been made in the Addis Ababa Action Agenda (AAAA), the Paris Agreement and intergovernmental processes by, for example, the Group of Twenty (G20) and the United Nations. This shows that political interest for this type of operations is growing.
- **The use of debt instruments to support the infrastructure and commercial sectors is growing, calling for increased attention to fiscal sustainability in countries most in need.** While grants by development co-operation providers are increasing moderately at a compounded annual growth rate (CAGR) of 2%, loans are increasing at a CAGR of 7%, i.e. more than three times faster than grants. Debt vulnerability is becoming a concern in the most vulnerable economies, with the number of developing countries in debt distress or at high risk of debt distress doubling from 12 to 24 between 2013 and 2017.
- **Of sector-allocable official development finance (ODF), 8% is implemented using sector budget support and 4% is channelled using pooled funding.** The Sustainable Development Goals (SDGs) call for increased policy coherence and more co-ordinated approaches. There is no definite answer to the question of how best to support sectors and cross-sectoral approaches using ODF, but pooled funding mechanisms and sector budget support can promote coherence and co-ordination across sectors and partners if well-funded and managed.
- **The untying agenda needs to be finished.** Of the USD 69 billion of sector-allocable official development assistance (ODA) commitments formally tied by Development Assistance Committee (DAC) countries in 2012-16, 58% are in social sectors. Moreover, two-thirds of ODA procured by DAC countries in 2015-16 were awarded to companies from the donor country in competitive procurement.
- **While channels of delivery may vary, depending on sector priorities and strategies, development effectiveness and good donorship need to guide development partners' efforts.** For example, in the social and humanitarian sectors, bilateral providers need to implement good funding practices with civil society organisations and multilaterals implementing projects in the most challenging contexts. This is particularly true for those highly dependent on bilateral resources.

5.1. The sector allocation of official development finance instruments

This section discusses the major trends shaping the sector allocation of ODF instruments.[1] It will first provide an overview of the different instruments used across sectors, including an overall thematic focus on instruments used in private sector operations. It will also present the main characteristics, challenges and opportunities arising from current trends related to specific instrument groups, i.e. grants, debt instruments, equity and investments.

5.1.1. A wide array of development finance instruments is used depending on the characteristics of each sector

ODF is provided through a wide variety of instruments

As indicated in Chapter 3, ODF consists of both concessional and non-concessional resources provided by bilateral and multilateral development partners. It can take the form of financial, technical or in-kind assistance (such as food aid and commodity). According to the OECD, ODF is provided using five main groups of instruments (see Figure 5.1):

- **Grants**: transfers in cash and in kind, where no legal debt is incurred.
- **Debt instruments**: transfers in cash and in kind where legal debts are incurred (e.g. loans, bonds and other securities) or could be incurred in certain events occur (e.g. reimbursable grants).
- **Equity**: a share in the ownership of a company or a collective investment scheme.
- **Mezzanine finance**: hybrid instruments, such as subordinated loans and preferred equity, that present risk profiles between senior loans and equity.
- **Guarantees/insurance**: risk-sharing agreements under which the guarantor agrees to pay part or all of a loan, equity or other instrument to the lender/investor in the event of non-payment by the borrower, or loss of value in case of investment.

While grants, debt instruments, equity investment and mezzanine finance are funded positions (i.e. there is an upfront transfer of resources), guarantees and insurance are unfunded, which means that the transfer of resources occurs only in certain conditions, mainly if a default of payment or other financial loss occur.

Figure 5.1. Simplified taxonomy of official development finance instruments

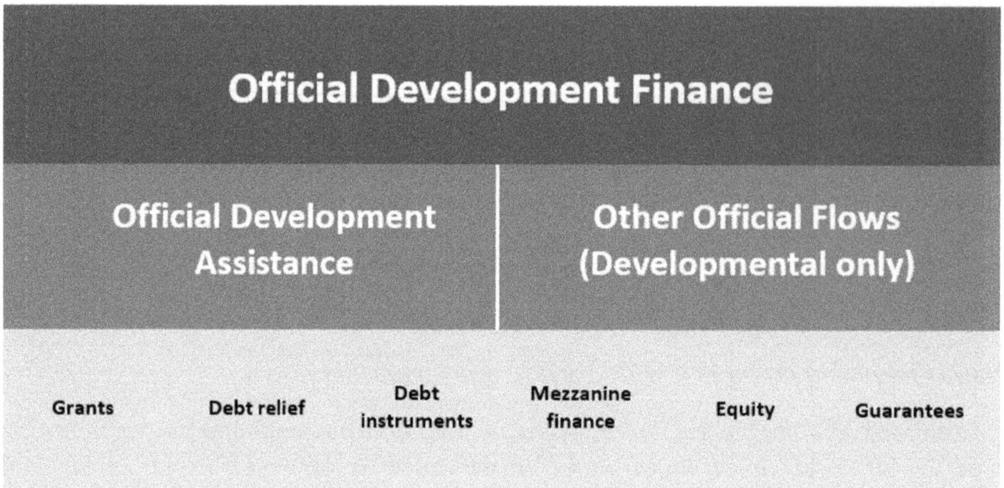

Source: Authors based on (OECD, 2018[11]), "Converged statistical reporting directives for the Creditor Reporting System (CRS) and the annual DAC questionnaire", https://one.oecd.org/document/DCD/DAC/STAT(2018)9/FINAL /en/pdf.

ODF instruments can have different levels of concessionality, which is a proxy for the level of subsidy or favourable treatment that development partners accord to public and private recipients. In this context, while grants are 100% concessional, the level of concessionality of the other instruments varies depending on their grant element, which is a proxy of concessionality compared to similar instruments available in the market. According to the new 2014 OECD DAC reform on loans, the concessionality of loans is calculated based on their interest rate, the grace period, the maturity and the discount rate (OECD, 2018[11]). The more these elements of loans are favourable for the recipients, the more the loan will be considered concessional.[2]

As shown in Chapter 4, the level of concessionality of ODF is generally higher for countries at a lower income level and with low fiscal and macroeconomic conditions. Favouring countries most in need is further encouraged in the new statistical framework agreed by the DAC in 2014.[3] This new framework revised the treatment of loan concessionality in OECD DAC statistics, attributing higher levels of concessionality for loans to least developed countries (LDCs) and other low-income countries (LICs) compared to loans provided at the same conditions to middle-income countries (OECD, 2014[2]). This is in line with the AAAA, which states that concessional resources need to be prioritised to countries with the greatest needs and the least ability to mobilise other resources, such as LDCs (United Nations, 2015[3]).

Overall, grants are mainly used in social sectors, whereas loans, equity and guarantees are mostly provided for the infrastructure and commercial sectors

Grant funding is the main source of ODF in social sectors whereas debt, equity and guarantees are mainly concentrated in infrastructure, business and banking and production sectors (see Figure 5.2). Grants are traditionally used in social sectors, which generate low or no returns to be financed through revenue-making instruments (e.g. loans). Grants are particularly important for the most vulnerable countries and population groups, where social needs are generally high and capacity to mobilise other types of resources is low. Conversely, the infrastructure, banking and business, and production sectors mainly rely on loans. This is for two reasons: the first is that costs in these areas are too high for scarce grant finance; the second is that investments can be recovered from public and private borrowers by increases in tax revenues from higher economic growth and future cash flows from users and consumers (e.g. fees and tolls). Similarly, equity investment and guarantees, which are instruments used to support private investment, are mainly in commercial sectors because they can generate revenue, such as in energy and banking and business.

Figure 5.2. Grants support social sectors whereas loans and equity support economic sectors

ODF by instrument and sector, average 2012-16, 2016 constant prices, USD billion commitments

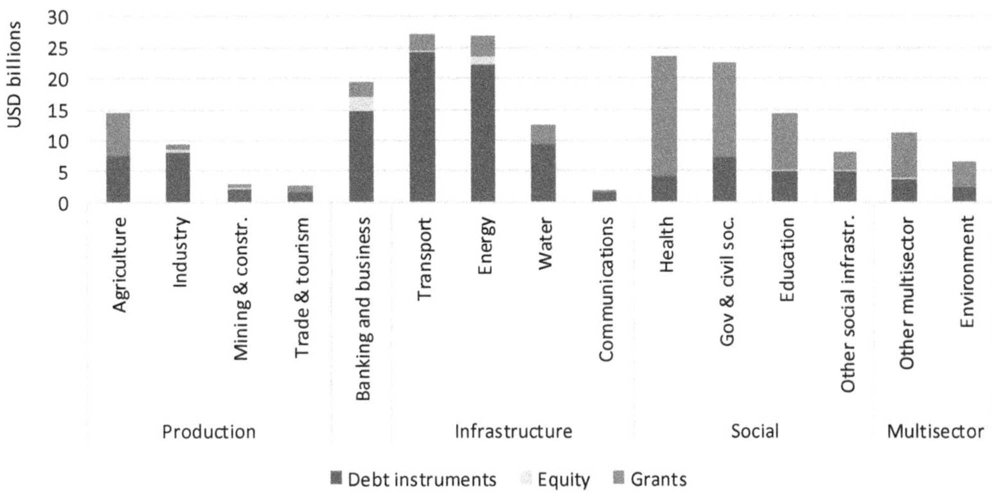

Source: (OECD, 2018[4]), "International development statistics (database)", http://www.oecd.org/dac/financing-sustainable-development/development-finance-data/idsonline.htm.

StatLink https://doi.org/10.1787/888933856036

Development partners' interest in instruments supporting the private sector is growing, particularly in areas where commercial opportunities exist

Development partners are engaging the private sector in a significant way, with an estimated annual amount that reached about USD 48 billion in 2016. This amount includes direct grants, interest subsidies, standard and syndicated loans, credit lines, direct investment in companies and participation in investment funds. However, it does not include the USD issuance value of credit enhancement and risk-mitigation instruments, such as guarantees and political risk insurance, as they are not financial flows. About two-thirds (60%) of these resources are loans, a fifth are grants and a fifth equity. Multilateral development banks (MDBs), particularly the International Finance Corporation (IFC) and the European Bank for Reconstruction and Development (EBRD) provided most of this financing (see Figure 5.3). Bilateral development finance institutions (DFIs) and aid agencies provided the remainder, with Nederlandse Financierings-Maatschappij voor Ontwikkelingslanden N.V. (FMO) being the largest DFI and the U.S. Agency for International Development (USAID) the largest aid agency.

Development partners channel resources to companies and financial institutions in areas with established commercial opportunities. These include banking and business, infrastructure and industry, which collectively receive more than two-thirds of total direct support for private-sector projects. Conversely, social sectors receive a tenth of the total, mainly from aid agencies, such as USAID and the United Kingdom government's Department for International Development (DFID). This shows that the vast majority of financing support for the private sector is used to mobilise commercial investment in sectors where the private sector is active. It is also worth noting that support for banking and business is provided for projects in infrastructure, manufacturing and agriculture via investment funds or banks that on-lend to private companies, especially small and medium-sized enterprises (SMEs). Therefore, the banking and business sector should also be seen as a channel for investment in infrastructure and various industries, in addition to being a sector on its own.

Figure 5.3. Development partners support the private sector in areas with established commercial opportunities

ODF in support of private sector operations, 2016, USD billion commitments

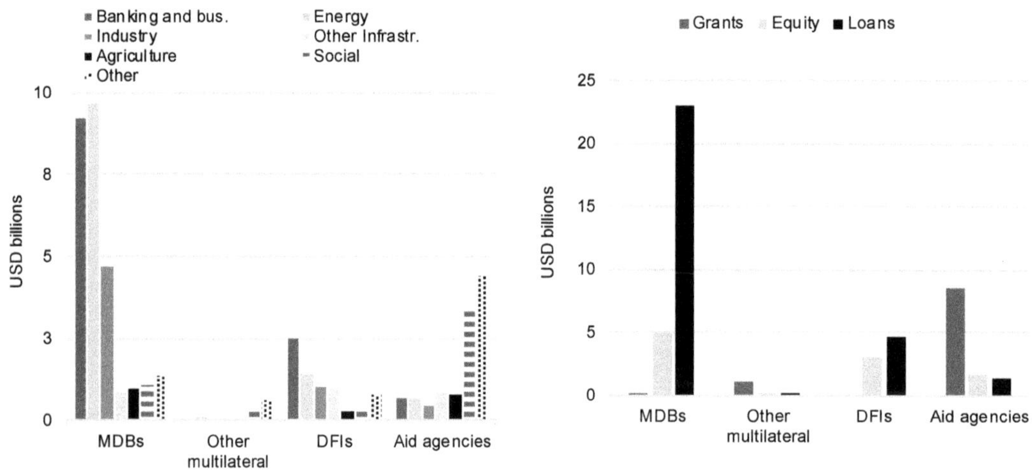

Note: some data include estimates from the author. See the Annex at the end of this report.

Source: (OECD, 2018[4]), "International development statistics (database)", http://www.oecd.org/dac/financing-sustainable-development/development-finance-data/idsonline.htm and annual reports.

StatLink https://doi.org/10.1787/888933856055

The increasing focus on private sector development is creating opportunities to mobilise additional finance for development

Mobilising additional private finance for development is one of the objectives of bilateral and multilateral development partners in their private sector development operations. However, amounts mobilised from the private sector through ODF instruments are still small when compared to the USD trillions that are needed to close the financing gaps to achieve the SDGs. In fact, according to a survey conducted by the OECD, amounts mobilised from the private sector accounted for an annual average of USD 20.3 billion between 2013 and 2015 (OECD, 2016[5]). Most of this financing was mobilised through guarantees and debt instruments, such as syndicated loans and credit lines, in areas with clear commercial opportunities, such as energy, banking and business, industry and mining and construction (see Figure 5.4). Conversely, equity instruments, such as direct investment in companies and shares in collective investment vehicles, mobilised less financing from the private sector compared to the other instruments, although they were used by a higher number of institutions.

The higher amounts mobilised through debt instruments and guarantees and lower levels from equity instruments can be explained by the fact that the magnitude of volumes and operations for loans and guarantees is much larger than for equity. In fact, as shown earlier in Figure 5.2, equity is only a small share of ODF from bilateral and multilateral development partners, whereas loans are the largest. For guarantees, it is more difficult to assess the potential of this instrument to mobilise resources as they are not financial flows, even though they do represent a risk for the provider. However, if one looks at the issuance value of the underlying instruments covered by guarantees, the magnitude of the operations would be much bigger than equity.

Figure 5.4. Amounts mobilised from the private sector by official development finance interventions are still small and concentrated in a few sectors

Amounts mobilised from the private sector by selected ODF interventions by sector, average 2012-15, current prices, USD billion commitments

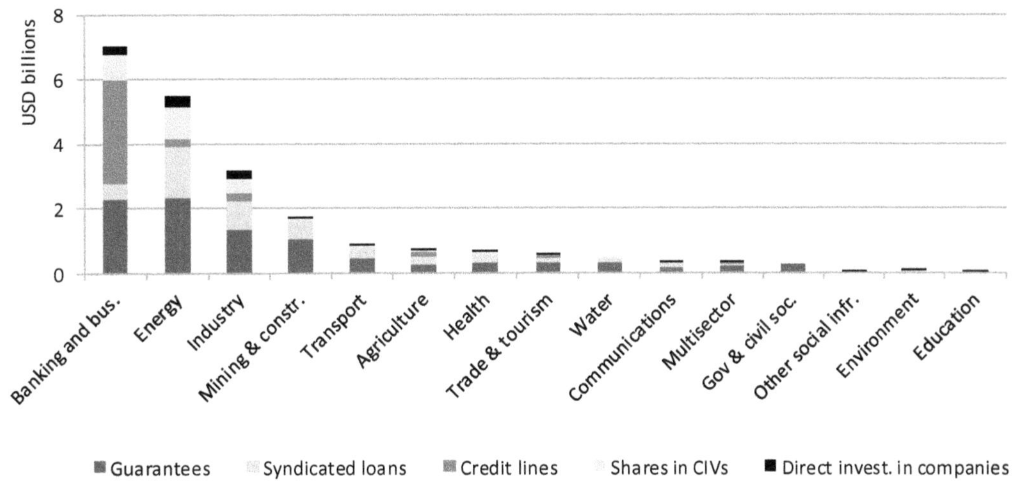

Source: (OECD, 2016[5]) "OECD DAC survey on amounts mobilised from the private sector by official development finance interventions 2012-2015", http://www.oecd.org/dac/financing-sustainable-development/development-finance-standards/mobilisation.htm.

StatLink https://doi.org/10.1787/888933856074

Albeit still relatively small, private amounts mobilised by ODF are set to grow considerably in the coming years. This is due to the increasing lending capacity of DFIs and MDBs as well as the increasing interest in commercial solutions for development. The AAAA, the Paris Agreement and intergovernmental processes at the DAC, the G20 and the United Nations clearly show a widespread political commitment to promoting commercial solutions for closing important financing gaps in infrastructure, climate change and social services [(United Nations, 2015[3]); (G20, 2017[6]); (OECD, 2017[7])]. Political commitment to increasing private finance is reflected in unprecedented capital reforms by MDBs to increase lending capacity, including joint targets at the G20 level (AIIB et al., 2017[8]). In the same vein, the financial capacity of bilateral DFIs is expanding considerably. For example, EDFI's annual commitments increased from USD 11 billion in 2005 to USD 36 billion in 2015 (EDFI, 2016[9]). This increase was mainly driven by government replenishments and reinvested earnings, and suggests a continued upward trend in the short to medium term. This trend is compounded by widespread interest of bilateral donors in providing commercial solutions for development, including through blended finance funds and facilities.

The growing interest in mobilising volumes of financing from the private sector points to the need for development partners to establish long-term strategies for addressing the needs of the private sector, including clear exit strategies and minimal use of concessionality. ODF can be strategically used to help private investment in development-related areas reach an appropriate scale. However, mobilisation strategies need to minimise the use of scarce concessional resources and envisage an exit strategy, so that private market financing can eventually self-sustain. This is in line with the recently agreed OECD blended finance principles, which state that blended finance operations should focus on commercial sustainability, minimise the use of concessional resources and have a clear strategy for the duration and exit of concessional finance [see Principle 2.c and 2.d in (OECD, 2018[4])].

5.1.2. Grants are mostly used for social sectors and agriculture in volumes that are stagnating

Development partners use grants for downstream projects mainly in social sectors and agriculture, in amounts that are stagnating

Grant funding is mainly concentrated in social sectors (including government and civil society), agriculture and multisector projects (including environment). The largest sectors are health and government and civil society. Beyond health[4] and multisector programmes, grants to other sectors are stagnating (see Figure 5.5).

Figure 5.5. Grants for sectoral programmes are stagnating

Share of grants over other instruments by official development partners (left hand chart) and volumes of grants by official development partners by groups of sectors (right hand chart), 2012-16, 2016 constant prices, USD billion commitments

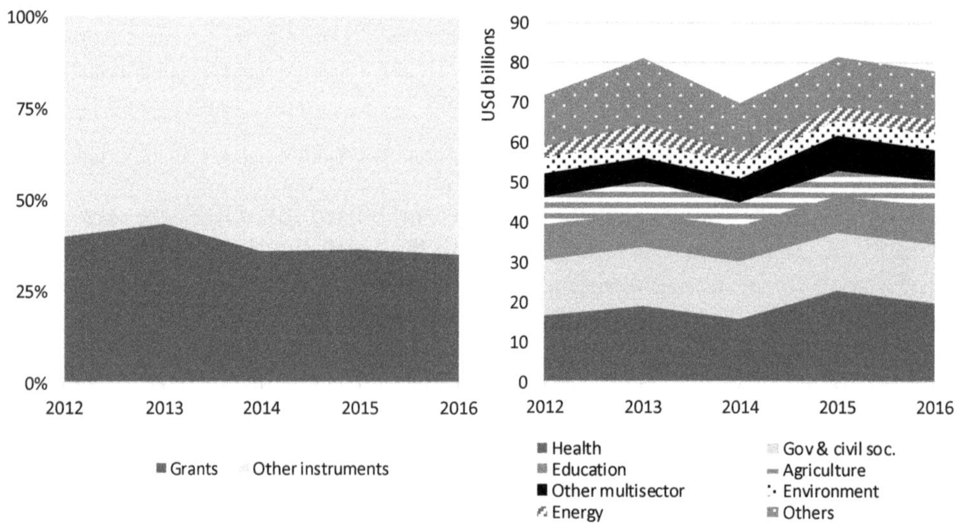

Source: (OECD, 2018[4]), "International development statistics (database)", http://www.oecd.org/dac/financing-sustainable-development/development-finance-data/idsonline.htm.

StatLink https://doi.org/10.1787/888933856093

In addition to the budget constraints faced by bilateral providers, the stagnation of grants to other sectors reflects an increased use of these resources for non-sector-allocable operations, in other words, contributions that are not allocated to specific development programme areas – examples include general budget support, debt relief, humanitarian assistance and in-donor refugee costs (see also Box 2.3 in Chapter 2). In fact, grants for non-sector-allocable operations increased from USD 28 billion in 2012 to USD 57 billion in 2016, and a large part of this financing was spent on addressing humanitarian crises. In particular, the share of grant support for humanitarian assistance and in-donor refugee costs, which are non-sector-allocable operations, more than doubled within total grant volumes from 14% in 2012 to 30% in 2016. This shows that an increasingly large proportion of grants is provided for short-term humanitarian response rather than long-term development, such as for sector programmes.

DAC members account for the vast majority (82%) of sector grant funding committed every year by all bilateral and multilateral development partners reporting to the DAC (Figure 5.6). Multilateral agencies and funds, such as the Global Fund, Gavi, the African Development Bank (AfDB) and the Global Environment Facility (GEF) provide most of the remaining portion. The largest providers of grants among all donors are by far the United States and European Union institutions. They allocate on average USD 20 billion and USD 11 billion of sector grant funding per year, respectively.

Figure 5.6. Bilateral donors and vertical funds provide the bulk of grant funding for sectoral operations

Grants from development partners by provider and sector groupings, average 2012-16, 2016 constant prices, USD billion commitments

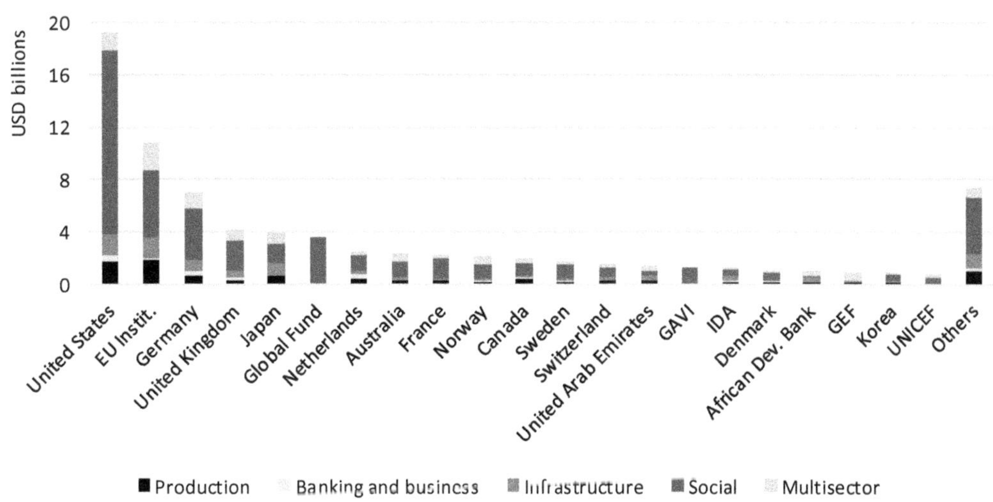

Source: (OECD, 2018[4]), "International development statistics (database)", http://www.oecd.org/dac/financing-sustainable-development/development-finance-data/idsonline.htm.

StatLink https://doi.org/10.1787/888933856112

Sector grant finance is mostly used to fund easily identifiable outputs and advisory services for policy and institutional development

Development partners provide large amounts of grant resources to cover physical inputs and services procured in projects. For instance, between half and two-thirds of the 2016 USD 20 billion of grant finance for health, which is the largest grant-funded sector, is for purchasing medical goods and services to prevent and control infectious diseases, such as HIV, polio, Ebola, Zika, malaria and tuberculosis. Notable examples include multibillion programmes that provide anti-retroviral drugs, anti-tuberculosis medicines and other medical commodities, such as the United States' President's Emergency Plan for AIDS Relief (PEPFAR) and Global Health Supply Chain programmes. Other examples include programmes supported by the Global Fund to fight AIDS, tuberculosis and malaria (see Box 5.1).

Box 5.1. United States' President's Emergency Plan for AIDS Relief

The United States' President's Emergency Plan for AIDS Relief (PEPFAR) is a multibillion global health programme started in 2003 by President George W. Bush. In the period 2004-17 PEPFAR provided about USD 70 billion of grants for HIV/AIDS and malaria programmes. This was done either bilaterally through United States agencies or via core and earmarked contributions to multilateral organisations, particularly the Global Fund. In 2017, grant funding from the United States under the PEPFAR programme amounted to USD 7 billion.

Slightly more than half (55%) of PEPFAR support is earmarked for health treatment, 15% for palliative care, 20% for prevention programmes and 10% for projects targeting orphans and vulnerable children, including babies. PEPFAR-funded activities mainly cover the provision of anti-retroviral treatment health care services and health care services to prevent and respond to HIV/AIDS.

PEPFAR is led and managed by the U.S. Department of State's Office of the United States' Global AIDS Coordinator and Health Diplomacy. Beyond the United States' Department of State, PEPFAR is implemented by seven US government departments and agencies, including: USAID, the U.S. Department of Health & Human Services; the U.S. Department of Defense; the Peace Corps; the U.S. Department of Commerce; the U.S. Department of Labor; and the U.S. Department of the Treasury.

Source: Authors based on [(Kaiser Family Foundation, 2017[10]) and (PEPFAR, 2016[11])].

Large portions of grant finance are also used to support advisory services as well as technical assistance for governance and democratic participation implemented by various public and private agencies. These include central governments, non-governmental organisations, multilateral agencies and private firms. In these situations, while projects are reported as supporting local governments, they may be implemented by large consulting firms providing technical expertise. Two-thirds of support for governance, which is the second-largest grant-funded sector, is for advisory services and technical assistance for:

- reforms on legal and judicial development and other public reforms (e.g. decentralisation, public financial management, modernisation of procurement)
- civilian peacebuilding, conflict resolution and stabilisation programmes
- human rights and democratic participation initiatives through core and non-core support to local non-governmental organisations.

Grant finance for policy and institutional development only accounts for a small portion of total grant resources to sectors, and is decreasing (see Figure 5.7). This includes technical assistance for policy reforms and institutional capacity building in areas such as public governance, environment policy, infrastructure policy and social sector policy. This could be explained by costs that are lower for technical assistance and other capacity-building activities than for physical inputs (e.g. medical drugs, machinery and social buildings). There is also an increased preference for donor support for specific projects with short-term and measurable impacts rather long-term, sector-wide approaches. However, more research is needed to better understand the reasons.

Figure 5.7. Sector grant finance for policy and institutional development is decreasing

Grant finance for policy and institutional development by sector (left hand chart) and by type of purpose (right hand chart), 2012-16, 2016 constant prices, USD billion commitments

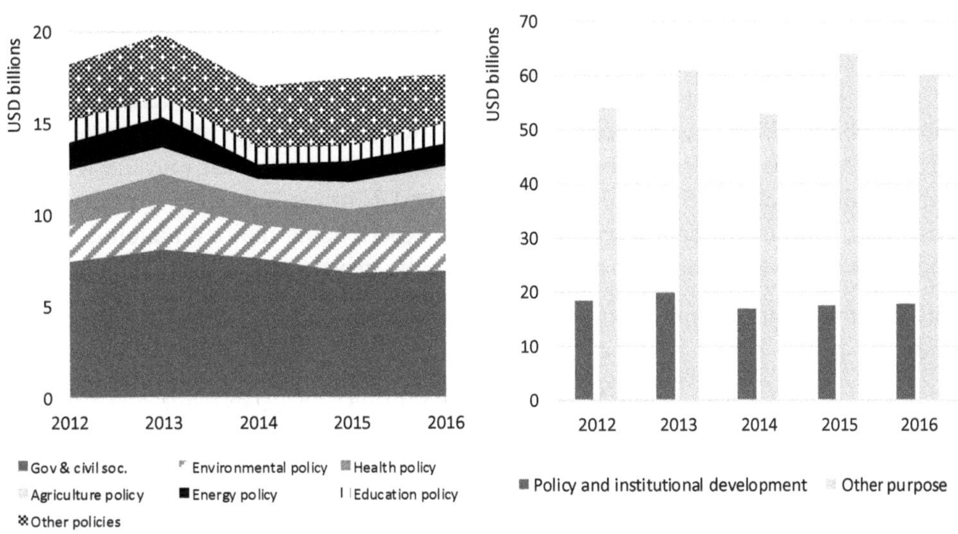

Source: (OECD, 2018[4]), "International development statistics (database)", http://www.oecd.org/dac/financing-sustainable-development/development-finance-data/idsonline.htm. See Annex for a list of purpose codes selected.

StatLink https://doi.org/10.1787/888933856131

Development partners are increasingly using grants for private-sector projects across sectors

Overall, development partners provided about USD 8 billion of grants directly to the private sector in 2016, most of which was from USAID, DFID and the European Union. Donors provide grant finance in their engagements with the private sector particularly to:

- mobilise additional private finance (i.e. blended finance)
- foster social and environmental impact (e.g. support innovative business models)
- promote job creation and entrepreneurship, including for micro and small enterprises (see Section 5.2 below).

One example of support for these three objectives is DFID's contribution to the Global Innovation Fund, the main goal of which is to promote social innovation. Another example is the European Union's grants to microenterprises, which mainly aim to increase the competitiveness of companies to support job creation. In blended finance projects, DAC members use grants to bring projects to commercial viability. They do this by subsidising loans and equity, providing partial protection against investment risks, and funding technical assistance and feasibility studies for project preparation (OECD, 2018[12]). While these objectives are not mutually exclusive, development partner grants may emphasise one objective over another.

Overall, the interest of development partners is mainly growing for the support of blended finance to increase the volumes of financing in specific areas, particularly renewable energy and SME finance, which are especially underfunded. Grant finance is increasingly provided for blended finance operations, both upstream through replenishments of DFIs and downstream via blended finance funds and facilities, generally managed by DFIs and MDBs. Between 2000 and 2016, a total of 167 blended finance funds and facilities were launched, with a combined size of approximately USD 31 billion, mainly financed by DAC members (OECD, 2018[12]).

In light of this trend – and as grants for sector programmes are stagnating (Figure 5.5) – it is vital to ensure that these scarce concessional resources are prioritised to support initiatives with the highest potential for the most vulnerable people across sectors. As mentioned above, this is in line with the AAAA, which states that the most concessional resources need to be prioritised for countries with the greatest needs and the least ability to mobilise other resources, such as LDCs (United Nations, 2015[3]). It is also true for those sectors, such as the social sectors, that are experiencing major financing challenges and have less capacity to mobilise resources from the private sector (see Chapter 3).

Prioritising the concessional resources for the sectors and projects that need it most includes:

- supporting business models and technology with more evident pro-poor impact (e.g. health technology, safe lighting, nutritious food and clean water)
- promoting entrepreneurship among the poorest, who normally lack the skills and the resources to start and run sustainable businesses.

For example, the United States' Helping Babies Breathe project mobilised private expertise to develop and implement evidence-based health-care practices to decrease neonatal mortality in 77 low-resourced countries. Early infant mortality was reduced by 47% and stillbirth by 24% in two years. Similarly, as mentioned in Chapter 3, mobile technologies promote financial inclusion by offering poor people previously inaccessible financial services. This has been shown by the development of mobile money transfer systems that are helping many poor people, including women, escape poverty and graduate from subsistence agriculture to small businesses (Suri and Jack, 2016[13]). In this context, M-Pesa is one of the most successful mobile money transfer systems. It increased financial access for millions of poor people in Kenya, and was kick-started with a GBP 1 billion grant from DFID (Martinez and McKay, 2011[14]).

5.1.3. The use of debt instruments to support the infrastructure and commercial sectors requires attention to fiscal sustainability in countries most in need

Multilateral development banks and a few large DAC members provide the majority of loans

Multilateral Development Banks (MDBs) and a few large DAC members provide the vast majority of concessional and non-concessional loans for development, mainly for the infrastructure and commercial sectors (see Figure 5.8). Among them, MDBs and Korea provided more non-concessional loans, whereas most DAC members, including the European Union, provide more concessional loans. In volume terms, loan amounts from the World Bank Group dwarf those of any other debt provider. They represent one-third of all concessional and non-concessional loans from bilateral and multilateral development partners reporting to the DAC. Moreover, while the concessionality of debt varies across sectors, the largest recipients are usually large middle-income countries, even when only concessional debt is taken into account. In fact, only a third of concessional debt was provided to LDCs and other LICs between 2012 and 2016. This can be explained by the fact that the volumes of financing needs are more important in countries with large and more advanced economies, because the volume of needs is higher and they have more capacity to absorb financing (see Chapter 3).

Figure 5.8. Multilateral development banks and a few DAC members provide the bulk of loans for development across sectors

Largest ODF providers of concessional and non-concessional debt by sector grouping (left hand chart) and sectoral distribution of ODF concessional and non-concessional loans (right hand chart), 2012-16 annual average, USD billion commitments

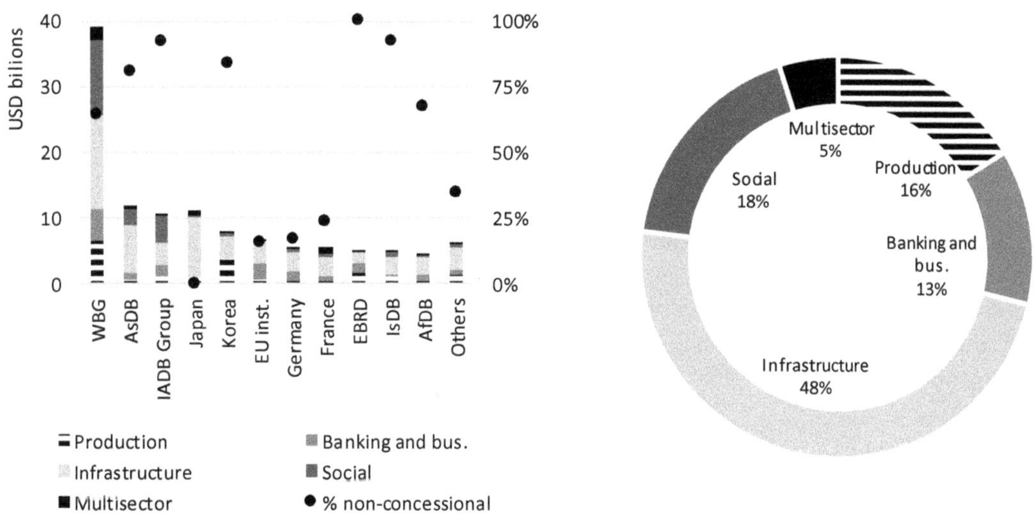

Source: (OECD, 2018[4]), "International development statistics (database)", http://www.oecd.org/dac/financing-sustainable-development/development-finance-data/idsonline.htm.

StatLink https://doi.org/10.1787/888933856150

Between a fourth and a fifth of debt instruments is provided by development finance providers to private companies and financial institutions in banking and business, infrastructure and production. Debt instruments make up the largest portion of ODF for private-sector projects, particularly from MDBs. Private-sector loans and other debt instruments account for about USD 31 billion in 2016 when estimates from development finance providers not reporting to the DAC are included. A third of the total is from the IFC and EBRD. Debt instruments from DFIs and MDBs to the private sector cover:

- large syndicated loans for infrastructure, including through public-private partnerships
- senior and subordinated loans to both SMEs and large companies in manufacturing, agriculture, and mining and construction
- credit lines to financial institutions that on-lend to SMEs in various industries
- project bonds from infrastructure companies and funds.

Debt instruments are the main financing mechanisms for MDBs and a few bilateral DFIs, such as the Overseas Private Investment Corporation (OPIC) or the Oesterreichische Entwicklungsbank AG (OeEB), and for aid agencies, such as the Agence Française de Développement (French Development Agency). For MDBs, loans are mostly non-concessional but they are usually provided at better terms and conditions than alternative options available to developing countries.

The use of loans is increasing in most sectors and income groups, particularly in the infrastructure and production sectors

While grants are increasing moderately, at a CAGR of 2%, loans are increasing at a CAGR of 7%, i.e. more than three times faster than grants (see Figure 5.9). In volume terms, the trend reflects a widespread boost of non-concessional loans by MDBs and a global upsurge of infrastructure finance by both bilateral and multilateral providers, including in LDCs and other LICs. This is reshaping the ODF architecture across income groups and sectors. While in 2012 two-thirds of sector-allocable ODF to LDCs and other LICs were in the form of grants, these instruments only accounted for slightly more than half in 2016. This trend was driven by minor increases of grants in most sectors and a significant rise in concessional and non-concessional loans for the infrastructure and social sectors. In middle-income countries, there is a significant upward trend in non-concessional debt, which boosts resources for the infrastructure and production sectors in lower middle-income countries (LMICs) and financing for every allocable sector, including social sectors, in upper middle-income countries (UMICs).

Figure 5.9. Loans are playing a bigger role in most sectors in the development finance architecture, particularly in infrastructure

Shares of concessional and non-concessional loans in total ODF from bilateral and multilateral development partners (left hand chart) and total of concessional and non-concessional loans by sector groupings (right hand chart), 2012-16, USD billion commitment

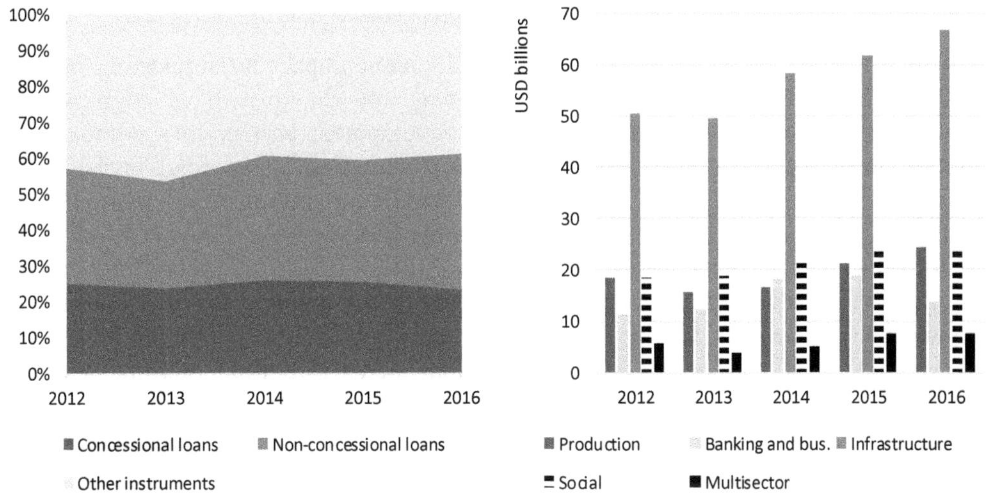

Source: (OECD, 2018[4]), "International development statistics (database)", http://www.oecd.org/dac/financing-sustainable-development/development-finance-data/idsonline.htm.

StatLink https://doi.org/10.1787/888933856169

Rising loans in the infrastructure and production sectors point to the need for increased attention to fiscal sustainability in countries most in need

Overall, the debt situation of developing countries is positive. External debt to gross domestic product (GDP) ratios declined significantly in the 2000s, thanks to high GDP growth, debt relief and countercyclical policies (Julks and Kawamura, 2017[15]). However, debt vulnerability is becoming a concern in the most vulnerable economies. The number of developing countries in debt distress or at high risk of debt distress doubled from 12 to 24 between 2013 and 2017 (IMF, 2018[16]). This can be explained by unproductive debt accumulation; the occurrence of shock, crises and disasters; and the hardening of loan terms and conditions for the poorest countries. The latter also borrow from the bond market and on semi-concessional terms from bilateral loan agencies, notably The Export-Import Bank of China and the Chinese Development Bank. This new debt composition in developing countries poses challenges both in preventing and resolving debt crises.

In this context, development partners need to continue to ensure the financial sustainability of their lending operations and provide technical assistance, including debt-management services and capacity building. Upstream policies,[5] sovereign risk frameworks[6] and other debt-assessment tools are used to evaluate countries' ability to take on debt. However, these assessments can be optimistic due to overly ambitious growth forecasts and unpredictable shocks, such as commodity price changes, conflicts, epidemics and fraud (IMF, 2018[16]); (Mooney and de Soyres, 2017[17]). Particular attention is required in countries most in need, e.g. small island developing states (SIDS) and conflict-affected countries, due to fragile fiscal and macroeconomic situations and vulnerability to shocks and disasters. In these countries, the AAAA encourages using debt relief or other risk-reducing instruments, including exchanges of public debt obligations for social or environmental expenditure. Examples include debt-for-health and debt-for-nature swaps, GDP-linked securities, or catastrophe and pandemic bonds (United Nations, 2015[3]).

5.1.4. Equity investments are used to boost innovative private solutions

Equity investments can have a significant development impact by supporting business innovation for development and paving the way for the growth of high-potential companies. First, the equity participation of a development partner in a company can boost the confidence of private investors, in turn attracting commercial investors and reducing the cost of capital. This was the case, for instance, in the European Commission's concessional equity investment in the Kenyan Lake Turkana Wind Power project via the Africa Infrastructure Trust Fund (OECD, 2018[12]). Second, investing in private equity funds that in turn support companies in developing countries can promote market-based solutions for development. This is especially the case when the fund targets areas with high positive social and environmental impact (e.g. seed funding or growth capital for SMEs, and funds investing in sustainable infrastructure).

Development partners provide equity instruments in private-sector projects with a much lower, but increasing, level of support compared to debt instruments (see Figure 5.10). OECD DAC data show that equity from bilateral and multilateral development partners increased from USD 4 billion in 2012 to USD 6 billion in 2016. If amounts from bilateral and multilateral development partners that do not report to the DAC are included, 16% of official support to the private sector is through equity instruments, particularly for funds investing in SMEs and infrastructure. The largest providers of equity are IFC, EBRD, CDC Group plc (CDC United Kingdom) and FMO (Netherlands).

Equity investments can support companies directly, particularly in manufacturing, and mining and construction. They can also support companies indirectly via collective investment schemes (such as investment funds providing seed funding or venture and growth capital for SMEs) or funds supporting energy and other infrastructure projects. The choice between direct investment in companies and investment in equity funds depends on a variety of factors, including:

- the degree of control and engagement
- risk-and-return profiles
- expertise with the required corporate governance skills
- country knowledge
- industry experience (IADB, 2017[18]).

Figure 5.10. Equity investments are small but growing

Equity investments of sector-allocable ODF by sector groupings (left hand chart) and by type of partner (right hand chart), annual average 2012-16, 2016 prices, USD billion commitments

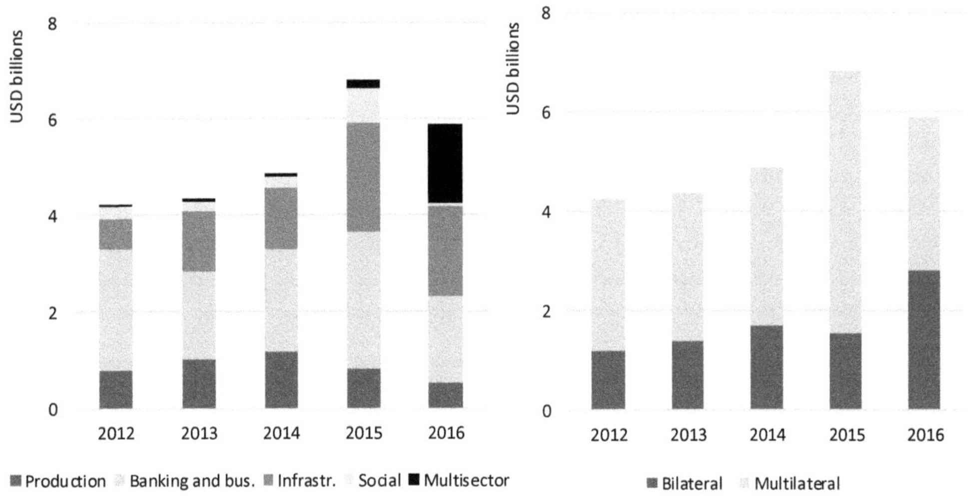

Note: amounts from DFIs and other development partners not reporting to the DAC are not included.
Source: (OECD, 2018[4]), "International development statistics (database)", http://www.oecd.org/dac/financing-sustainable-development/development-finance-data/idsonline.htm.

StatLink https://doi.org/10.1787/888933856188

While most MDBs provide low shares of equity compared to loans, the picture within most bilateral DFIs is more nuanced. For instance, the CDC (United Kingdom), Norfund (Norway), the Swiss Investment Fund for Emerging Markets (SIFEM) and the Investment Fund for Developing Countries (IFU; Denmark) invest more through equity than debt instruments. The FMO (Netherlands), the German Investment and Development Company (DEG), the Compañía Española de Financiación del Desarrollo (COFIDES; Spain), the Società Italiana per le Imprese all'Estero (SIMEST Spa; Italy), the Belgian Investment Company for Developing Countries (BIO) and the Société Belge d'Investissement International (BMI-SBI ; Belgium) provide an even mixture of debt and equity (EDFI, 2016[9]). Examples of innovative equity investments include the Global Energy Efficiency and Renewable Energy Fund (GEEREF), which is advised by the European Investment Bank (EIB). GEEREF is a fund-of-funds that supports private equity funds investing in renewable energy and energy efficiency in developing countries. Another example of innovative equity investment by multilateral agencies is the EBRD Equity Participation Fund. It mobilises funds from global institutional investors to participate in 20%-30% of EBRD's new direct equity investments above EUR 10 million.

5.1.5. Guarantees can boost private finance mobilisation in infrastructure and production sectors, but lack the appropriate incentive structure to be promoted

Guarantees and other risk-mitigation instruments are used by development partners to cover defaults of payments or other financial losses incurred by a lender or other investor. Risk-mitigation instruments include political risk insurance, foreign exchange risk mitigation or partial credit guarantees. The latter also serve to reduce default exposure and spread on project bonds in infrastructure funds and companies.

The main sectors in which guarantees are used are infrastructure and production. The largest provider of guarantees and risk-mitigation instruments is by far the World Bank Group's MIGA. It provides insurance against political risks such as expropriation or civil disturbance, or partial risk guarantees to cover government non-payments. While smaller in size, other MDBs [e.g. IFC, the Asian Development Bank (AsDB), the Inter-American Development Bank (IADB), the African Development Bank (AfDB), the Islamic Development Bank (IsDB)], DFIs [e.g. Overseas Private Investment Corporation (OPIC), CDC, FMO, OeEB, Proparco and Norfund] and aid agencies (e.g. USAID) provide guarantees and other credit-enhancement facilities. For instance, the AsDB provides partial credit guarantees in local currencies to reinsure financial institutions' first loss default exposure to project bonds issued by infrastructure project companies. Another example is USAID's Development Credit Authority, which uses partial credit guarantees to cover loans for entrepreneurs who align with USAID's priorities in agriculture, education, energy, the environment, health, infrastructure, SMEs, trade and water (OECD, 2016[19]).

There is certainly an interest from the development community in ensuring an appropriate level of guarantees for development. Nevertheless, achieving this objective has been hampered by lack of understanding and incentives for providing these instruments. Understanding and measuring the impact of guarantees has been notoriously challenging given that, unlike grants, loans and equity, guarantees are unfunded positions. In fact, unless guarantees are activated, there is no financial flow. At the same time, guarantees entail a cost for the providers that use these instruments, such as DFIs and MDBs among others, since they represent a financial exposure that limits space for new investment in the same way as loans would do. Since guarantees appear to be particularly complex instruments, development partners prefer providing loans as they are better known, more standardised and easier to manage. Therefore promoting the use of guarantees to mobilise finance in the highly underfunded infrastructure and production sectors will require a change in the incentive structure for guarantee providers. This could include:

- using set-aside equity capital funds
- providing incentives to staff to encourage the use of guarantees
- reducing the equity capital allocation required for certain classes of guarantee (particularly partial/political risk guarantees)
- unilaterally reducing pricing for guarantees (Humphrey and Prizzon, 2014[20]).

5.2. Improving financing approaches and channels within and across sectors

5.2.1. An integrated development agenda requires financing approaches that are coherent within and across sectors

The integrated nature of the SDGs reinforces the need to adopt coherent approaches based on country needs. For this reason, this subsection will highlight the challenges and opportunities arising from a growing development finance architecture, such as more financial resources for development and the emergence of competing and particularistic interests. Some topical areas will be discussed in more detail, such as the importance of sector budget support, pooled funding mechanisms and the untying agenda as ways to promote coherence within and across sectors and actors.

While a growing number of development partners increases sector financing for development, it also makes coherent and co-ordinated approaches more difficult

The development finance architecture is becoming increasingly complex as the number of development finance providers and intermediaries is growing (see Figure 5.11). Resources from taxpayers and private endowments are used to support country governments directly or are channelled in multiple ways through intermediaries such as CSOs and multilateral organisations or through private channels (such as companies and financial institutions). A growing galaxy of intermediaries is expanding resources for development operations as these institutions can pool financing upstream from a variety of public and private sources or by reinvesting earnings from revenue-making operations, such as loans. For instance, since the inception of their operations, the World Bank Group's International Bank for Reconstruction and Development (IBRD) and IFC unlocked USD 900 billion of financing (mostly loans) with only USD 19 billion of paid-in capital (World Bank, 2018[21]). Capital was built through internal income, such as through capital markets and loan repayments.

Figure 5.11. The increasing complexity of development finance architecture

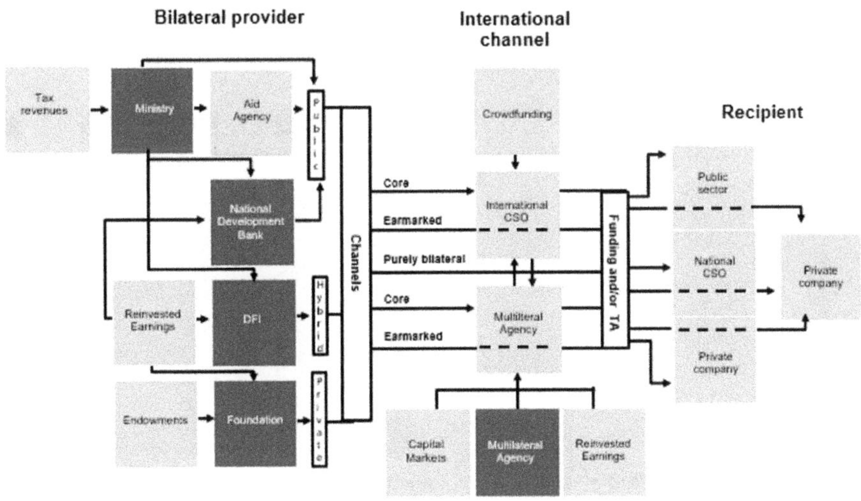

Source: Author's own stylised representation
Note: the representation above aims to show the potential complexity of the involvement of a galaxy of providers and intermediaries in the delivery of development finance, rather than being a comprehensive description of the entire development finance architecture. TA stands for technical assistance.

At the same time, a proliferation of actors and sources of finance brings new ways of working and potentially diverging interests into the development landscape. This might challenge co-ordinated approaches for development across sectors. For example, preliminary findings from an upcoming OECD report on multilateral development finance show that private sources and philanthropies are increasing resources for multilateral organisations in some sectors, particularly for health. However, the financing is piecemeal and often provided for areas that follow their own priorities rather than the strategic priorities of multilateral organisations (OECD, Forthcoming[22]). Similarly, an increased reliance on companies and financial institutions can leverage significant amounts of private financing in areas with established commercial opportunities. But this requires attention in balancing the commercial motives of private projects and the development objectives of official support provided for these initiatives [(OECD, 2018[4]); (OECD, 2018[12])].

The 2030 Agenda requires increasing support through approaches that enhance policy coherence, such as sector-wide financing and joint funding mechanisms

Development partners allocate most of their sector financing for specific projects. The interest of development partners in supporting specific projects could be explained by the need to control resources and the preference for delivering outputs that are quantitatively measurable. This development finance paradigm is exemplified in results-based aid modalities, in which tranches of financing are disbursed when measurable outcomes are achieved. By contrast, development partners provide low shares of their resources as sector budget support and through pooled funding mechanisms (see Figure 5.12). However, sector budget support and pooled funding could increase policy coherence and better serve the achievement of an integrated development agenda if well designed and implemented.

Figure 5.12. Project-type interventions are prevalent in most sectors

ODF volumes for sectoral programmes by type of intervention (left hand chart) and shares of ODF for sectoral programmes by type of intervention and sector grouping (right hand chart), annual average 2012-2016, 2016 prices, USD billion commitment

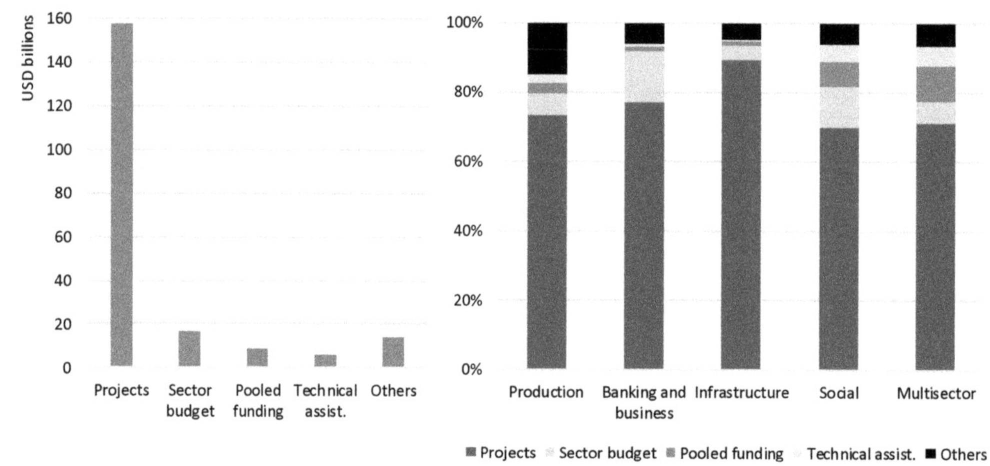

Source: (OECD, 2018[4]), "International development statistics (database)", http://www.oecd.org/dac/financing-sustainable-development/development-finance-data/idsonline.htm.

StatLink https://doi.org/10.1787/888933856207

Sector budget support can foster sector coherence, but policy conditionality needs to be aligned with country priorities

Only 8% of sector-allocable ODF is implemented through sector budget support, which is about loans, grants and technical assistance provided for the implementation of national sector strategies of recipient governments (e.g. energy, health and education). Resources are generally provided through the recipient government's system, usually the ministry of finance. They are then channelled to the sector ministry or public agency responsible for budget execution (Williamson and Dom, 2010[23]). While policy conditionality is set at a broad thematic level, there is no earmarking on specific projects. In sector budget support (as well as in general budget support) donors and recipient governments negotiate overarching principles of reform and performance assessment frameworks to provide indicators for monitoring the implementation of reforms.

Sector budget support is mostly provided by multilateral organisations, particularly MDBs and the European Union (see Figure 5.13). MDBs mainly provide concessional and non-concessional loans for sector budget support, in amounts that are increasing. For instance, the World Bank provides development policy loans to support policy reforms in infrastructure, financial policy and public governance (e.g. public financial management, decentralisation and investment laws). Grant finance for sector budget support is less than loans and mainly provided by the European Union. Examples of grant-funded sector budget support includes the USD 1 billion committed by the European Development Fund in 2016 to support broad-based agricultural policy reforms to promote food security and agricultural development in Burkina Faso, Mali, Niger and Rwanda.

Figure 5.13. Sector budget support is mostly provided by multilateral development banks and EU institutions

ODF volumes for sector budget support by provider and sector (left hand chart) and shares of ODF for sector budget support by sector grouping (left hand chart), annual average 2012-16, 2016 prices, USD billion commitment

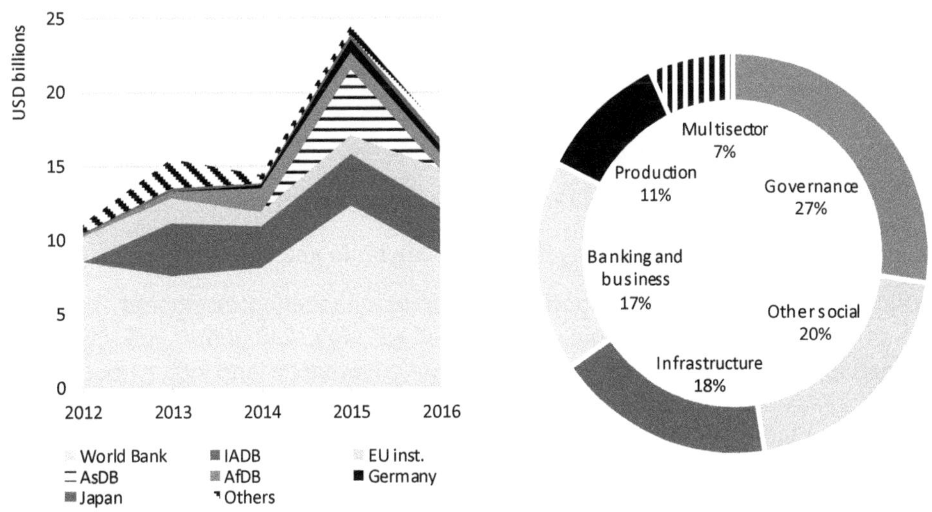

Source: (OECD, 2018[4]), "International development statistics (database)", http://www.oecd.org/dac/financing-sustainable-development/development-finance-data/idsonline.htm.

StatLink https://doi.org/10.1787/888933856226

Proponents of sector (and general) budget support point out that this type of financing increases national ownership, aligns with domestic sector strategies, and allows for harmonisation among donors. However, detractors emphasise that it can lead to corruption and misappropriation of funds in contexts with high political and fiduciary risks. Nevertheless, a comprehensive review of general and sector budget support evaluations of donors suggests that evidence is needed to confirm the assumed risks of corruption of budget support (Orth et al., 2017[24]). However, evidence shows that this type of support improves public financial management and the provision of public goods and services when there is the institutional capacity and political will for reform of the recipient government (Orth et al., 2017[24]).

Pooled funding mechanisms can promote cross-sector approaches if well-funded and managed

Pooled funding mechanisms are financing vehicles that earmark or blend resources to support sector, integrated or system-wide programming and implementation. Providers contribute resources to an autonomous account, managed jointly with other providers and/or the recipient, or through more complex fund structures similar to multilateral institutions. The account or other fund has specific purposes, modes of disbursement and accountability mechanisms. Pooled funding mechanisms are generally administered by a multilateral agency or by a sector ministry in developing countries through basket funds. Their configurations can be quite diverse in terms of sector scope, geographic eligibility, financing model, funding governance, administration and implementation channels.

While far from being a panacea, pooled funding mechanisms can support a cross cutting and integrated development agenda, but need good governance and financing structures to succeed. These mechanisms offer the opportunity to increase the quantity and the quality of financing by:

- consolidating scattered earmarked funding
- promoting innovation
- fostering policy coherence and co-ordination
- increasing financial mobilisation (OECD, 2015[25]).

However, they can:

- increase transaction costs and fragmentation
- need governance mechanisms that ensure country ownership and co-ordination
- require donor financing streams that are predictable and flexible.

In a similar way to sector budget support, resources channelled as pooled funding are small (4% of total ODF to sectors) and concentrated among a few donors, mainly bilateral providers and the European Union institutions, in governance and other social sectors (Figure 5.14). These amounts do not include support provided as core finance from bilateral donors to large multilateral pooled funds, such as Gavi or the Global Fund, as the large size and institutional complexity of these mechanisms make them more like multilateral organisations than pooled funds.

Amounts of pooled funding increased significantly in 2015 and 2016 thanks to increased support from the European Union through multisector trust funds in Africa. Multilateral pooled funding is much larger than support through basket funds, accounting for 81% of all resources channelled through pooled funding. Multilateral pooled funding mechanisms support a large set of activities across development, humanitarian and peacebuilding programmes, mainly created and managed by the United Nations and the World Bank. While United Nations pooled funds are mainly used for humanitarian and peacebuilding work, the World Bank's managed or administered trust funds[7] focus on health, environment, infrastructure, agriculture and SME finance.

Figure 5.14. A few DAC members provided most of pooled funding, mainly for governance, other social sectors and multisector projects

ODF for sector programmes channelled through pooled funding mechanisms by sector groupings (left hand chart) and by provider (right hand chart), annual average 2012-2016, 2016 prices, USD billion commitments

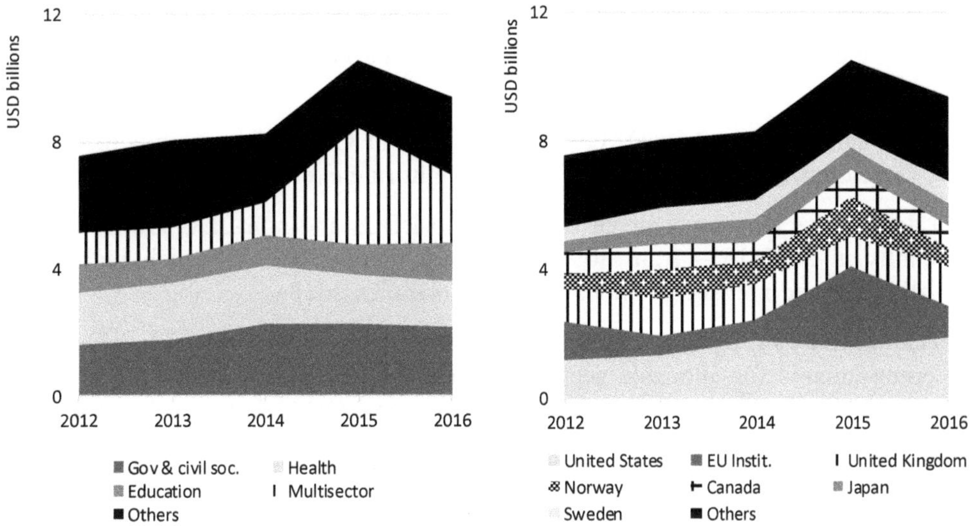

Source: (OECD, 2018[4]), "International development statistics (database)", http://www.oecd.org/dac/financing-sustainable-development/development-finance-data/idsonline.htm.

StatLink https://doi.org/10.1787/888933856245

Interest in the use of multilateral pooled funds is growing, especially in the United Nations. In fact, the upcoming United Nations reform aims to double the share of financing received from donor through multi-donor trust funds in various sectors and themes in order to reduce the very high level of funding earmarked by donors at the project level. One of the initiatives for achieving this objective is to boost the SDG Fund. This international multi-donor and multi-agency development mechanism (created in 2014) pools resources from various donors in order to support multi-sector programmes and partnerships in various SDG-relevant themes.

Bilateral donor support for their national companies can stifle appropriate sector allocations if they prevail over assessments of local needs

The success of the 2030 Agenda will require supporting appropriate sector allocations based on country needs. In contrast to this, tied aid, which is ODA that can only be used to buy goods and services from the provider country, can stifle appropriate sector allocations of resources if motivated by the national interest of the provider rather than the local needs of developing countries. In fact, while case-by-case analysis is needed to evaluate the development impact of tied ODA, the risks are:

- bias towards sectors of interest for donor companies rather than priority sectors of developing countries
- reduced ownership of national development policy by the recipient countries
- higher project costs due to uncompetitive procurement (Miyamoto and Chiofalo, 2017[26]).

DAC countries have significantly reduced formal restrictions in their procurement processes in the last decade. DAC members have committed to untie bilateral ODA to the greatest extent as suggested by:

- a 2001 DAC recommendation on untying aid to LDCs, which was extended to non-LDC heavily indebted poor countries (HIPCs) in 2008
- the aid effectiveness principles agreed in Paris and reiterated in Busan and Nairobi
- the indicators used in DAC peer reviews and Global Partnership for Effective Development Co-operation (GPEDC) monitoring exercises.

OECD data shows that the share of tied ODA to LDCs and non-LDC HIPCs decreased significantly in 2005-15 – from 30% to 12% of bilateral ODA (which includes both sector-allocable and non-sector-allocable ODA) (OECD, 2018[27]).

However, the untying agenda seems to have slowed in recent years. The share of tied ODA commitments for allocable sectors to all ODA-eligible countries remained at an average of 18% of their total sector-allocable bilateral ODA[8] between 2012 and 2016. Most (58%) of the USD 69 billion of ODA commitments formally tied by DAC countries in 2012-16 are for social sectors. Slightly less than half is for government and civil society, with the rest being equally split between health and education. Beyond social sectors, a fifth of sector-allocable tied ODA is for infrastructure (mainly transport), a tenth is for multisector projects and 5% is for agriculture. In terms of providers, about half (53%) of sector-allocable tied ODA from DAC countries is from the United States, and about a third (29%) is provided by Germany (16%), Japan (13%) and Korea (7%). Sector-allocable tied ODA from the United States is mainly spent on legal and judicial development and various disease-control interventions. From Germany it is spent on education, and from Japan and Korea on transport and other infrastructure.

Moreover, by looking beyond formal tying, OECD data show that a very high share of ODA is still awarded to companies from the donor country in competitive procurement. Tying generally refers to a legal/formal restriction for companies to participate in ODA-funded procurement based on nationality (*de jure* tying). But it can in fact also take place through various informal restrictions that favour companies from provider countries (*de facto* tying which is tying by default). Examples include advertising the tender in the donor country's language or setting criteria that only certain firms can meet (Meeks, 2017[28]). In particular, about two-thirds of ODA procured by DAC countries in 2015-16 were awarded to companies from the donor country in competitive processes (OECD, 2018[27]). Case-by-case analysis is needed to demonstrate *de facto* tying practices. Meanwhile, the very high share of ODA procured to donor country companies raises some issues about financing awards in open procurement processes and points to the need for further analysis in this area.

5.2.2. Development effectiveness and good donorship need to guide development partners' efforts, even if channels of delivery vary, depending on sectoral priorities and strategies

Development partners use different channels depending on their priorities, knowledge and country needs. This subsection will highlight the salient characteristics and issues of the sector financing channels, including by comparing bilateral and multilateral development partners. While the use of different channels is justified by the sector specialisation of development partners, this subsection argues that development effectiveness principles always need to guide development partners' efforts.

Operations with country governments are mainly financed and implemented by multilateral (rather than bilateral) development partners in both the economic and social sectors

Bilateral development partners implement most of their ODF using channels other than governments, particularly in social sectors. By contrast, multilateral development partners channel most of their financing to governments. In fact, only a third of concessional and non-concessional finance from bilateral development partners reporting to the DAC was channelled to country governments between 2012 and 2016. This was mainly in infrastructure and to LMICs and UMICs rather than to LDCs and other LICs (see Figure 5.15). The remaining two-thirds of bilateral development finance beyond country governments is almost equally split between (i) donor agencies; (ii) external intermediaries, such as CSOs and multilateral organisations; and (iii) the private sector. Low levels of support through country governments beyond infrastructure may be explained by sector specialisations of implementing channels in certain sectors (e.g. companies in the production sectors). They may also be explained by mixed results in the public financial management agenda in some developing countries.

Figure 5.15. Large portions of bilateral development finance are provided beyond national governments, particularly in social sectors

ODF from bilateral development partners by channels (left hand chart) and sector groupings (right hand chart), annual average 2012-16, 2016 prices, USD billion commitments

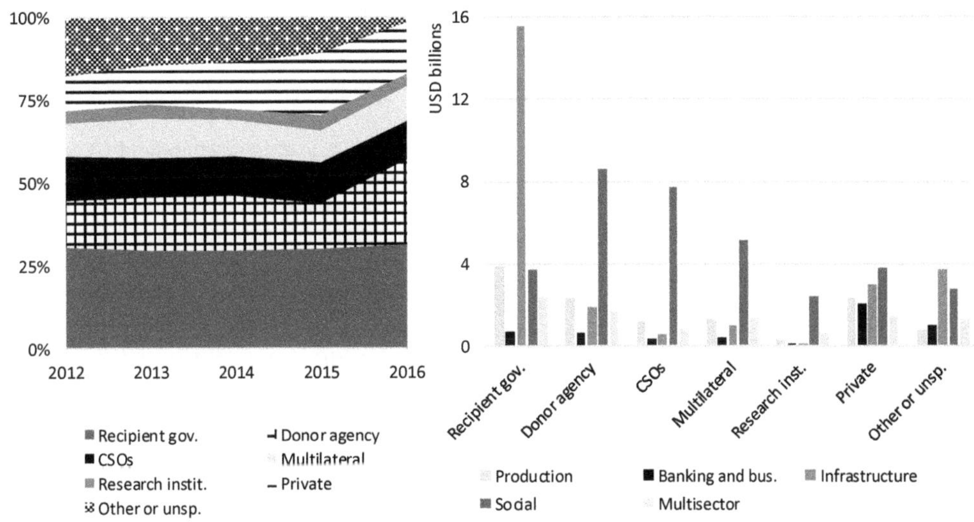

Source: (OECD, 2018[4]), "International development statistics (database)", http://www.oecd.org/dac/financing-sustainable-development/development-finance-data/idsonline.htm.

StatLink https://doi.org/10.1787/888933856264

Conversely, multilateral organisations provide higher shares of their sector-allocable ODF to developing country governments than bilateral providers (see Figure 5.16). This could be explained by the specialised knowledge of multilateral organisations in certain sectors (e.g. infrastructure), in policy and institutional reforms, as well as their extensive country presence. Multilateral organisations, particularly MDBs, are the largest providers of public sector loans for infrastructure. They are also the biggest providers of project loans and of sector budget support in social sectors.[9] Moreover, the European Union provides large amounts of grants to governments for policy and institutional development in infrastructure sectors, the financial sector and for agriculture. In particular, the European Union is the largest provider of grant finance for policy and institutional development among all bilateral and multilateral development partners.

Figure 5.16. Multilateral organisations channel most of their financing to country governments, mainly in the infrastructure and social sectors

Shares of ODF for sectoral programmes from multilateral development partners by channel (left hand chart) and ODF volume for sectoral programmes by channel and sector groupings, annual average 2012-16, 2016 prices, USD billion commitments

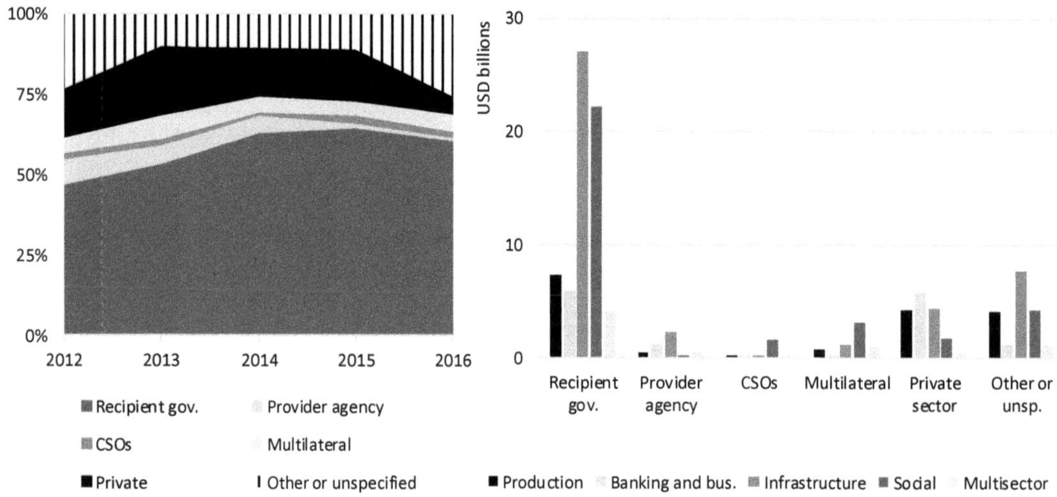

Note: Amounts behind bar charts are annual averages. Amount from EU institutions through EIB were moved from multilateral to provider agency. "Other or unspecified" might also include the private sector.
Source: (OECD, 2018[4]), "International development statistics (database)", http://www.oecd.org/dac/financing-sustainable-development/development-finance-data/idsonline.htm.

StatLink https://doi.org/10.1787/888933856283

A large use of CSOs and multilateral institutions in the most challenging contexts by bilateral development partners point to the need for strong policy dialogue and good funding practices, particularly with institutions highly dependent on their resources

As shown above, large portions of ODF from bilateral development partners are channelled beyond national governments. About half of bilateral development finance within sectors is implemented by donor agencies (17%), CSOs (14%), multilateral organisations (10%) and research institutions (4%). In the most challenging contexts, bilateral development partners prioritise implementation through external agencies, such as CSOs and multilateral agencies, rather than their own agencies. In fact, the share of financing channelled through CSOs and multilateral agencies in LDCs and other LICs is much higher than through donor agencies (see Figure 5.17).

Figure 5.17. Bilateral development partners use multilateral and CSOs in their priority sectors and in LDCs and Other LICs

Shares of ODF for sectoral programmes channelled by bilateral development partners through donor agencies by sector group and income group (top chart), multilateral organisations (middle chart) and CSOs (lowest chart), 2012-16 annual average, 2016 prices, USD billion.

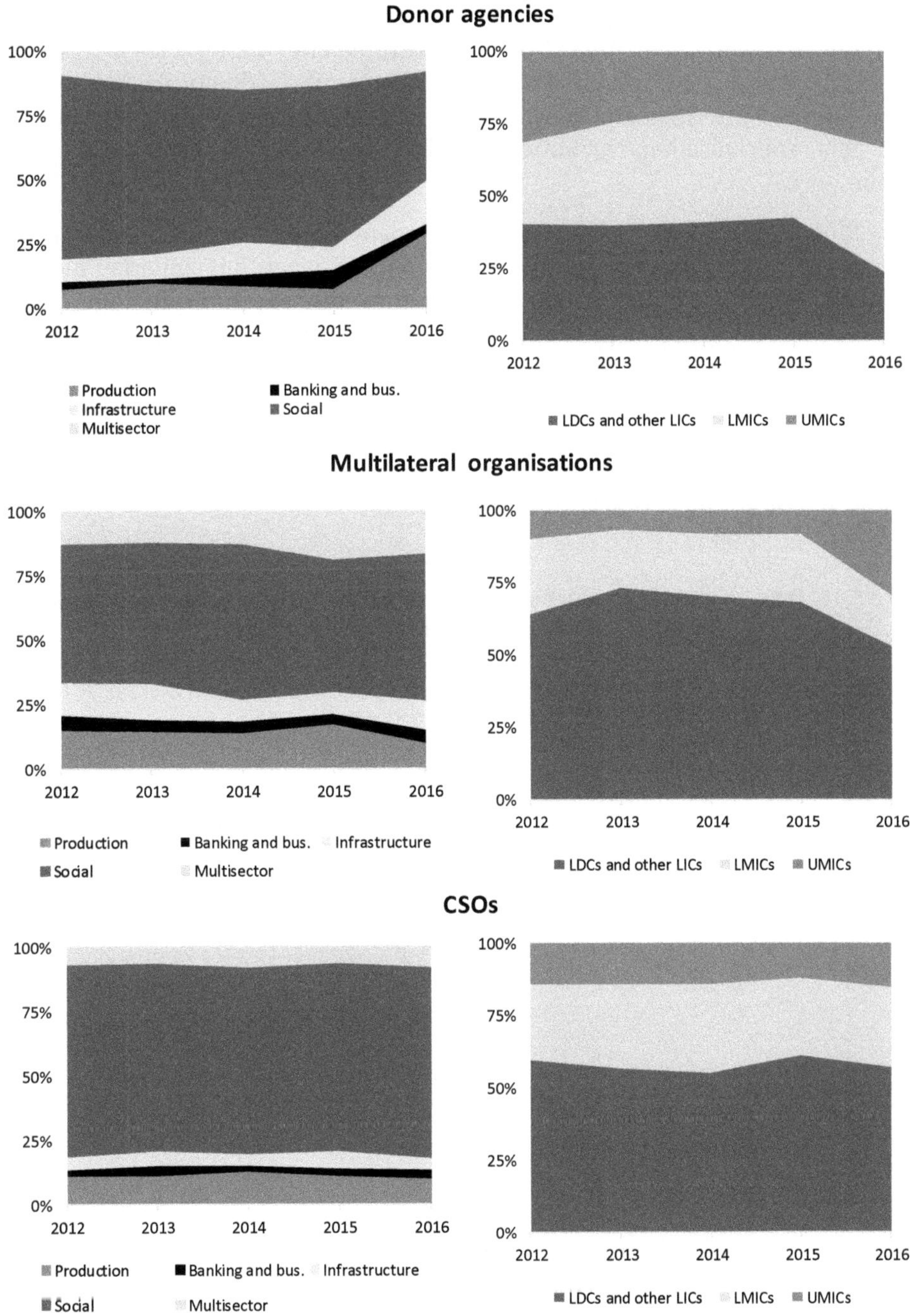

Note: shares by income group only include amounts allocated to specified income groups.

Source: (OECD, 2018[4]), "International development statistics (database)", http://www.oecd.org/dac/financing-sustainable-development/development-finance-data/idsonline.htm.

StatLink https://doi.org/10.1787/888933856302

A greater use of external implementing agencies in the most challenging contexts could be seen as a risk-management approach. This allows donors to transfer part of the programmatic and fiduciary risk to the implementing agencies (with their greater thematic and country knowledge) while retaining some degree of control (OECD, 2012[29]). Previous OECD research shows that DAC members value CSOs as partners when they have grass-roots knowledge of needs in developing countries and expertise in specific sectors and themes (e.g. poverty, environment, governance and human rights) (OECD, 2012[29]). Similarly, the 2018 OECD Survey on Multilateral Aid Policies and Allocations (OECD, Forthcoming[22]) shows that DAC countries partner with multilateral organisation that share national priorities and have a perceived comparative advantage in terms of expertise and specialisation, including in risky environments and LDCs (OECD, Forthcoming[22]).

The delegation of operations by bilateral development partners to CSOs and multilaterals in the most challenging contexts is particularly visible when humanitarian aid is taken into account. Figure 5.17 above does not capture this, as humanitarian aid is not considered an allocable sector in the DAC reporting system. As shown in Figure 5.18, DAC countries channelled significantly higher amounts to humanitarian assistance through CSOs and multilateral organisations than through their donor agencies and other channels. Amounts channelled by DAC countries through multilateral agencies and CSO for humanitarian assistance increased significantly from 2012 to 2016. The largest increases in funding were through multilateral channels, doubling from USD 5 billion in 2012 to USD 10 billion in 2016.

Figure 5.18. DAC countries channel most of their ODA for humanitarian programmes through multilateral organisations and CSOs

DAC countries' ODA for humanitarian programmes by channel, 2012-16 annual average, 2016 prices, USD billion commitment

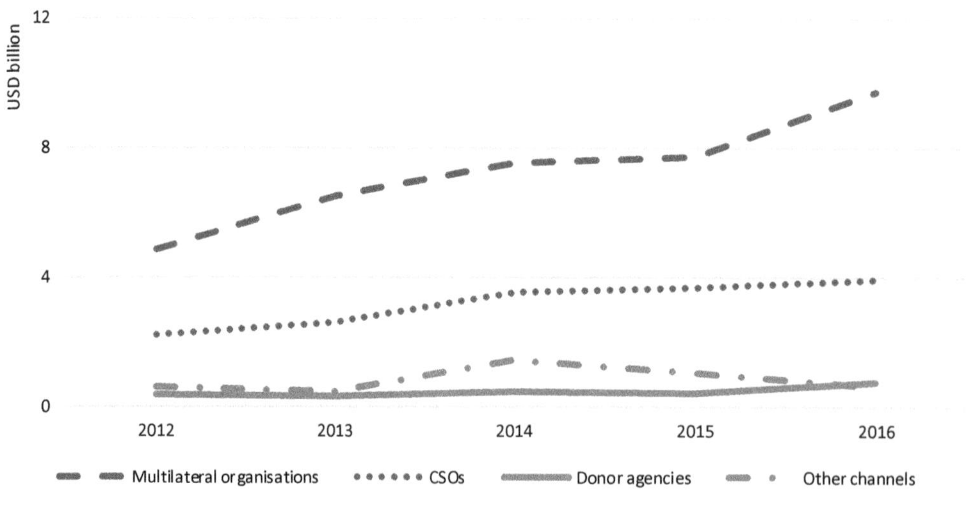

Source: (OECD, 2018[4]), "International development statistics (database)", http://www.oecd.org/dac/financing-sustainable-development/development-finance-data/idsonline.htm.

StatLink https://doi.org/10.1787/888933856321

Increasing the delegation of bilateral development partners to multilateral organisations and CSOs in priority sectors and challenging contexts raises the question of establishing effective funding polices and partnerships among donors and intermediaries. This is particularly evident for CSOs and multilaterals that rely heavily on bilateral donor assistance to fund their budgets, because they may feel constrained to accept resources for operations that are not entirely aligned with their mandate and strategy. This challenge is particularly prominent in the United Nations development system – 80% of the revenue of its agencies and institutions is in the form of piecemeal earmarked contributions (United Nations, 2017[30]).

Multilateral organisations and funds can act as donors in their own right and use other multilateral organisations as intermediaries for project implementation

Multilateral development partners also use the multilateral system for project implementation, even if they do so to a lesser extent than bilateral donors. On average, 12% of concessional ODF from multilateral development partners is channelled through other multilateral organisations and 0.2% for non-concessional operations in 2012-16. However, sector-specific or thematic vertical funds and a few United Nations agencies allocate very high shares of their sector resources through the multilateral channel (Figure 5.19). By only taking into account concessional ODF, Gavi, GEF, the Climate Investment Funds, the International Labour Organization, the Nordic Development Fund and the Green Climate Fund (GCF) channel most of their financing through other multilateral organisations.

Figure 5.19. Vertical funds and a few United Nations agencies allocate very high shares of their sector resources through the multilateral channel

Sector-allocable ODA volumes from multilateral agencies through other multilateral agencies by sector grouping (left hand chart) and shares of sector-allocable ODF from multilateral agencies through other multilateral agencies by sector grouping (right hand chart), average 2012-16, 2016 prices, USD billion commitment

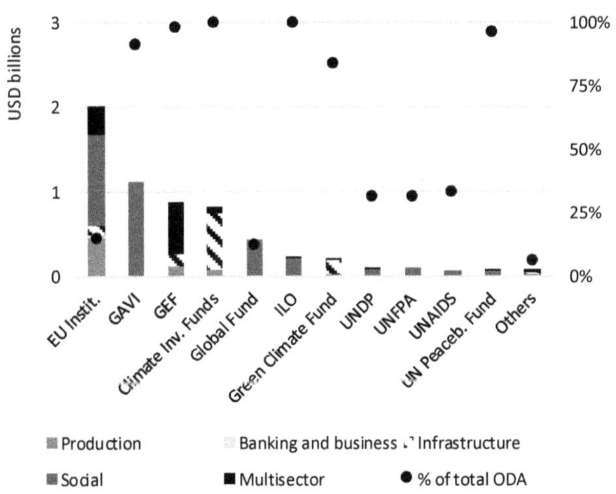

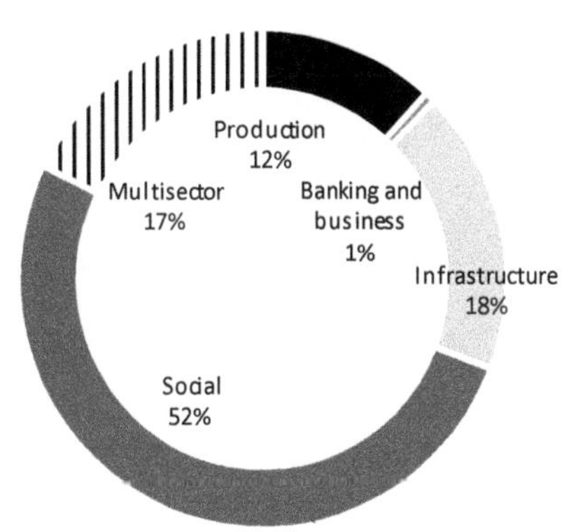

Note: concessional finance channelled by the EU inst. through EIB is not included.
Source: (OECD, 2018[4]), "International development statistics (database)", http://www.oecd.org/dac/financing-sustainable-development/development-finance-data/idsonline.htm.

StatLink https://doi.org/10.1787/888933856340

The main implementing agency for the European Union is United Nations Development Programme (UNDP; 10% of total outflows through the multilateral channel), for Gavi it is the United Nations Children's Fund (UNICEF; 84%), for the GEF is UNDP (41%), for the Climate Investment Funds it is IBRD (33%) and AsDB (30%), and for the Green Climate Fund it is EBRD (34%).

Contributions from multilateral organisations are increasingly significant as a source of revenue for other multilateral organisations, particularly for those working on social sectors that rely on grants, such as United Nations entities. The upcoming OECD Multilateral Development Finance Report shows that multilateral organisations account for a fifth of resources to the United Nations development system (OECD, Forthcoming[22]). For example, the European Union provided 10% of all funding to the UNDP and 5% to the Global Fund in 2016 (OECD, Forthcoming[22]). Therefore multilateral organisations, like their bilateral donors, need to provide resources that are adequate, predictable, flexible and aligned with the mandate of the recipient multilateral institution.

Development partners also use private channels for their development co-operation across sectors

Development partners use the private sector to increase the quantity and development impact of their resources. These operations can be quite diverse, reflecting a wide variety of partnerships with micro firms, SMEs, large industrial companies, multinational groups, banks and financial institutions of various sizes. Overall, the reasons why development partners engage with the private sector include:

- **Mobilising private finance:** mobilisation is mainly carried out by DFIs and MDBs through blended finance approaches that attract private investment in sectors with clear commercial opportunities – such as energy, manufacturing and SME finance. Operations in social sectors also exist but are less prominent due to limited commercial opportunities. Examples include DFI and MDB lending and derisking operations, coinvestment platforms and blended finance funds and facilities. While in these operations debt, equity and guarantees are sourced from capital markets and reinvested earnings of commercial operations, significant amounts of grants are provided by DAC members through DFI replenishments, blended finance funds and facilities, and direct credit enhancement.
- **Fostering innovation for social and environmental impact:** this objective is pursued to support business models with high social and environmental impact. Development partners can provide financial assistance (e.g. grant seed finance) or mentoring and technical assistance to companies with innovative business models and technologies. Examples include challenge funds, such as DFID's Africa Enterprise Challenge Fund and the Swedish International Development Cooperation Agency's Innovations Against Poverty Programme. These give grants to eligible companies to promote innovative business models in poverty reduction via competitive selection, particularly in agriculture and financial inclusion. Other examples include support from vertical funds (such as the GCF, the GEF, Gavi and the Global Fund) to companies with innovative business models and technology in the areas of environment and health.
- **Promoting entrepreneurship for job creation and poverty reduction:** this objective aims to increase the productivity of local companies in order to promote local private-sector development and job creation (Miyamoto and Chiofalo, 2017[26]). Direct financial assistance and capacity building target companies,

including small ones employing poor or disadvantaged people, e.g. in smallholder farming and informal manufacturing. For instance, Germany helps SMEs in developing countries through vocational training and by supporting business membership organisations, such as chambers of commerce and business associations, to foster investment and economic activity. Other donors channel resources to CSOs that work with small companies and farmers, such as the Netherlands and the United States supporting the Acumen Fund, which is a CSO supplying smallholder farmers in East Africa with asset-based financing and agricultural training services to reduce hunger and poverty.

As for any other channel of delivery, engaging with the private sector requires focusing on development results and supporting local priorities

Engaging with the private sector is needed to mobilise financial resources and expertise for development. At the same time, projects involving the private sector need to be inclusive and sustainable, and prevent social and environmental harm to local communities, just like any other development project. A priority in this regard is the implementation of environmental and social safeguards (ESS), which are policies, procedures and guidelines set by development partners to avoid, minimise or manage environmental and social risks in their operations. This is particularly true in large-scale infrastructure, which can have major impacts on local communities. While the need to comply with ESS is crucial for both public and private projects, it is increasingly recognised as a key element in the mobilisation of private finance. However, poor ESS monitoring and evaluation (M&E) by DFIs and MDBs means that they sometimes support private-sector projects that cause evident social and environmental damage for the local population [(Roasa, 2017[31]); (Geary, 2015[32])]. This is all the more complex in engagements with financial intermediaries, as an extended chain of intermediation makes M&E more difficult [(Geary, 2015[32]); (Roasa, 2017[31]); (CAO, 2017[33])].

Beyond ESS, private-sector engagements necessitate funding policies and practices responsive to local needs rather than the interest of donors and/or the private sector. This includes prioritising development over commercial objectives and investing in the local private sector rather than in donor country companies. DFI and MDB mandates may lack the explicit requirement of engaging with local governments and/or local stakeholders (e.g. local CSOs), threatening country ownership and alignment with local priorities (Pereira, 2016[34]). While alignment with local priorities is important in any sector, it is even more important in those with evident business opportunities where commercial motives could subdue development objectives. For instance, evidence from the mapping of private-sector partnerships in Uganda shows that the effectiveness of private partnerships decreases in sectors with stronger business opportunities – i.e. it is lower in financial services, medium in energy and higher in agriculture. This is due to low targeting of marginalised people, lack of systematic engagement with the government and poor M&E (see Box 5.2).

Moreover, the need to ensure the financial sustainability of DFIs and MDBs may push these entities to implement "bank-like" operations rather than development projects. This could explain why most of the operations of bilateral and multilateral DFIs are in UMICs and in sectors/projects with robust business cases, particularly in energy and financial services. In this regard, more effort is needed to support the riskiest projects, which include targeting the poorest countries and the poorest people. In blended finance, this will require a change of the incentive structure of DFIs and MDBs to prioritise the increase in development impact for the most vulnerable people over the increase in financial volumes from the private sector. This will also imply adapting skills sets and administrative processes to fragile contexts and addressing higher financial and programmatic risks for these projects.

Box 5.2. Developing the effectiveness of private-sector partnerships at sector level

The Global Partnership for Effective Development Co-operation (GPDEC) assesses the effectiveness of development co-operation projects and partnerships with the private sector. A mapping of 66 private-sector engagement (PSE) platforms at global, regional and sector levels found that sector approaches were more inclusive and country-owned, more likely to have an in-built monitoring and accountability function, and focused more on development results. Given that sector PSE platforms are often more focused and local in nature, these findings may not be surprising. Case studies subsequently conducted in Bangladesh, Egypt, El Salvador and Uganda echo the need for greater development effectiveness at the sector level as well. For example, a comprehensive review of 192 projects in Uganda in which the private sector has the implementation role finds that for agriculture, energy and financial services:

- **Only a limited number of the projects examined explicitly targeted the most marginalised people.** This is the case for 44% of projects in agriculture, a critical sector for poverty eradication in Uganda. The figures are substantially lower for financial services (8.6%) and energy (2.3%). While other projects may still benefit those left behind, findings suggest that they do not focus enough on poverty impact and development additionality.
- **Most projects do not systematically involve the Government of Uganda or other local stakeholders as partners**. This is the case in agriculture (40% involve local stakeholders, 11% the government), energy (16% engage local stakeholders, 12% the government) and financial services (1.7% involve both local stakeholders and the government).
- **There are significant information gaps in M&E**. At best, 9% of projects in energy provide activity-level monitoring and 11% in agriculture are evaluated. The figures are even lower for the financial sector, suggesting considerable transparency gaps in PSE efforts in Uganda.

Sources: Authors based on (GPEDC, 2017[36]); (GPEDC, forthcoming[37]).

Finally, the impact and inclusiveness of private-sector engagements will require M&E systems that track and assess the link between private-sector engagements and the development results. However, the commercial nature of these engagements and the ensuing complexity and confidentiality of these operations make them difficult to monitor and assess. For example, many DFIs invest in funds located in offshore financial centres and tax heavens, which makes M&E even more challenging (Pereira, 2016[34]). In addition, further evidence is needed to prove the leveraging effect and in particular the development additionality of blending practices [(OECD, 2018[12]); (Pereira, 2016[34]); (Oxfam, 2017[35])]. Development partners need to create systems that ensure financial allocations towards projects based on stronger evidence of financial mobilisation and development impact. These systems need to incorporate the effectiveness principles agreed in Paris and Busan, and more recently in the OECD blended finance principles (OECD, 2018[4]).

Notes

[1] The statistical data for Israel are supplied by and under the responsibility of the relevant Israeli authorities. The use of such data by the OECD is without prejudice to the status of the Golan Heights, East Jerusalem and Israeli settlements in the West Bank under the terms of international law.

[2] While rules for calculating the concessionality of loans were well established in the 2014 reform, calculating the concessionality of other instruments (such as equity investments, mezzanine finance and guarantees) is still part of the ongoing process of modernisation of the DAC reporting system.

[3] The statistical framework is currently in a test phase and will be applicable in 2019 on 2018 flows.

[4] The increases of health financing in 2015-16 should be seen in the context of the Ebola crisis at the end of 2014, so the upward trend in this sector may not be structural, but rather related to the response by providers to this specific outbreak.

[5] E.g. the International Monetary Fund (IMF) debt limits policy and the World Bank's non-concessional borrowing policy.

[6] E.g. the IMF-World Bank debt sustainability framework.

[7] Such as financial intermediary funds, recipient-executed trust funds and World Bank-executed trust funds.

[8] The share of sector-allocable tied ODA decreased slightly over the five years, from 19% of sector-allocable bilateral ODA from DAC countries in 2012 to 16% in 2016. While European Union institutions provide high amounts of tied ODA, which is procured to European Union member countries' companies, it is not included in the calculation as it is a multilateral organisation.

[9] Including governance.

References

AIIB et al. (2017), *Joint MDB Statement of Ambitions for Crowding in Private Finance*, https://www.bundesfinanzministerium.de/Content/DE/Downloads/G20-Dokumente/Hamburg_Genannte_Berichte/Joint-MDB-Statement-of-Ambitions.pdf?__blob=publicationFile&v=1. [8]

CAO (2017), *Third Monitoring Report of IFC's Response to: CAO Audit of a Sample of IFC Investments in Third*, http://www.cao-ombudsman.org/newsroom/documents/documents/CAOMonitoringReport_FIAudit_March2017.pdf. [33]

EDFI (2016), *Investing to Create Jobs, Boost Growth and Fight Poverty*, EDFI, Brussels, https://www.deginvest.de/DEG-Documents-in-English/Download-Center/EDFI-Flagship-Report-2016.pdf. [9]

G20 (2017), *Principles of MDBs' strategy for crowding-in Private Sector Finance for growth and sustainable development*, http://www.bundesfinanzministerium.de/Content/DE/Downloads/G20-Dokumente/principles-on-crowding-in-private-sector-finance-april-20.pdf?__blob=publicationFile&v=2. [6]

Geary, K. (2015), *The suffering of others*, https://www.oxfam.org/en/research/suffering-others. [32]

GPEDC (2017), *Mapping results and platforms, partnership and initiatives review framework*, http://dx.doi.org/www.effectivecooperation.org/wp-content/uploads/2018/01/Mapping-Private-sector-engagement-initiatives.pdf. [36]

GPEDC (forthcoming), *Private Sector Engagement through Development Co-operation in Uganda*. [37]

Humphrey, C. and A. Prizzon (2014), *"Guarantees for development: A review of multilateral development bank operations"*, ODI, London, UK, https://www.odi.org/sites/odi.org.uk/files/odi-assets/publications-opinion-files/9398.pdf. [20]

IADB (2017), *"Comparative Study of Equity Investing in Development Finance Institutions"*, Inter-American Development Bank, Washington, D.C., https://publications.iadb.org/bitstream/handle/11319/8207/Comparative-Study-of-Equity-Investing-in-Development-Finance-Institutions.pdf?sequence=8. [18]

IMF (2018), *"Macroeconomic Development and Prospects in Low-Income Developing Countries (2018)"*, International Monetary Fund, Washington, D.C., http://www.imf.org/en/Publications/Policy-Papers/Issues/2018/03/22/pp021518macroeconomic-developments-and-prospects-in-lidcs. [16]

Julks, A. and H. Kawamura (2017), *Global context for achieving the 2030 Agenda for Sustainable Development: International financial flows and external debt*, United Nations Department of Economic and Social Affairs, https://www.un.org/development/desa/dpad/wp-content/uploads/sites/45/publication/dsp_policy_10.pdf. [15]

Kaiser Family Foundation (2017), *The U.S. President's Emergency Plan for AIDS Relief (PEPFAR)*, http://files.kff.org/attachment/Fact-Sheet-The-U.S.-Presidents-Emergency-Plan-for-AIDS-Relief-(PEPFAR). [10]

Martinez, M. and C. McKay (2011), "Emerging Lessons of Public Funders in Branchless Banking", *CGAP Focus Note* 72, http://www.cgap.org/sites/default/files/Focus-Note-Emerging-Lessons-of-Public-Funders-in-Branchless-Banking-Jul-2011.pdf. [14]

Meeks, P. (2017), *Unravelling Tied Aid*, https://eurodad.org/files/pdf/1546810-unravelling-tied-aid-1530880935.pdf. [28]

Miyamoto, K. and E. Chiofalo (2017), "Development Co-operation for Private Sector Development: Analytical Framework and Measuring Official Development Finance", *OECD Development Co-operation Working Papers*, No. 32, OECD Publishing, Paris, http://dx.doi.org/10.1787/ded2028f-en. [26]

Mooney, H. and C. de Soyres (2017), *Debt Sustainability Analyses for Low-Income Countries: An Assessment of Projection Performance*, International Monetary Fund, Washington, D.C., http://www.imf.org/~/media/Files/Publications/WP/2017/wp17220.ashx. [17]

OECD (2018), *"2018 Report on the DAC Untying Recommendation"*, OECD, Paris, https://www.oecd.org/dac/financing-sustainable-development/development-finance-standards/DCD-DAC(2018)12-REV2.en.pdf. [27]

OECD (2018), *"International development statistics (database)"*, OECD, Paris, http://www.oecd.org/dac/financing-sustainable-development/development-finance-data/idsonline.htm. [4]

OECD (2018), *"Converged statistical reporting directives for the Creditor Reporting System (CRS) and the annual DAC questionnaire"*, OECD, Paris, https://one.oecd.org/document/DCD/DAC/STAT(2018)9/FINAL/en/pdf. [1]

OECD (2018), *Making Blended Finance Work for the Sustainable Development Goals*, OECD Publishing, Paris, http://dx.doi.org/10.1787/9789264288768-en. [12]

OECD (2017), *"DAC High Level Communiqué, 31 October 2017"*, https://www.oecd.org/dac/DAC-HLM-2017-Communique.pdf. [7]

OECD (2016), *"OECD DAC survey on amounts mobilised from the private sector by official development finance interventions 2012-2015"*, OECD, Paris, http://www.oecd.org/dac/financing-sustainable-development/development-finance-standards/mobilisation.htm. [5]

OECD (2016), *Private Sector Engagement for Sustainable Development: Lessons from the DAC*, OECD Publishing, Paris, http://dx.doi.org/10.1787/9789264266889-en. [19]

OECD (2015), *"Multilateral Aid 2015: Better Partnerships for a Post-2015 World"*, OECD Publishing, Paris, http://dx.doi.org/10.1787/9789264235212-en. [25]

OECD (2014), *"DAC High Level Meeting - Final Communiqué - 16 December 2014"*, OECD, Paris, http://www.oecd.org/dac/OECD%20DAC%20HLM%20Communique.pdf. [2]

OECD (2012), *Managing Risks in Fragile and Transitional Contexts: The Price of Success?*, Conflict and Fragility, OECD Publishing, Paris, http://dx.doi.org/10.1787/9789264118744-en. [29]

OECD (Forthcoming), *Multilateral Development Finance Report 2019: Towards a New Pact on Multilateralism to Achieve the 2030 Agenda Together*, OECD Publishing, Paris. [22]

Orth, M. et al. (2017), *What we know about the effectiveness of budget support. Evaluation Synthesis*, https://www.deval.org/files/content/Dateien/Evaluierung/Berichte/2017/DEval_Synthesen_Bericht_2017_EN_bffinal.pdf. [24]

Oxfam (2017), *Private Finance Blending for Development*, https://www.oxfam.org/sites/www.oxfam.org/files/bp-private-finance-blending-for-development-130217-en.pdf. [35]

PEPFAR (2016), *PEPFAR: U.S. President's Emergency Plan for AIDS Relief*, https://www.pepfar.gov/documents/organization/252516.pdf. [11]

Pereira, J. (2016), *"The development effectiveness of supporting the private sector with ODA funds"*, https://www.ituc-csi.org/IMG/pdf/tudcn-dfi_study_web_en.pdf. [34]

Roasa, D. (2017), *Reckless Development: The IFC's Dodgy Deals in Southeast Asia*. [31]

Suri, T. and W. Jack (2016), "The long-run poverty and gender impacts of mobile money", *Science*, Vol. 354/6317, pp. 1288-1292, http://dx.doi.org/10.1126/science.aah5309. [13]

United Nations (2017), *Repositioning the UN development system to deliver on the 2030 Agenda – Ensuring a Better Future for All: Report of the Secretary-General*, http://digitallibrary.un.org/record/1473546/files/A_72_684%26E_2018_7-EN.pdf. [30]

United Nations (2015), *"Addis Ababa Action Agenda of the Third International Conference on Financing for Development"*, http://www.un.org/esa/ffd/wp-content/uploads/2015/08/AAAA_Outcome.pdf. [3]

Williamson, T. and C. Dom (2010), *Sector Budget Support in Practice: Good Practice Note*, https://www.odi.org/sites/odi.org.uk/files/odi-assets/publications-opinion-files/5802.pdf. [23]

World Bank (2018), *"Sustainable Financing for Sustainable Development"*, World Bank, Washington, D.C., http://siteresources.worldbank.org/DEVCOMMINT/Documentation/23776700/DC2018-0002_PSustainableFinancing421.pdf. [21]

Annex A. Technical note

This technical note describes the various parameters and estimates used in this publication. It has six different sections: data sources, scope of actors, data coverage, definition of broad sector categories, main data limitations, and the authors' estimates and exclusions.

Data sources

Three main data sources were used:

- The (OECD, 2018[1]) Creditor Reporting System (OECD CRS) database, which includes both concessional and non-concessional official flows, i.e. official development assistance (ODA) and other official flows (OOF).
- The (OECD, 2016[2]) Development Assistance Committee survey on *Amounts Mobilised from the Private Sector by Official Development Finance Interventions* 2012-15.[1] Amounts for 2016 were estimated using the annual growth rate of private finance mobilised for the period 2012-15.
- The (OECD, 2017[3]) survey on *Private Philanthropy for Development* 2013-15.[2] 2012 data were estimated using 2013 data and 2016 data were estimated using 2015 data as the survey only covered the period 2013-15.

Additional sources were used, including from the International development statistics (IDS) online databases (OECD, 2018[4]) and are specified in the relevant sections of the report (e.g. in the notes of certain graphs, figures and boxes).

Scope of actors

This report aimed to use the maximum amount of information reported to the Development Assistance Committee (DAC) by sector, including all OECD CRS reporters: DAC members, non-DAC reporters and multilateral organisations. We also added the four philanthropic foundations that have reported to the OECD CRS since 2016 and others that responded to the OECD survey on Private Philanthropy for Development 2013-15 (OECD, 2017[3]).

The report includes analyses using the following three donor groupings:

DAC countries: Australia, Austria, Belgium, Canada, Czech Republic, Denmark, Finland, France, Germany, Greece, Hungary, Iceland, Ireland, Italy, Japan, Korea, Luxembourg, Netherlands, New Zealand, Norway, Poland, Portugal, Slovak Republic, Slovenia, Spain, Sweden, Switzerland, United Kingdom, United States.

Non-DAC providers: Algeria, Bulgaria, Croatia, Cyprus[3], Estonia, Iraq, Israel[4], Kazakhstan, Kuwait, Latvia, Libya, Liechtenstein, Lithuania, Malta, Qatar, Romania,

Russian Federation, Chinese Taipei, Thailand, Turkey, United Arab Emirates. Saudi Arabia was not included in this analysis due to the lack of detail reported by country and sector (see more details in the section "Estimates and exclusions").

Multilateral organisations: Adaptation Fund, African Development Bank, African Development Fund, Arab Bank for Economic Development in Africa, Arab Fund for Economic Social Development, Asian Development Bank Special Funds, Asian Development Bank, Asian Infrastructure Investment Bank, Caribbean Development Bank, Climate Investment Funds, Council of Europe Development Bank, European Bank for Reconstruction and Development, European Union Institutions[5], Food and Agriculture Organisation, Gavi (the Vaccine Alliance), Global Environment Facility, Global Fund, Global Green Growth Institute, Green Climate Fund, Inter-American Development Bank, Inter-American Development Bank Invest, Inter-American Development Bank Special Fund, International Atomic Energy Agency, International Bank for Reconstruction and Development, International Development Association, International Finance Corporation, International Fund for Agricultural Development, International Labour Organisation, International Monetary Fund (Concessional Trust Funds), Islamic Development Bank, Joint United Nations Programme on HIV and AIDS, Montreal Protocol, Nordic Development Fund, Organization of Petroleum Exporting Countries Fund for International Development, Organization for Security and Co-operation in Europe, United Nations Children's Fund, United Nations Development Programme, United Nations Economic Commission for Europe, United Nations Environment Programme, United Nations High Commissioner for Refugees, United Nations Peacebuilding Fund, United Nations Population Fund, United Nations Relief and Works Agency for Palestine Refugees in the Near East, World Food Programme, World Health Organisation, World Tourism Organisation.

Private foundations: Bill & Melinda Gates Foundation, Dutch Postcode Lottery, People's Postcode Lottery, Swedish Postcode Lottery. Flows from other philanthropic foundations were aggregated under the name "Other foundations".

Data coverage

This report mainly focuses on the concept of official development finance (ODF), which is a broad measure of developing countries' official receipts for developmental purposes. Developing countries are those on the DAC List of ODA Recipients (OECD, $2018_{[5]}$).

ODF is defined as the sum of:

- Bilateral ODA flows
- Bilateral OOF except for OOF grants and loans for commercial purposes (i.e. grants to developing countries for representational or essentially commercial purposes as well as official loans to private exporters in the donor country and subsidies [grants] to the private sector to soften its credits to developing countries)
- All grants and loans by multilateral development institutions, irrespective of the grant element of the loans.

The dataset excluded core contributions to multilateral organisations in order to avoid double counting with their outflows. Export credits and OOF grants were also excluded to ensure that the dataset only included developmental flows.

When analysing sectoral allocations, "sectoral ODF" was used (and "sectoral ODA" where relevant), which is limited to purpose codes below 50000.[6]

Commitments were used as the basis for the measurement of flows. Commitments reflect the direct political will of providers; they benefit from very good data coverage for ODA and OOF flows for the period of study; data on private finance mobilised and markers are measured on a commitment basis.

The period of study was mostly 2012-16, with estimates made where necessary (e.g. for amounts mobilised and philanthropic information as indicated above).

The types of finance and types of aid were based on the DAC code lists (OECD, 2018[6]).

In order to deliver key messages and detailed analyses, the following sources for **regional and country groupings were used**:

- For income groups, the World Bank classification (2017)[7]
- For groups of countries most in need: for least developed countries, see (OECD, 2018[5]); for landlocked developing countries, the UN list of landlocked countries was used[8]; for small island developing states, see the OECD DAC list[9] and for fragile contexts, see (OECD, 2018[7])
- For regions, see (OECD, 2018[8]), Annex 8.

Definition of broad sector categories

Sectors were compiled with the following methodology:

Table A A.1. Sector compilation methodology

Sectors	Relevant purpose codes
Education	11xxx
Health and population	12xxx and 13xxx
Water	14xxx
Government and civil society	15xxx
Other social sectors	16xxx
Transport and storage	21xxx
Communications	22xxx
Energy	23xxx
Banking and business	24xxx and 25xxx
Agriculture	311xx, 312xx, 313xx and 43040
Industry	321xx
Mining and construction	322xx and 323xx
Trade and tourism	331xx and 332xx
Environment	41xxx
Multisector	43xxx except 43040

In this report, the broad sector categories comprise the following subsectors:

- **Social sectors** cover education, health and population, government and civil society, and other social services, but not water
- **Infrastructure** includes water, transport and storage, communications, and energy

- **Banking and business** is a sector on its own
- **Production sectors** are agriculture, industry, mining and construction, and trade and tourism.
- **Multisector** comprises environment and multisector. General environmental protection activities are classified under the multisector/cross-cutting sector broad sector category in the DAC classification. It covers activities related to conservation, protection or amelioration of the physical environment without sector allocation. As a result, these activities do not reflect the totality of the donors' investments targeting the environment but only the part that cannot be allocated to a single sector.

Main data limitations

The OECD CRS database provides a large amount of information regarding sectoral allocations of official development finance flows. However, some of the flows provided in the context of development co-operation cannot be analysed by sector. For example, "general budget support" activities (purpose code 51010) are by nature unearmarked contributions to the government budget and cannot be allocated to a sector. They therefore do not appear in sector-allocable ODF as defined in this report. However, these funds will ultimately target one or more specific sectors in the recipient country. General budget support only represents a small fraction of total ODA.

Another limitation of the data provided in this report relates to the fact that the OECD CRS database includes information recorded as multisector (purpose code 43010). Activities recorded under this purpose code by the provider of development co-operation cannot be disaggregated by sector. To address this issue, the authors included a multisector category in the graphs where relevant to provide the reader with estimates of the activities reflecting this limitation. The multisector category in this report includes both multisector activities and activities recorded under the environment purpose code, which is very much cross-cutting in nature.

Finally, although the reporting by development co-operation providers has improved over the last few years, it is worth noting that support provided through non-governmental organisations is not always clearly allocated to a sector by OECD CRS reporters, and is often reported as "unspecified". The OECD DAC Secretariat is working with members to improve the allocation by sector of funding channelled through non-governmental organisations. This is done via an annual report on OECD CRS reporting issues.

Estimates and exclusions

The following estimates were made in the context of this publication:

- **With regards to non-DAC information:** for the sake of comparability and robustness regarding the quality of reporting, the OECD DAC Secretariat has used gross disbursements as a proxy for analysing the sectoral allocations wherever commitments were not available. Saudi Arabia only provided information on its development co-operation programme on an aggregate basis. As this did not allow for a sectoral breakdown, Saudi Arabia was not included in the analysis.

- **Multilateral organisations**
  - Gross disbursements were used as a proxy for commitments for the Arab Bank for Economic Development in Africa, Gavi (the Vaccine Alliance), International Atomic Energy Agency, Montreal Protocol, United Nations Environment Programme, United Nations Population Fund, and World Food Programme due to incomplete reporting on a commitment basis.
  - For the African Development Fund and Climate Investment Fund: commitments were used for ODA and gross disbursements for OOF, due to specific reporting issues.
  - For the Council of Europe Development Bank: gross disbursements were taken as a proxy for commitments in 2013 to fill the data gap.
- **Philanthropic foundations:** in order to respect the confidentiality of data by foundations, these were aggregated by year, recipient, income group, channel of delivery, type of finance and broad sector.
- **Mobilisation:** the OECD DAC survey on amounts mobilised from the private sector by ODF intervention (OECD, 2016[2]) covers the period 2012-15. In order to respect confidentiality agreements with data reporters, information on private finance mobilised was aggregated by year, recipient code, income group, category, type of finance and broad sector. Amounts for 2016 were estimated using the annual growth rate of private finance mobilised for 2012-15.
- **Figure 3.17 on shares of financing needs in infrastructure in developing countries by region and Figure 3.18 on annual expenditures and financing gaps in key sectors in developing countries**
  - Shares of financing needs in infrastructure in developing countries by region (Figure 3.17) were calculated using estimates in (McKinsey, 2017[9]). Estimates might include some countries that are not ODA eligible.
  - The annual expenditures and financing gaps in infrastructure in developing countries (Figure 3.18) are based on estimates made by UNCTAD (2014[10]) through a meta-analysis that combines estimates made by several studies available in the literature. As UNCTAD 2014 provides ranges of current investments and financing gaps in each infrastructure sector, Figure 3.18 shows the average of these ranges. Amounts include only capital expenditure and not operating expenditure.
- **Figure 3.19. Concessional support for policy and institutional development (2007-16):** to create Figure 3.19, only sectors related to policy and institutional development were selected. These include the following OECD Creditor Reporting System purpose codes:
  - **Governance:** public-sector policy and administrative management (15110); public finance management (15111); decentralisation and support to subnational government (15112); anti-corruption organisations and institutions (15113); domestic revenue mobilisation (15114); legal and judicial development (15130); conflict, peace and security (152xx).
  - **Budget support:** general budget support (51010).

- **Social infrastructure:** social/welfare services (16010); employment policy and administrative management (16020); housing policy and administrative management (16030); statistical capacity building (16062).
- **Environment**: environmental policy and administrative management (41010).
- **Others:** education policy and administrative management (11110); health policy and administrative management (12110); population policy and administrative management (13010); water policy and administrative management (14010); transport policy and administrative management (21010); communications policy and administrative management (22010); energy policy (231xx); financial policy and administrative management (24010); monetary institutions (24020); agricultural policy and administrative management (31110); forestry policy and administrative management (31210); fishing policy and administrative management (31310); industrial policy and administrative management (32110); mineral and mining policy and administrative management (32210); construction policy and administrative management (32310); trade policy and administrative management (33110); tourism policy and administrative management (33210).

- **Figure 5.3 in Chapter 5 on the use of private-sector instruments in areas with established commercial opportunities:** amounts channelled to private-sector companies by bilateral and multilateral development partners in 2016 are actual and estimated figures representing amounts for private-sector operations. Figures for the following are for 2015: African Development Bank, Asian Development Bank, Belgian Investment Company for Developing Countries, CDC Group Plc (formerly the Commonwealth Development Corporation), Compañía Española de Financiación del Desarrollo, European Bank for Reconstruction and Development, Finnfund, Investment Fund for Developing Countries, Islamic Development Bank, Nederlandse Financierings-Maatschappij voor Ontwikkelingslanden N.V., Norfund, Oesterreichische Entwicklungsbank AG, Sociedade para o Financiamento do Desenvolvimento, Società Italiana per le Imprese all'Estero, Société Belge d'Investissement International and Swiss Investment Fund for Emerging Markets.

  The amounts were calculated using various methods depending on the data available from the OECD Creditor Reporting System and secondary data, in particular:

  - Measuring amounts channelled through the private sector (channel parent category 60000) in the OECD Creditor Reporting System was the default method for estimating amounts for private-sector operations.
  - Amounts from African Development Bank and Asian Development Bank were calculated using OECD Creditor Reporting System data with the channel parent category 90000 ("Others") as their private-sector operations were reported through this channel.
  - International Finance Corporation amounts were considered to be 100% channelled to the private sector as the institution did not report on channels in 2016 and because it works predominantly with the private sector.
  - Amounts from Belgian Investment Company for Developing Countries, CDC Group Plc, Compañía Española de Financiación del Desarrollo, Finnfund, Investment Fund for Developing Countries, Nederlandse Financierings-Maatschappij voor Ontwikkelingslanden N.V., Norfund, Oesterreichische Entwicklungsbank AG, Sociedade para o Financiamento do Desenvolvimento,

Società Italiana per le Imprese all'Estero, Société Belge d'Investissement International and Swiss Investment Fund for Emerging Markets are estimates calculated by converting figures in euros from (EDFI, 2016[11]) to US dollars. The shares of sectors and instruments provided in the report were then applied to the US dollar amounts.

- Corporación Andina de Fomento figures were estimated using data from the 2016 annual report (CAF, 2017[12]).

Notes

[1] http://www.oecd.org/dac/financing-sustainable-development/development-finance-standards/mobilisation.htm.

[2] http://www.oecd.org/dac/financing-sustainable-development/development-finance-standards/beyond-oda-foundations.htm.

[3] Note by Turkey: the information in this document with reference to "Cyprus" relates to the southern part of the Island. There is no single authority representing both Turkish and Greek Cypriot people on the Island. Turkey recognises the Turkish Republic of Northern Cyprus (TRNC). Until a lasting and equitable solution is found within the context of the United Nations, Turkey shall preserve its position concerning the "Cyprus issue".

Note by all the European Union Member States of the OECD and the European Union: The Republic of Cyprus is recognised by all members of the United Nations with the exception of Turkey. The information in this document relates to the area under the effective control of the Government of the Republic of Cyprus.

[4] The statistical data for Israel are supplied by and under the responsibility of the relevant Israeli authorities. The use of such data by the OECD is without prejudice to the status of the Golan Heights, East Jerusalem and Israeli settlements in the West Bank under the terms of international law.

[5] The EU Institutions are also a DAC member.

[6] Please see (OECD, 2018[6]) for more information on code lists.

[7] See (World Bank, s.d.[13])

[8] http://unohrlls.org/about-lldcs/country-profiles-2/

[9] See Table 1 in (OECD/The World Bank, 2016[14])

References

CAF (2017), *"Annual Report 2016"*, CAF, Caracas, http://scioteca.caf.com/handle/123456789/1079. [12]

EDFI (2016), *"Investing to Create Jobs, Boost Growth and Fight Poverty"*, EDFI, Brussels, https://www.edfi.eu/wp/wp-content/uploads/2017/10/EDFI-Flagship-Report-2016.pdf. [11]

McKinsey (2017), *"Bridging Infrastructure Gaps: Has The World Made Progress?"*, https://www.mckinsey.com/industries/capital-projects-and-infrastructure/our-insights/bridging-infrastructure-gaps-has-the-world-made-progress. [9]

OECD (2018), *"Converged statistical reporting directives for the Creditor Reporting System and the annual DAC questionnaire - Annexes - modules A, B, and C"*, OECD, Paris, https://one.oecd.org/document/DCD/DAC/STAT(2018)9/ADD1/FINAL/en/pdf. [8]

OECD (2018), *"DAC List of ODA recipients"*, OECD, Paris, http://www.oecd.org/dac/financing-sustainable-development/development-finance-standards/daclist.htm. [5]

OECD (2018), *"International development statistics (database)"*, OECD, Paris, http://www.oecd.org/dac/financing-sustainable-development/development-finance-data/idsonline.htm. [4]

OECD (2018), *"OECD DAC and OECD CRS code lists"*, OECD, Paris, http://www.oecd.org/dac/financing-sustainable-development/development-finance-standards/dacandcrscodelists.htm. [6]

OECD (2018), *"States of Fragility Framework"*, OECD, Paris, http://www.oecd.org/dac/conflict-fragility-resilience/statesoffragilityframework2018.htm. [7]

OECD (2018), *"Creditor Reporting System"*, OECD, Paris, https://stats.oecd.org/Index.aspx?DataSetCode=crs1. [1]

OECD (2017), *"OECD Survey on Private Philanthropy for Development 2013-15"*, OECD, Paris, http://www.oecd.org/dac/financing-sustainable-development/development-finance-standards/beyond-oda-foundations.htm. [3]

OECD (2016), *"OECD DAC survey on amounts mobilised from the private sector by official development finance interventions 2012-2015"*, OECD, Paris, http://www.oecd.org/dac/financing-sustainable-development/development-finance-standards/mobilisation.htm. [2]

OECD/The World Bank (2016), *Climate and Disaster Resilience Financing in Small Island Developing States*, OECD Publishing, Paris, http://dx.doi.org/10.1787/9789264266919-en. [14]

UNCTAD (2014), *"World Investment Report 2014: Investing in the SDGs, an Action Plan"*, United Nations, http://unctad.org/en/PublicationsLibrary/wir2014_en.pdf. [10]

World Bank (s.d.), *"World Bank Country and Lending Groups"*, World Bank, https://datahelpdesk.worldbank.org/knowledgebase/articles/906519-world-bank-country-and-lending-groups. [13]

ORGANISATION FOR ECONOMIC CO-OPERATION AND DEVELOPMENT

The OECD is a unique forum where governments work together to address the economic, social and environmental challenges of globalisation. The OECD is also at the forefront of efforts to understand and to help governments respond to new developments and concerns, such as corporate governance, the information economy and the challenges of an ageing population. The Organisation provides a setting where governments can compare policy experiences, seek answers to common problems, identify good practice and work to co-ordinate domestic and international policies.

The OECD member countries are: Australia, Austria, Belgium, Canada, Chile, the Czech Republic, Denmark, Estonia, Finland, France, Germany, Greece, Hungary, Iceland, Ireland, Israel, Italy, Japan, Korea, Latvia, Lithuania, Luxembourg, Mexico, the Netherlands, New Zealand, Norway, Poland, Portugal, the Slovak Republic, Slovenia, Spain, Sweden, Switzerland, Turkey, the United Kingdom and the United States. The European Union takes part in the work of the OECD.

OECD Publishing disseminates widely the results of the Organisation's statistics gathering and research on economic, social and environmental issues, as well as the conventions, guidelines and standards agreed by its members.

OECD PUBLISHING, 2, rue André-Pascal, 75775 PARIS CEDEX 16
(03 2018 25 1 P) ISBN 978-92-64-30770-4 – 2018

www.ingramcontent.com/pod-product-compliance
Ingram Content Group UK Ltd.
Pitfield, Milton Keynes, MK11 3LW, UK
UKHW051501290926
15471UKWH00008B/1344